Man Without a Gun

Man Without a Gun

One Diplomat's Secret Struggle
to Free the Hostages, Fight Terrorism,
and End a War

Giandomenico Picco

TIMES BOOKS

RANDOM HOUSE

Copyright © 1999 by Giandomenico Picco
Map copyright © 1999 by Jeffrey L. Ward

All rights reserved under International and Pan-American Copyright Conventions. Published in the United States by Times Books, a division of Random House, Inc., New York, and simultaneously in Canada by Random House of Canada Limited, Toronto.

Grateful acknowledgment is made to Alfred A. Knopf, Inc., for permission to reprint four lines from "Pity the Nation" from *The Garden of the Prophet* by Kahlil Gibran. Copyright © 1933 by Kahlil Gibran and copyright renewed 1961 by Mary G. Gibran. Reprinted by permission of Alfred A. Knopf, Inc.

Library of Congress Cataloging-in-Publication data is available.

ISBN 0-8129-2910-1

Designed by Michael Mendelsohn at MM Design 2000, Inc.

Random House website address: www.atrandom.com
Printed in the United States of America on acid-free paper

9 8 7 6 5 4 3 2

First Edition

SPECIAL SALES
Times Books are available at special discounts for bulk purchases for sales promotions or premiums. Special editions, including personalized covers, excerpts of existing books, and corporate imprints, can be created in large quantities for special needs. For more information, write to Special Markets, Times Books, 201 East 50th Street, New York, New York 10022, or call 800-800-3246.

LIBRARY
ALMA COLLEGE
ALMA, MICHIGAN

To my son, Giacomo,
who lives his life with dignity,
bravery, and grace beyond his years

"There is properly no history;
only biographies."

—Ralph Waldo Emerson

Acknowledgments

I come from northeastern Italy, a place where empires, kingdoms, and so-called ethnic tribes have intersected and clashed for centuries. The former Yugoslavia is a twenty-minute drive from where I was born; Vienna, Budapest, Prague, and Belgrade are closer to my hometown than Rome is.

My first awareness of the world beyond my small corner of it came in 1956, when Hungarians rose up in pursuit of freedom only to be crushed by military forces under Soviet control. I was eight years old. My political life, in a sense, was conceived in that moment of high international drama. I would grow up, study at university and beyond, even achieve some fleeting celebrity as a result of my diplomatic duties, but the seeds of my belief system were planted then: that might should not make right and that the *hope* for justice is an indispensable ingredient of peace. Justice itself may not be of this world, but the hope for justice is.

Early on, I learned that violence against the individual in civil society is a handicap from the past, not a recipe for the future. By the age of eighteen, I wanted to be a part of something that could stop violent conflicts and save human lives. The United Nations gave me the chance to fulfill that dream in cities like Teheran and Baghdad, Beirut and Damascus.

This book is not a field guide for dealing with wars and terrorism; it is an account of how one person was able to deal with these realities of the late twentieth century in ways that may or may not be repeated in the twenty-first. I never held a gun in my hands. My story proves that to a large extent the real enemy behind hatred and wars is intolerance. Intolerance, in whatever form, simply creates more of the same.

While the United Nations as an organization offered me the platform to pursue my dreams, it was Javier Pérez de Cuéllar, the fifth secretary-general of the United Nations, who made it possible for me to have one of the most rewarding careers in the international body. He was a mentor and then some, giving me confidence, trust, support, and the freedom to do what I believed in and to make a contribution at both the political and human level.

The United Nations of Pérez de Cuéllar was, in retrospect, the most successful since the organization's founding. It was during his administration that the Geneva agreement on Afghanistan made it possible for the Soviet troops to withdraw from that troubled land. It was on his watch that the cease-fire agreement for the bloody Iran-Iraq war was brokered at a time when some still wanted the conflict to continue. His United Nations played a pivotal role in ending the El Salvadoran civil war, implementing the agreements for the independence of Namibia, and reshaping relations among the Security Council's permanent members after Mikhail Gorbachev arrived on the scene. And, of course, Pérez de Cuéllar, without any mandate from the United Nations itself, stepped into a space individual governments had never imagined for the secretary-general and authorized a plan to free the hostages from Lebanon—a plan that I was privileged to devise and carry out for him. He was successful because he delegated responsibility to individuals rather than to offices. In effect, we operated as commandos who used an institution for logistical support to do what needed to be done.

To me, history is not an operative concept. Biography is. I take my text from the book La Storia—History—by Elsa Morante. To this great Italian writer, history is what each of us lives in real time. There may be big biographies or small biographies, but they are what I think of as history. To some extent, the concepts of history, like those of religion, ethnicity, culture, and even institutions, are used as an excuse to hide the responsibilities of individuals. History does not kill, religion does not rape women, the purity of blood does not destroy buildings, and institutions do not fail. Only individuals do these things.

This book is an account of my individual decisions, minor as they may have been; my responsibilities, for better or worse; and my contributions, positive or negative, during the twenty years I spent at the United Nations. The scope of my activities included the Cyprus dispute, the Afghan crisis, the cease-fire negotiations for an end to the Iran-Iraq war, and, finally, the liberation of the Western hostages in Beirut—an operation that in its execution represented, I believe, the United Nations at its best. By the time I went into the lion's den of the Islamic Jihad in Lebanon, the United Nations was no longer a job for me; it was a mission.

On July 17, 1992, when I left the UN Building through the same gate I had entered two decades earlier, my sense of idealism was stronger than ever. I had been part of something that had stopped wars and saved human lives, and in that respect I had fulfilled my aspirations. I also was convinced that, as this story will prove in part, living according to your principles is much more important than life itself.

Many people helped me with this book, and they need to be recognized. Diane Munro provided advice, wisdom, and reason as she helped me rescue a disastrous first version of the manuscript that was not me or my story. She grounded many of my thoughts when I wanted to ramble on about my fears and emotions over the years, and she endured the pressure even when I drove her to exhaustion. Michael Ruby brilliantly edited a much longer version of the book without making me feel that he had chopped years off my life. His eleventh-hour intervention was indispensable: he got the sense of my story, my idiosyncrasies, and my unavoidable arrogance, and did so in a very short time and with great human and intellectual tact. Michelle Franssen, my assistant, transcribed more tapes than she will ever do again in her life, deciphering my pronunciation and, I'm sure, improving the text in the process. Ron Nazzaro helped her in that operation and even claimed he enjoyed it. Kate Cooney went through the uncorrected galleys with care and wisdom. Alberto Vitale, then chairman of Random House, believed in me and my story and gave me the opportunity to tell it. The burden of editing fell on Peter Bernstein, who took it in stride, and Luke Mitchell, who made things look easy even when they were not. Nancy Inglis and Lynn Anderson gave their professional touch to the text.

My UN colleagues, I hope, will feel some measure of vindication in a true story that proves how valuable their work can be and how little critics of the organization know about it. Judith Karam—at different times my secretary, assistant, colleague, adviser, and friend—was irreplaceable as I roamed around the Near and Middle East. Her moral solidity, midwestern common sense, and wise counsel got me through some tough spots. Maria and Steiner Bjornsson and Butch Waldrum were my family and operating center in Damascus; they must have violated any standing operating procedures of UN peacekeeping to suit my secrecy and my continuous changes of plans, and to protect me as best they could. Lieutenant Colonel Timo Holopainen and Major Jens Nielsen of Observer Group Beirut were the faces waiting for me at night when I would return from my unorthodox trips into "Jihadland." I could not have done anything in Lebanon without them.

I had many traveling companions in Afghanistan, Pakistan, the former USSR, Iran, Iraq, Syria, Lebanon, Israel, Britain, the United States, and Germany, but I think it's probably in their best interests that they go nameless here. Without the help of some of them, I wouldn't be alive to tell this story. They taught me about life and death and commitment, about human bonding across religious, national, cultural, and ethnic boundaries. So did Terry Anderson, who became a good friend after we both walked out of Lebanon.

Lorenzo Attolico pushed me, as only a good friend can do, to finish the manuscript. John Connorton, John Alfieri, and Danilo Noventa all helped from a distance more than they will ever know.

And, of course, Javier Pérez de Cuéllar has a special place. He opened doors for me, he trusted me, he encouraged me, he supported me, he let me do what I believed was right.

I wrote this book mostly for my son, to complete a story of which he has heard only fragments. Though he perhaps understood some of the reasons for my long absences, he nevertheless paid a price. This is my imperfect way of telling him why I was not with him when I should have been.

—Gianni Picco, January 1999

Contents

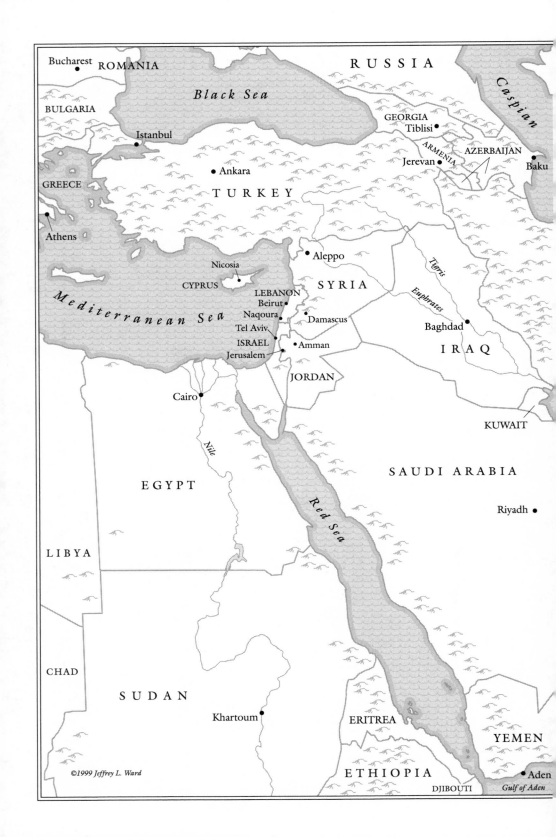

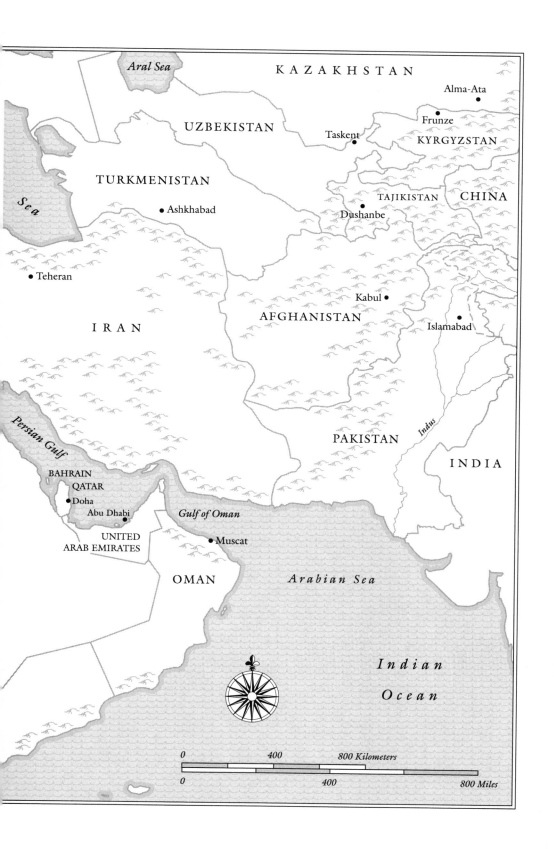

Man Without a Gun

Washington, Damascus, Teheran

Spring 1992

It was my third visit to the White House in as many months, and the omens were not good. In January and March, I had gone to Washington to see Brent Scowcroft, the retired air force general serving as George Bush's national security adviser and a man with a well-earned reputation as a strategic thinker. My mission was at once simple and delicate. For years, I had been telling the Iranian authorities in Teheran that the American president would reciprocate in some way, would reach out to the Islamic Republic, if they used their influence in Lebanon to win the freedom of the American hostages. Bush had used the words "Goodwill begets goodwill" in his inaugural address of January 20, 1989, and he had meant it as a signal to those who might help in Beirut. It was directed, I reminded the Iranians early and often, at them. Now it was nearly four months since Terry Anderson, the last of the American hostages in Beirut, had been freed, and the Iranians were growing restless. It was time for Washington to deliver its part of the implied quid pro quo.

Scowcroft had intimated at our first two meetings that the United States might have some difficulty living up to its "promise" of three years earlier. Even so, I held out hope that the administration would give me *something* I could take to the Iranians. Perhaps I was in denial: the idea that a word given would not be kept was unacceptable to me, since my credibility had been essential to the success of my work. Indeed, it had saved my life more than once. I did not even hint to Teheran that I was facing problems securing reciprocity from Washington. In retrospect, maybe I should have because Scowcroft made it official in April: the timing was not propitious; there would be no gesture toward Iran anytime soon. Was it the upcoming presidential election? Perhaps. After all, could the incumbent risk looking soft on a country that still tarred America as "the Great Satan"? Could he appear to pay off a government that had essentially taken over the U.S. Embassy in Teheran in 1979? Whatever the reasons, a three-year operation in Beirut built on a foundation of trust had suddenly turned to sand. Unwittingly—naively, as it turned out—I had misled an entire government.

I made one more run at Scowcroft. Iran, I learned, had approached a European company for spare parts that did not fall under the NATO embargo on trade with Teheran. Nevertheless, no NATO country would authorize such a sale without a green light from Washington. So I tried to dope out another way, something that might get us out of the bind. What if the United States simply ignored the sale? The ambassador from the European country involved could call on Scowcroft to raise the issue. Given that the spare parts were not on the blacklist, the White House would neither sanction nor reject the proposal. In other words, the ambassador would receive no official comment. White House officials could then properly say, if asked, that they had never given formal consent even as the sale went through. The Europeans, in effect, would act as the conduit for the goodwill gesture to Iran. I, in turn, would suggest to Iran that the White House had allowed that to happen, making good on George Bush's words of January 20, 1989.

Good play, unresponsive audience: Scowcroft rejected the proposal. There would be no deal. That left me with a broken promise, two German hostages still in Beirut, no clue to the fate of the missing Israeli pilot Ron Arad, and, painfully, my credibility—the most important thing, which had enabled me to spring nine Western hostages and ninety-one Lebanese prisoners—in tatters. Time had run out. My failure to deliver the American side of the deal with the Iranians essentially rendered me a liar, and I had to face up to the fact if I were to have any chance to reclaim my integrity, one more trip would be required. I could hardly expect the United Nations' new secretary-general, Boutros Boutros-Ghali, to understand or to pop for a ticket to Teheran. But this was personal now: going to Teheran was exactly what I had to do. I had to look into the eyes of President Ali Akbar Hashemi Rafsanjani and acknowledge my inadvertent deception. Nothing less would do, not if I wanted to salvage what I could of my professional and personal credibility. Without it, I knew, I was a nonentity.

My chance came quickly. In late spring, I was in Damascus working on the release of the last two German hostages in Lebanon. I made arrangements with the Iranians to fly to Teheran on one of the many flights linking it to the Syrian capital. The two countries were close politically: Damascus was then a tourist destination for families of Iranians who had been killed in the war against Iraq, as well as a city for political pilgrims. Buses would take tourists from the Syrian capital to the border of the occupied Golan Heights to gaze down upon the enemy: Israel.

In Teheran, I met with Javad Zarif, the Iranian diplomat I had worked with for years. He knew that I had asked to see the president to deliver an important message. He also knew that I had been to the White House and was expecting information about the goodwill gesture. At about 4 P.M., Zarif took me to see Rafsanjani. We met in his private office, more spartan than the official office where I had met with him and UN Secretary-General Pérez de Cuéllar in years past. It was our first meeting since all the American hostages had returned home from Lebanon.

There were few pleasantries. I looked straight into the president's eyes, which is considered somewhat impolite in Eastern cultures, and said in English that I had come to Teheran with news of broken promises. I explained that although the hostage operation had been based on the assumption that a goodwill gesture from America would be offered, I had been informed by Washington that no reciprocity would be forthcoming.

At first, Zarif declined to translate the bad news. When he hesitated, I told him to put my words into Farsi.

"You want me to say this?" Zarif couldn't quite believe it. "Do you understand what you are saying?"

"Yes," I said, "I want you to tell the president of Iran that I lied to him, although unknowingly. The principle is more important to me than the consequences."

Rafsanjani followed our exchange, bemused and curious, since he did not speak or understand English. Finally, he seemed almost embarrassed by the obvious tension between his two guests.

Eventually I said, "If you don't translate, I'll sit on the floor." It had just popped into my mind, something that would make the point to Zarif and increase his uneasiness. Zarif finally agreed, and I repeated my message sentence by sentence so that he would translate word for word and would not summarize.

Rafsanjani looked at me, then paused, giving himself time to collect his thoughts before responding. I had no idea what would come next, but the difficult part for me was over. I had spoken the truth.

"My government has had always good relations with you," he began. "We have known you for a long time. We have assisted you in Lebanon out of respect for the United Nations secretary-general. We have taken many political risks in our cooperation with you. Not everybody was in favor of such cooperation. Nevertheless, we went ahead. Since we engaged in this effort we have listened carefully to what you told us, including all the various assurances. You understand, Mr. Picco, that you are putting me in a very difficult position. In fact, it may be a very difficult position for both of us."

I understood him loud and clear. Rafsanjani was Iran's most pragmatic political leader, and he must have played a valuable chip convincing those in Teheran who opposed him that helping in Beirut would pay off in an American goodwill gesture. Now he had just been told the bet was worthless.

"The first thing I could do here is to decide never to let you leave Teheran," Rafsanjani said. The potential menace was clear.

"I came to do what I had to do," I told him. "To me, my job is done. I understand that you will have to do yours."

I waited for the translation and kept looking at his face for any reaction or any hint of what would happen next. I thought about Evin prison, the infamous place where the shah's secret police had tortured its opponents and where the Islamic Revolution had incarcerated many others. Yet I had no regrets. I actually felt relieved because I did not have to make any more decisions. It was now up to others or to the Almighty. It was almost ironic that, having played a part in putting an end to the Iran-Iraq war in 1988, having survived the scrutiny of the Islamic Jihad in Beirut, having spent more hours with a hood over my head than I care to remember, I could now end up in a Teheran prison.

The translation complete, Rafsanjani was ready. "I am sad to hear that this is the reason you came," he said, Zarif translating the Farsi into English. "The relationship we have had goes back for years. I think it is best if you leave Teheran very, very quickly. The news of what you have told me will travel fast to other quarters, and they may decide not to let you go."

It was time for the last retreat. Rafsanjani and I shook hands very politely, neither of us smiling. Leaving his private office, I heard no noise and no voices. I cannot say if that was because there were none or simply because I was in a different dimension, numb to the immediate reality. "You are mad to come here and say these things," Zarif scolded on the way out. He was very worried about the domestic consequences for Iran's president. My troubles might be over, but Rafsanjani's and those of other Iranian officials who had spent political capital to help free the Beirut hostages were just beginning.

As we were going to the airport, I reflected on the city that had been so central to my professional life for so long. Between 1982 and 1992, I had been to Iran more often than I had been to Italy, my home country. My activities in Afghanistan had an Iranian connection, my work in Iraq was part of the war with Iran, and my last operation for the United Nations, securing the release of the Western hostages from Beirut, had been done together with Iran. There is no doubt in my mind that I survived the dangers of Beirut because of Teheran's cooperation and assistance.

In the end it had come to this. I was angry then, not at Scowcroft, a true professional and the greatest strategist I have ever met, and not at President Bush, whose political predicament I understood and whose Middle East policy had been on many occasions quite courageous, wise, and good for America. Further, I was fully aware I had created new problems in Iran for President Rafsanjani. What made me mad was the fact that the foreign policy of any country can fall victim to domestic politics, that other lives in Lebanon might hang in the balance, and that I could do very little about it. My only consolation—and it wasn't much—was that I had taken for granted early on that governments could change positions and leave us out in the cold. That was why the hostage deal had been made principally on a quid pro quo that had depended only on myself and the UN secretary-general. It was probably the reason why I was still alive and free and most of the Western hostages had gone home.

I would continue my work for another month, helping to free two German hostages held in Beirut and finishing up some odds and ends at UN headquarters in New York. But as Zarif and I headed for the airport, I could hear the sound of a door closing. My life at the United Nations, my time as one of Pérez de Cuéllar's unarmed commandos, was over.

Part One

The author (*at right*) with Javier Pérez de Cuéllar.

CHAPTER 1

The Making of an International Civil Servant

The Cold War Incubation

I DEALS HAVE TO BE SET HIGH ENOUGH that you can walk comfortably underneath them. On the morning of May 14, 1973, I first set foot in the building that would be my home for almost twenty years. By the time I left, my idealism still intact, I had fulfilled my dream of pursuing diplomatic initiatives that helped to end wars and regional conflicts and, in the process, may even have contributed to saving some lives.

There were few Italians working in the UN Secretariat at that time; since the United Nations strives for geographical balance among its employees, I may well have been the equivalent of an affirmative action hire. I certainly was inexperienced, having come directly from the cloistered world of the academy—first as an undergraduate in Padua at one of Europe's oldest universities, then as a graduate student in international relations at one of America's newest (the University of California at Santa Barbara), and finally as a postgraduate at the Free University of Amsterdam for a last degree in European history. The United Nations paid me accordingly: my first job ranked at the lowest professional grade, providing a net income of $756 a month.

I began as a trainee at UN headquarters in New York in what was called the "Soviet Department." Actually, it was officially known as the Department of Political and Security Council Affairs, but it owed its nickname to the fact that a Soviet national was always in charge, the result of some early Cold War maneuvering. In 1950, shortly after the Korean War had begun, the Security Council had authorized a military operation against the North mainly because the Soviet representative chose to be absent at the time of the vote. Moscow, to put it mildly, was not happy, and made sure thereafter that one of its own would control the department that services the Security Council. This, in turn, meant that the rest of the UN Secretariat went out of its way to ensure that our department was like a branch without life.

My first regular job was to start a digest of the international press for internal consumption. It had never been done before because it had to be acceptable reading to all nationalities, which meant that the selection of the items and the terminology used to describe them would have to satisfy both Eastern and Western sensibilities. It was, in other words, an impossible task. Perhaps I was asked to start the news digest because as a very junior officer I was both naive and expendable. As it turned out, I succeeded by using a bit of Italian imagination—perhaps inbred because Italy, with its pro-Western government and a strong Communist opposition, seemed a microcosm of the larger Cold War struggle.

The challenge, as I saw it, was to invent new terminology to report events in a manner that would be found politically correct by all recipients no matter their nationality, ideology, or political commitment. This was easier said than done. During the Cold War, geographical names especially had a political connotation. One could not say "Berlin" or "West Berlin" without offending East or West Germany as well as Washington or Moscow. In reporting on the Arab-Israeli conflict, any use of the words "Palestine Liberation Organization" was unacceptable to the United States and Israel. The Soviet "invasion" of Afghanistan was unacceptable to the Russians; it became the Soviet "intervention." The politics of terminology became my first field of expertise at the United Nations.

My boss, a Soviet named Arkady Shevchenko, would send down complaints to me about my choice of items or wording, and a Mr. Vladimir Kuzmin, who was generally assumed to be the KGB man in his private office, would arrive to chastise me. So I began to skirmish with the front office of the department, first almost unknowingly, then consciously as I tried to report events that were in the United Nations' interest but not necessarily in the Soviet Union's. Words such as "imperialist" and "Communist" were replaced by "progovernment" and "opposition"—or vice versa, as the case might be. The disarmament proposal of one side was always reported with a reference to the latest proposal of the other. It was obviously much trickier to report what Moscow considered to be a "domestic" issue—and therefore unreportable according to the front of-fice—even when the issue involved a major uprising or civil war in a pro-Soviet country. Human rights issues in Communist countries, of course, were difficult to report in the digest, as were Arab editorials describing "Western plots" against their countries. Proxy wars between East and West represented another challenge.

Shevchenko, as the world was soon to learn, was not what he seemed. In 1977, after I left his department, he sought political asylum in America; he had been a double agent for sixteen years and remains the highest-ranking Soviet official to defect to the West. In naming names, Shevchenko fingered Valdik Enger, one of his assistants and an ex-colleague of mine. Enger, a Soviet national from Latvia, was arrested in New Jersey in the act of picking up some U.S. Navy secrets in a milk carton. During Christmas 1979, he was one of five Soviet agents to be exchanged for the Russian refusenik Anatoly Sharansky, now in Israel as Natan Sharansky.

So our little cell had, in descending order of importance, a Soviet double agent, an active spy, and a very naive Italian of twenty-four. That was my apprenticeship in the world of international diplomacy during the Cold War.

My Soviet years, as I called them, were good training. And my familiarity with Italy's polarized politics, a society divided by what I still think of as the Catholic and Marxist churches, helped me maintain my equilibrium in the Cold War environment. My village of Enemonzo in the eastern Alps had as many Communists as Christian Democrats. I had been educated as a Catholic, but I had also read Marx and Lenin. I was steeped in the need for social justice early on and acutely aware of the perversity of cultural and racial prejudices.

In a sense, my background helped me to understand the basic components of the United Nations as they then were. Just as the Soviet Department had gained its nickname from the country that most influenced it, the office that attended to the diplomatic business of the General Assembly, the United Nations' largest legislative body, was known as the "American Department" after the nation that controlled it. This mirrored the duality in which I had been raised, and it seemed perfectly natural to operate under these guidelines.

In time, I discovered that for most people the Cold War was less involved with political opinions, despite its hostile rhetoric, and more with personal lives. A file about me was being compiled in Moscow, I learned, and personal details of my life were a part of it. One of my Soviet colleagues said that this was unavoidable in the Cold War reality. A diplomat who receives instructions on a political matter does not act on his own and is rarely a decision maker. But the weak spots in his personal life, both covert and overt, become matters of state for his adversaries and even for bureaucratic rivals on his own side. They want to know his vulnerabilities, particularly in the arenas of sex, money, and health, which provide the three principal types of information that can be used against him. Any opponent who knows about these most personal matters gains an edge in blackmail, which was a major tool of the Cold War, influencing behavior in the most profound ways even when it was not actually used.

I came to know accidentally about one Eastern European diplomat who had a very sick child. The father had felt that if he remained in the United States, unable to afford the child's expensive care, the Americans might at some point try to compromise him by offering him money for treatment in New York. He had no evidence that this would happen, but he assumed it might and was terrified. That was enough for him to decide to leave. Tragically, the daughter died soon after the diplomat returned home. That was a very personal price paid by one foot soldier in the Cold War.

Surveillance was a way of life. On one trip to an Eastern European country with the secretary-general during the early 1980s, we were carrying a cryptofax machine that sent its signals through a standard telephone. Interruptions kept garbling our messages. Exasperated, one of my colleagues picked up the phone and spoke into it: "Please let me send the fax, and then I will give you a copy." The fax quickly went through. In Baghdad, we assumed that the hotel rooms were bugged not only for sound but for video. In America they were less intrusive: we all could spot the small boats constantly patrolling the East River, ostensibly for security, and assumed they carried listening devices beamed at the UN buildings between First Avenue and the river's edge.

I feared that one day I might find myself compromised even though I had not come to the United Nations from government service and had no roots in any official establishment. Indeed, if I had come from the government service of any European nation, I would have been trained to spot real and imagined dangers and possibly warned about them. But with no support network to fall back on in case of trouble, I found myself isolated and often did not know who was working for whom. My natural reaction was to avoid making friends or developing personal relationships except on a superficial level; in fact, at times, my only confidante was my wife.

Geography and natural resources are facts. Culture, religion, and ideology are all relative concepts. Ethnicity is in many cases an illusion, given population movements across continents and oceans over the centuries. Consider the Balkans. In Bosnia, an ethnic war was waged in the name of mythologized history and the purity of blood. Yet until 1991, 40 percent of the marriages were interethnic, between Serbs and Croats and Muslims. The Muslims of Bosnia are Serbs who converted to Islam in the 1500s and 1600s. The very concept of a pure ethnic group is a blasphemy against fact and common sense, at least in Europe. The huge migrations that have taken place over the last thousand years as a result of famines, plagues, and economic dislocations make a mockery of any theory based on purity of blood in the heart of the continent. The human species will never advance if we believe that good is on only one side of the river and bad on the other, and that leaders need to invent an "enemy" in order to rule.

After two and a half years in my "Soviet" job, I was eager to take on something more operational. The most coveted place to work at that time was the small Office of Special Political Affairs led by Under Secretary Brian Urquhart, a legendary Brit admired for his charm, intelligence, and creativity. Urquhart, a daring paratrooper in World War II and a close associate of Secretary-General Dag Hammarskjöld, had joined the United Nations at its inception in 1945 and played a major role, with Lester Pearson of Canada, in developing UN peacekeeping operations. His department was considered the elite of political offices, working mainly in the Middle East.

The office was fast moving and compact, composed of about ten people. It was staffed with dedicated individuals. F. T. Liu from prerevolutionary China, James Jonah from Sierra Leone, and George Sherry from the United States were Urquhart's principal deputies. George turned out to be the best teacher I ever had at the United Nations. He had started his career as an interpreter from Russian into English and later became an expert on Cyprus, which was the first conflict I experienced firsthand. Brian, by contrast, was never a teacher even though I learned from him— "despite him," as I once told him. The peacekeeping forces, or the Blue Helmets, as they were widely known, were by then the most successful UN operation. The office was involved in the first UN truce observation mission, which went back to 1948 and 1949, after the first Arab-Israeli war and in the war between India and Pakistan over Kashmir that began in the same period.

Decisions to deploy peacekeeping forces were made by the Security Council, but managing their deployment fell to the secretary-general and the Office of Special Political Affairs, which had a fair amount of freedom for maneuver in diplomatic activities. That was its major attraction: I knew by then that the deskbound bureaucracy of the United Nations in New York was not for me. This most independent arm of the secretary-general's office, I thought, offered me the chance to have it both ways—to make a political and intellectual contribution as well as to get involved more directly in conflict resolution at ground level. My expectations did not go unmet.

Cyprus was my first assignment in the field, my introduction to the manual labor of mediation. Not only did it teach me how to use the hand tools of diplomacy; by the kind of luck that makes careers, it also placed me under Javier Pérez de Cuéllar, a Peruvian diplomat then serving as a UN special representative for Cyprus at the request of Secretary-General Kurt Waldheim. The mandate on this issue given by the Security Council to the secretary-general allowed him to exercise his own diplomacy through his representatives and to make his own proposals.

Since Cyprus's independence from the British in 1960, the island's Greek and Turkish communities had had a difficult coexistence. Greek Cypriots outnumbered Turkish Cypriots by four to one. The Cyprus Constitution of that time was aimed at creating a functioning executive branch that would protect the rights of the smaller community but not be tyrannized by it. It was not to be so. The two concepts clashed, and the story of Cyprus evolved into a series of attempts to right one wrong with another. Today, thirty-eight years after independence, thirty-five years after Greek Cypriots sought to modify the original Constitution in their favor, and twenty-four years after the Turkish Army intervened to protect the Turkish Cypriot community, the island remains divided. As in other cases, the Turkish side in 1974 won the battle but lost the peace. Turkish

Cypriots are now free from possible Greek Cypriot pressure or control, but they get only a fraction of the economic benefits received by the Greek Cypriot community, whose per capita income is higher than that of some Western European nations.

I landed in Cyprus on a very hot day at the end of September 1976, for what was supposed to be a two-year tour of duty. Instead, I would remain involved in the problem of Cyprus until January 1985. Cyprus provided me with a lesson in the value of pride over money, right over might, and the indomitable hope for justice no matter how faint the prospect. But my exit from the scene would not be honorable.

The line that has separated the two sides in Cyprus since 1974 is called the Green Line. It runs through the capital city of Nicosia and from east to west across the treeless fields of the central plain and the foothills of the mountains. (In the wide space of the Mesaoria plain, the trees were cut down by the Venetians in the 1500s during their brief century-long stay on the island to better observe the approaching Ottoman Army. It did not help much.)

The UN Peacekeeping Force in Cyprus (UNFICYP) was deployed along the Green Line. In addition to a military contingent of about seven thousand soldiers separating the two sides, there were a press officer from Iraq and two political officers, one from the East (Poland) and one from the West (myself).

Most of my duties consisted of mediating minor problems between the opposing military forces and solving the daily problems of the population. Many problems stemmed from the military partition itself, which had cut family farms in half and divided schools from their students, hospitals from their patients, workers from their businesses.

Only diplomats and UN officials were allowed to cross the Green Line freely. For Greek Cypriots and Turkish Cypriots to do so, negotiations had to be conducted by a UN official. These minor mediations were hardly noticed anywhere else, but they made daily life more bearable for those Cypriots affected by the war. Still, nothing in Cyprus was easy. Harvesting a field across enemy lines was a sensitive political matter that became a battleground for power plays. The easiest way to show power was to destroy something or to refuse cooperation. That is pretty much what happened in Cyprus in those days. Saying no, to show power! Why anybody derived pleasure from making somebody else's life more difficult was, and is, beyond me. My job was essentially to convince Turkish

Cypriot or Greek Cypriot officials that they would look more powerful by saying yes. I was just learning how important a role a mere individual can play in complex political events. In that vein, it was essential to develop personal relationships with the individuals involved on both sides. One-on-one conversations proved essential in breaking through official positions. I learned how to personalize every matter, which frankly isn't all that hard for an Italian.

It became our job to help protect the remaining Greek Cypriots in the north and Turkish Cypriots in the south. We helped children cross military lines to go to school, the elderly to receive health care across checkpoints, farmers to attend to their fields that were under the control of an enemy army. As we arranged to satisfy both sides through a series of reciprocal gestures, the ledgers became more complicated. A demand for water to irrigate parched crops on one side might be made in recompense for restoring a power outage that had occurred several months earlier.

Keeping the accounts was the task that fell to the United Nations' "good offices" if demands could not be matched at a precise point in time. In Cyprus, the Turkish Cypriot side always appeared uncompromising. The Greek Cypriot side, by contrast, projected an image of flexibility on almost any issue. These initial positions, it turned out, were not useful in predicting outcomes, since the Greek Cypriots would often discuss ad nauseam rather than decide and the Turkish Cypriots would reverse course without a hint of advance notice.

Negotiations were also complicated by unwritten rules from the UN Secretariat; we had to take the position of each side at face value, New York suggested, without saying so directly, to ensure impartiality. This was, and remains, a guiding principle in UN circles. I did not realize at the time that impartiality is not a useful concept. Any side to a conflict would necessarily accuse the mediator of partiality to test him, both on his principles and on his commitment to his mandate. Impartiality applies only to mirror-image situations, which rarely exist in nature or negotiations. Only later did I come to realize that what both sides of a conflict want from a mediator is not impartiality but credibility—the ability to deliver the goods.

The impact of individuals in a place like Cyprus is magnified, and I began to see in the faces of the island's people that my work was making a difference—not a huge difference, certainly, but a change for the better. The gratification was tremendous. My role was limited to the tasks of day-to-day living, not the larger Cyprus problem, which was considered outside the reach of a junior officer. I would soon enough play a role in grander diplomacy, but I knew then that I had chosen the right career and that the United Nations could be a flexible tool for good in the hands of those who worked in the field. I intended to return to New York to get a new assignment working in the Middle East. That would come eventually, but not before some adventures elsewhere.

CHAPTER 2

Afghan Tales

The Last Battle of the Cold War

T HE YOM KIPPUR WAR and the Arab oil embargo. The end of the Vietnam
War. The skyrocketing oil prices and the shocks to Western
economies. The rise of political Islam and the seizure of America's embassy in Teheran. The 1970s and 1980s were a tumultuous time of conflict, of shooting wars by proxy between the United States and the Soviet
Union. But Afghanistan had a special importance. There, in the rugged
mountains and on the barren steppes of Central Asia, East met West in a
decade-long struggle that marked the last battle of the Cold War.

Through much of the nineteenth century, imperial Russia had jousted
with Britain for primacy in the region, but Afghanistan had gained an independence of sorts in 1907. After World War II, it played the role of
buffer between Soviet Russia and its pro-Western neighbors to the south
and east—Pakistan and Iran. By the mid-1970s, however, two things were
clear: the shah of Iran and a new Afghan government were very cozy, and
the shah was a staunch ally of America. Moscow was not amused. In 1978,
a pro-Communist coup installed Noor Mohammed Taraki; twenty months
later, Soviet troops were "invited" by a successive pro-Soviet government
headed by Babrak Karmal to stabilize the situation.

Soviet troops entered Afghanistan on December 26, 1979. Western
governments, particularly the United States, reacted predictably: they
backed the Islamic holy warriors—the mujahideen—who had taken on
the Communist government even before the Soviets arrived. Washington's objective was not so much victory as it was entanglement: keep the
arms flowing to the mujahideen and hobble Moscow for as long as possible. In this enterprise, the Americans found themselves with some sur-

prising new friends. Most Islamic nations and many Third World countries sided with the West against the Soviet Union, a traditional ally for many of them. (The mujahideen, it turned out, were not quite the great freedom fighters portrayed by the Reagan White House and in much of the Western press. Some would later side with Saddam Hussein in his invasion of Kuwait. Others turned against the West by training terrorist cadres.)

The UN Security Council could do little, of course; the Soviet Union was a permanent member and quickly made clear that it would exercise its veto if the Security Council tried to act. Then it did just that. The General Assembly, however, passed a resolution—backed, significantly, by most Third World countries, which often sided with Moscow—condemning the Soviet intervention; but this could hardly be expected to have much impact on the Red Army.

I had returned from Cyprus in 1978; serendipitously, Javier Pérez de Cuéllar had been named to share the leadership of the Office of Special Political Affairs with Brian Urquhart. Urquhart continued to focus on the coveted Middle East portfolio. Pérez de Cuéllar, meanwhile, got the thankless Afghan brief. I longed for a piece of the Middle East, but by that time I had become an assistant of Pérez de Cuéllar, and I cast my fate with my mentor. In retrospect, it proved a pretty wise decision.

When Pérez de Cuéllar asked me to write a brief on "what we should do on Afghanistan," I felt I had received the best assignment available in the entire organization. Of course, the odds of devising a successful diplomatic approach, "selling" it to the secretary-general, then selling it to the parties involved, and eventually carrying it out were not very good. The Soviets and the Americans were at each other's throats in places all over the world, and few people considered the UN secretary-general a serious political player in the conflicts. Waldheim's tenure also was coming to a close, and thinking of ways to expand the secretary-general's role was hardly Topic A in diplomatic quarters anywhere.

But then we caught a break in Pakistan, a Muslim country that shares a long border with Afghanistan and that eventually would shelter millions of Afghan refugees. On January 6, 1981, at a New Year's reception for the diplomatic corps in Islamabad, Pakistani President Mohammed

Zia ul-Haq and the Soviet ambassador exchanged a few words about the possibility of negotiations; the Soviet envoy agreed in principle. Pakistani diplomats conveyed this information to the UN secretary-general, suggesting that he take diplomatic soundings about arranging contacts between Afghan and Pakistani officials. We knew it was the opening we had been waiting for. Pérez de Cuéllar told me to get to work.

He also gave me a deadline. Waldheim was going to an important meeting of nonaligned foreign ministers in New Delhi in early February, and both the Afghan and Pakistani foreign ministers would be there. Pérez de Cuéllar wanted my draft proposal by mid-January, in time to work out the kinks before the secretary-general headed for India. My paper was entitled "Possible Course of Action." It included a package of four elements for negotiation: noninterference and nonintervention in each other's internal affairs; the return of refugees; withdrawal of foreign troops; and international guarantees.

Eventually, these four elements became the components of the final agreement reached in 1988, ending the war. But getting there wasn't easy. From the outset, even the order of points in the package was disputed by all sides. At first, the Afghan-Soviet side objected to including the withdrawal of troops as part of the negotiations. The Pakistanis, meantime, demanded a fifth point: they explicitly wanted the right of self-determination of the Afghan people to be included, implying a change of government in Kabul. The reality of the UN structure was that we could negotiate only among governments that had seats at the United Nations, and at that time the Soviet-backed Kabul government was acting as the legitimate Afghan government. Interestingly enough, this position was never challenged by Washington or any other Western country in the context of the United Nations. Accordingly, there was no role in these talks for the guerrilla opposition. Pakistan had to speak for itself and the Afghan mujahideen it supported. In the end, the frontline negotiators would be Pakistan, the United States, and the Soviet-installed Afghan government, with one wrinkle: since the Pakistanis did not recognize the Kabul government, they would negotiate with Afghan officials only as members of the ruling party. Other nations—"countries directly and indirectly involved in the crisis" (read Iran)—would be "consulted" by the secretary-general. Pakistan balked at holding any direct talks with Kabul, so we had to resort to indirect negotiations, or "proximity talks" in the diplomatic lexicon. This involved UN intermediaries shuttling between the two parties in different locations. It was a technique pioneered a half century ago by the legendary Ralph Bunche, who helped to end the first Arab-Israeli war in 1949, an effort for which he was awarded the Nobel Peace Prize.

In Cyprus, I had learned the subtle differences between a "mediator" and a "good officer," distinctions little understood by the uninitiated. A full-fledged mediator usually has a mandate and the independence to make his own proposals regardless of the positions of the parties. A good officer technically cannot make his own proposals but can only encourage the two parties to stretch their positions until they touch. For years, "good officer" was the favored description for the secretary-general because it connoted his limited ability to negotiate and the circumscribed scope of his initiatives.

But this theoretical difference between mediator and good officer can easily dissolve in the real world. It's fine to emphasize the good-officer role of the secretary-general, but then it's up to each of his representatives to stretch the confining rubber band as far as possible without snapping it. This is critical to understanding what we did in Afghanistan. The Soviets had rejected the General Assembly resolution; they would never accept it as a mandate for negotiation. So we never suggested that it was. On the other hand, we never said to the Pakistanis that we were *not* acting on the basis of the General Assembly's resolution. Accordingly, one side viewed the role of the secretary-general as the consequence of a mandate given him by the General Assembly while the other side saw it as the exercise of his good offices. The proposed package for negotiation came from the secretary-general.

In the spring of 1981, it was time to see if the four-point program we had developed in New York had any purchase in the region itself. Pérez de Cuéllar, his wife, and I headed first for Islamabad and our first meeting with Pakistani President Zia ul-Haq and his government. We then flew to Kabul—my first trip to Central Asia—in a six-seat prop plane requisitioned from UNMOGIP, the UN observers deployed since 1949 in the disputed Kashmir area between India and Pakistan. The plane was so small it had to detour south through Baluchistan to avoid the Pamir Mountains between Kabul and Islamabad.

The Soviet presence was evident even before we landed. The airport was under military control, and we could see antiaircraft batteries along the landing path. Soviet planes were using the airport for troops, supplies, and other visitors. Kabul wasn't exactly a city under siege, but it was plainly under Soviet control. Even though our escorts did everything possible to avoid contact, we saw plenty of armored personnel carriers (APCs) on patrol. Russian-made Niva cars—four-wheel-drive, jeep-type vehicles that were standard issue for intelligence officers and secret police—cruised down the streets. Oddly, though, Kabul's buildings seemed little the worse for war. In fact, the decade-long Soviet conflict would do scant damage to the city's structural integrity. Widespread destruction came later, after 1989, when the mujahideen and then the Taliban forces took control of the country.

We were cosseted in a villa inside what used to be the Royal Compound in Kabul—totally protected, isolated, but still only a few minutes from the Presidential Palace and the Foreign Ministry, where our meetings would take place. The key figures became clear soon enough. The Soviets had a huge embassy in Kabul, befitting an occupying power, but the ambassador was something of a figurehead. The real power was his proconsul, a deputy named Vassily Sofronchuk, who had an office right next to the Afghan foreign minister's. Pérez de Cuéllar and I knew Sofronchuk, or at least knew of him, from an earlier time when he had served at the Soviet Mission to the United Nations. In the late 1980s, he would become the under secretary-general for Security Council affairs at the UN Secretariat, and I would learn that this stocky figure was a jovial fellow with a good sense of humor and a great knowledge of world affairs. But then he seemed every inch the hard-line Soviet bureaucrat who had stage-managed arrangements for the entry of Soviet troops in 1979. By contrast, Mohammed Shah Dost, the foreign minister of the Kabul regime, was an old-time diplomat of the Kingdom of Afghanistan, tall and as distinguished as his noble lineage, a presence who seemed somehow unconnected to the regime he represented.

Then there was President Babrak Karmal, a founding father of Afghan communism who had served as ambassador to Prague during the previous two years, while another Communist faction controlled the government. Our first meeting with him, in the Presidential Palace, amounted to no more than a detailed rehash of the Soviet version of the events leading to the "invitation" to Moscow. The problem, he insisted, was Pakistan, which had launched attacks along the border as an antidote to Pashtu tribal nationalism. Most Afghans were Pashtu, and in Karmal's view of events, the Pakistanis worried that Pashtu nationalism might overwhelm their northwest provinces. This would grow old fast, since Karmal opened almost every meeting in the years to come with the same litany of Pakistani aggression and infiltration. Indeed, by the third telling, I found myself nodding off. This, needless to say, might have been an embarrassment on any number of levels, not least because I was supposed to take notes for our official record. Besides, note takers cannot remain idle lest the principals think their words are being ignored. In any event, I had developed a system of fake writing, jiggling my pen up and down on the pad so that the result looked like an EKG.

In those days, Kabul seemed a Central Asian city of another era, Kipling country, and we wanted to experience it—or at least I did. We asked to be taken to the marketplace, where I left the official party for a stroll through the bazaar. Seeing ordinary Afghans up close would help me to form my own impression of the country, I thought, to fit pieces into the puzzle in ways that couldn't be done in diplomatic meetings. That first visit also fed my growing passion for carpets—awakened first in Cyprus by Turkish traders—that became my excuse on future trips to break away from official duties and wander the city. I visited some shops on Chicken Street—the major thoroughfare for tourists in past times—and others in town. Checking out the goods gave me the opportunity to strike up conversations with shopkeepers that I renewed on subsequent trips. If the trips are frequent enough, you can take the pulse of a place and measure changes in behavior. Prices and the quantity of products in street markets can be key barometers of a country's economy.

Many shopkeepers were working for the regime; others had family members who were active in the opposition. Going from shop to shop, I tried to learn a bit about the current situation and the country. I browsed shops that carried lapis lazuli, carpets, and furs from Himalayan wolves. In explaining his trade, a jeweler may give a sketch of reality by telling you how easily the stones had been brought to him. Likewise, the selection of carpets would indicate if the traffic to Hamburg—a main commercial hub for Afghan carpets—was still going strong or not. A furrier would speak about prime hunting locations or the difficulties of hunting in a given area because of the fighting.

By the end of May 1981, Pérez de Cuéllar had resigned as under secretary-general when rumors of his bid for the top job in the United Nations began to circulate. As I accompanied him out of the UN Building on that last day of May, I told him, more as wishful thinking than as a prophecy, that he would return in the top job.

Despite his formal resignation, he retained his role as envoy to Afghanistan, and we remained in contact on this issue. We visited Pakistan and Afghanistan again in August 1981, this time Pérez de Cuéllar, his secretary, and me. Our objective was to reach an agreement on the agenda items for the negotiations, which would be a first step forward that could be reported to the General Assembly in the fall. If one side wanted to add an item to our four-point agenda and the other side wanted to subtract one, perhaps we could work toward a compromise.

As sometimes happens in the throes of a major crisis, side issues related to the main subject matter came up. Kurt Waldheim had been questioned and reprimanded by the Soviet ambassador in New York, Oleg Troyanovsky, about a former Afghan diplomat now employed at the UN Secretariat. Mir Abdul Siddiq had quit the Afghan government and signed up at the United Nations. But the Soviets and their comrades in Kabul—unwilling to let a defector get away if they could stop him—were insisting that he had embezzled money from the Afghan Mission and could not work for the United Nations since he was legally still a government employee. Traditionally, matters that could upset a major power and lead to a dispute were given not to an official with Pérez de Cuéllar's high rank but rather to a junior staff member; this provided political cover for the top negotiator.

The issue came up after our official dinner in Kabul with Shah Dost, the Afghan foreign minister. The meal had been set for 6 P.M., early enough so that everyone could eat, talk, and still get home before the curfew went into effect. Afterward, Dost agreed to talk to me alone in a corner of the huge reception hall for what he clearly intended to be a very brief chat. Siddiq had never resigned from the diplomatic service of Afghanistan, the minister said, so he was not eligible for a UN job. I said that he had signed a formal declaration that he had resigned, and we had it on file. We therefore considered him an individual and not the representative of a member country. I also pointed out that the relationship between a staff member and the United Nations is a matter for an individual and not his government. Dost cited Article 2 of the UN Charter, which forbids the United Nations from interfering in the internal affairs of its member nations. I cited Article 101, proclaiming the independence of the international civil service and its employees from pressures by their own or other governments.

With an eye on the clock, Dost then threatened that relations between Kabul and the secretary-general would be strained if the dispute were not resolved. This was no small threat, since we had not even started peace talks and he would be one of the principal interlocutors when we did. I replied that I understood his predicament but that if he persisted, relations between the UN secretary-general and Kabul might become even worse.

Dost wanted to cut the conversation short, pleading the curfew. I insisted on clearing up the whole thing, pointing out that surely the curfew was not an impediment for a foreign minister. By this time, I was probably beyond my brief: if the Afghans and especially their powerful Soviet masters wanted to play this out, they could do real damage to my career. But 90 percent of diplomacy is a question of who blinks first, and Dost did. The foreign minister made it clear to me that he would have to raise the matter again, but he agreed to do so with me. It was a way to save face. There would be no escalation of the issue. We would talk more about it, but no action was expected on either side. Siddiq continued as a UN staff member for many years, long after Dost completed his service as foreign minister, well after Ambassador Troyanovsky ended his career, indeed even after the Soviet Union came to an end. For me, the episode marked the point when I started to shed my Continental skin and think distinctly un-European thoughts—that there are a right and wrong in most matters, for example, and not an inevitable middle ground that sacrifices principle. My on-the-job education in diplomacy was moving into secondary school.

The Afghan bazaar taught me some valuable lessons as well. I had become hooked on Afghan carpets, none of them individually expensive, each a new piece of my life. One kilim, for instance, was a unique souvenir of the Soviet occupation. It had been placed on the street so the traffic could "age" it—standard operating procedure for Kabul merchants—and I saw a Soviet armored personnel carrier rumble over it. I bought it for $50.

The housekeeper at the government guest residence where we stayed in Kabul gave me tips on how to buy carpets: Court a carpet as you would a woman, he explained with broken English, hand gestures, and the help of any passersby who spoke a bit of English. Take your time and never reveal your intentions. You shouldn't pause when you first see something you like, but continue your inspection of the merchant's entire stock. Then concentrate on a carpet you have no intention of buying and pronounce it excellent but too expensive. It is permissible to take another look at the carpet you really want, but say nothing and courteously take your leave. A few days later, return to the shop and resume discussions with the merchant, ensuring that the carpet you really want is still there. When the negotiations on the unwanted carpet come to a crunch, refuse the price offered to you and name your lower price for second best, which is, of course, the carpet you really want. In other words, focus your interlocutor's attention on something you aren't really interested in while you remain focused on your objective—a lesson I also learned from a master of the technique named Saddam Hussein. We began negotiations with the Afghan-Soviet side by focusing on items other than the withdrawal while always keeping it on the table.

In December 1981, Javier Pérez de Cuéllar was elected secretary-general of the United Nations, and as he began his first term he asked me to join his private office. It was a great opportunity for two reasons. First, it put me in the center of the political decision-making process in the UN Secretariat, and second, it gave me the chance to transform my own ideas into diplomatic proposals and eventually into reality. But for Pérez de Cuéllar, it wasn't an easy time. The United Nations itself was almost under siege, and very few people thought that a new or expanded role for the secretary-general was necessary. Indeed, with tensions between them at a peak, the two superpowers seemed to have little use for the United Nations and seemed to consider its leader irrelevant. On the one hand, the Reagan administration considered the United Nations worthless at best and patently anti-American at worst, and its ambassador, Jeane Kirkpatrick, reinforced the point with her apparent disdain for the Secretariat and its people. On the other, the Russian gerontocracy in charge of Soviet foreign policy saw the United Nations as a tool of the West and the New York Secretariat as an agent of U.S. intelligence. Each side, in effect, thought the other guys were in control.

Neither side seemed to realize that the world was changing. For the first time since 1945, the Iranian revolution had demonstrated that something existed beyond the Cold War; for the first time since 1945, both superpowers were supporting the same side, Iraq, against Iran in a war that had begun in 1980 and was expanding rapidly. This had not escaped our analysis on the thirty-eighth floor of the UN Building, and it encouraged us to accelerate our rethinking of the secretary-general's office. We figured we had nothing to lose: since no one was paying much attention to the secretary-general anyway, a more political role for him might not even be noticed at first. It was simply too implausible.

Afghanistan became the first testing ground, but the steps we took would also have an impact in other arenas over the decade ahead. We believed it was necessary to conduct political negotiations directly from the secretary-general's own office. By making his office the real political center, Pérez de Cuéllar was assaulting the United Nations' fiefdoms, particularly those of the top under secretaries normally in charge of the political issues. The potential for internal conflict was considerable. I was fully aware of the hazards, but I was also convinced that unless he were willing to go for broke and seize control of some of the negotiations, he could not hope to change his standing with the superpowers or increase his political clout in world affairs.

Going for broke also meant a personal commitment that required people who shared it—and in February 1982, Pérez de Cuéllar's choice for his envoy on Afghanistan fit the bill. Diego Cordovez was a longtime UN official. He was also an Ecuadorian national, which made him a bold choice by definition, given the hostility between his country and the secretary-general's native land of Peru. But for reasons unknown to me, the Soviets were initially opposed to Cordovez. Pérez de Cuéllar did not want to be vetoed in his first appointment as secretary-general, so I was charged with "selling" Cordovez to the Soviets. I did it by telling them that the secretary-general intended to keep a close eye on Cordovez and that he would do so by putting me at his appointee's side.

Cordovez took on his new duties exactly as we expected—with tremendous professionalism and dedication. In trying to launch a round of proximity talks, he began a gradual enlargement of the four-point agenda. What began as four lines became four lines with an additional paragraph attached to each. Over the years, the paragraphs became a set of articles, then a more complete text, and eventually each item became an individual legal instrument that represented a long chapter of the entire agreement. Cordovez's pursuit of progress was aided in part by changes in the Soviet Union. Leonid Brezhnev died early in 1982, nearly two decades after taking power, and a new man, Yuri Andropov, was in charge in Moscow.

Andropov was the former head of the KGB, but the American press made him sound like a Russian James Bond—a worldly spymaster who favored jazz, Western literature, and Scotch whiskey. In fact, what he did possess was a keen understanding of his country's strengths and weaknesses; he knew that the Soviet Union had made a serious mistake in its Afghan adventure, and he clearly wanted to disengage. It was no coincidence that from the winter of 1982 to July 1983, the proximity talks, which had begun a year earlier in Geneva at the Palais des Nations, got a big boost. UN negotiators would meet with the Afghan contingent in the morning and with the Pakistani team in the afternoon. Andropov had appointed a Soviet shadow negotiator, who would consult with UN representatives at the same time the proximity talks were going on. Ambassador Nikolai Gavrilov would come to the Palais to meet with Cordovez on a regular basis before and after meetings between the Afghan delegation and the United Nations. In reality, progress in the talks was achieved through him, then reflected later in positions taken by the official Afghan delegate, Foreign Minister Dost.

With Andropov in the Kremlin, we were beginning to think a solution might be within reach. But Gavrilov died of a heart attack in June 1983, and Andropov's own health began to fade in July—and with it hopes for a breakthrough. Suddenly, negotiations on the Afghan crisis were on hold. Andrei Gromyko was in charge of Soviet foreign policy—and he had long before been nicknamed "Dr. Nyet."

Gromyko had been the public face of Soviet foreign policy for more than a generation and was considered by many in the West to be the man of détente. But did the long-serving foreign minister really shape foreign policy? Probably not. He was, by all accounts, a man who followed orders and would make no decisions and take no risks on his own. That was certainly our experience with the Afghan crisis, where he stalled and stalled and stalled. During the two years that included Andropov's illness and subsequent death and the brief interregnum of Konstantin Chernenko, Gromyko did not move a comma or propose any new step that might have taken advantage of the power vacuum in Moscow. Though very little transpired, I did manage to come to know Gromyko a bit. I saw him lie blatantly to Pérez de Cuéllar in private. At many meetings with the secretary-general, in both Moscow and New York, he would point to me and ask jokingly, "What is the tall Italian doing here?" I stand six feet, four inches; Gromyko, it seemed, could not imagine a tall Italian.

What the meetings lacked in substance they certainly made up for in a style of their own. In Moscow they sometimes took place in ornate, gilded Kremlin rooms—visual reminders of czarist Russia's glories. And they were unvaryingly formal and long—in part because Gromyko needed time to repeat the party line in great detail, in part because he insisted on saying everything in Russian even though he was fluent in English. He preferred the long delays needed to translate his words into English and ours into Russian so he could hear everything twice.

There is a great negotiating advantage in letting an opponent know you have all the time in the world. Learning how to exhaust an opponent proved valuable, and learning how to focus over the long haul served me well during the long nights in Beirut seven years later, when I was negotiating for the release of the Western hostages.

In 1982 and 1983, Cordovez and I visited Afghanistan several times, always staying at the same guest house in Kabul adjacent to other diplomatic residences. The Afghan housekeeper who had helped to educate me about his country's carpets and how to bargain for them now served me well in another way. I had begun to take early-morning runs through the

streets of Kabul, in part because I needed the daily exercise, in part because it was a way to see the city and perhaps learn a bit more about it. The
housekeeper spoke no English, but when he realized running was my
hobby, he managed to learn enough to knock on my door every morning
at six and say, "Picco run!" In effect, he forced me to run every day
whether I felt like it or not; not to run would have violated his hospitality.

The Afghans plainly enjoyed the spectacle of this tall foreigner jogging through their streets at 6:30 in the morning, particularly since I was
never alone. Security agents armed with automatic weapons followed at
a walk when I went out the first time, then broke into a run trying to
keep up. The resulting racket didn't do much for their image, and the
next day, they retreated to a car. Periodically, they would invite me to ride
back to the guest house, hoping to get the silliness over with as quickly
as possible. I always declined.

The other routine feature of my trips was a visit to the Italian Embassy,
which naturally served up the best pasta in town. But the real attraction was
Father Angelo Panigatti, an embassy chaplain and unofficial Vatican envoy
in Kabul. Father Panigatti was a short, portly man with a round face, small
eyes, and little hair left on his head. He looked like a village priest, but the
knowledge and alertness in his face conveyed a worldliness beyond his
humble position. He had gone to Afghanistan in the late 1960s. He had become a feature in the markets and teahouses, spoke the languages of
Afghanistan, had traveled the countryside, had even been named, despite
his Roman Catholic collar, an honorary Muslim. He knew more about the
country and its peoples than many intelligence services did.

Father Panigatti explained how the Afghans covered their political
bets. Every family with a member working for the Communist government made sure that it also had another relative working with the opposition across the Pakistani border in Peshawar, a city of Kiplingesque
political intrigues. He also warned me that the mujahideen leaders in Peshawar had made the mistake of ignoring tribal lines, in part because
they had been chosen by Pakistan, which knew it could never control
people whose primary loyalty was to their tribe and not to their paymasters. This had helped to hot-wire the civil war because the leaders in Peshawar lacked the tribal base to become leaders at home. Propped up by
money and weapons from the West, they bullied their way through the
tribal system. "This will be the end of Afghanistan," lamented Father
Panigatti, and he turned out to be right.

The single most important factor in the end of the Afghan war was not the fighting—the mujahideen could never have won a decisive victory, even with the Stinger missiles supplied by the United States—but the emergence of a man whose policies would change the world.

Mikhail S. Gorbachev became general secretary of the Communist Party of the USSR in March 1985, and almost immediately, Soviet foreign policy began to change. Pérez de Cuéllar got an early sign of what was to come at the funeral of Konstantin Chernenko, Gorbachev's predecessor, when the new general secretary of the Soviet CP asked to see the secretary-general of the United Nations. Gorbachev said that he would remain in close contact with Pérez de Cuéllar and that he had a keen desire to resolve the Afghan crisis. Within a few months, Moscow named a highly regarded diplomat, Nikolai Kozyrev, to be unofficial Soviet negotiator; in effect, he would conduct the real negotiations with the UN team, even as it continued the formal talks with the Afghans. Kozyrev would remain on the case for nearly three years, until the Geneva agreement ending the Afghan war was signed on April 14, 1988.

With Gorbachev at the helm, there was no more shadowboxing on the issue of withdrawal; he openly referred to the Soviet intervention in Afghanistan as a mistake.

Afghanistan was a "bleeding wound" on the flank of the Soviet Union, and it had to be sealed off, the Soviet leader said. He intended to take his troops out of Afghanistan, and the UN negotiations seemed the right channel to get it done.

His cooperation with the secretary-general would continue on other fronts as well. By 1987, in fact, Pérez de Cuéllar and his representatives had become deeply involved not only in the Afghan crisis but in cease-fire negotiations between Iran and Iraq. A plan we had devised five years earlier to create a new activist role for the secretary-general was showing visible results. Even Washington was paying attention. For us, the Cold War had ended.

Soon after the meeting with Gorbachev, Yuri Vorontsov, a deputy foreign minister, was appointed Soviet ambassador to Kabul with one brief: to close the file on Moscow's Afghan debacle. Vorontsov's high rank was a signal of how seriously the new leadership was taking the issue. We were already into the endgame, and everything was coming together to put greater pressure on the Soviets—the Stinger missiles provided to the resistance by Pakistan and the United States, the huge financial drain, the continuous opposition of former allies in the Third World. And there was a unique factor for the Soviet government: domestic opposition. The body bags being shipped back from Kabul had brought the war home to the Russians, and a genuine antiwar movement was building, with demonstrations in the streets of Moscow.

All of this gradually helped to undermine the Soviet Union's diplomatic position. The issue of whether Soviet troops had been invited or had invaded was no longer relevant; the focus now, even by Moscow, was on the timing and manner of troop withdrawal. Diego Cordovez had worked indefatigably to construct as complete an agreement as possible, each section crafted into a legal instrument over eight years of negotiations with the Pakistanis, the Soviets, and the Afghan government, now headed by President Nasrullah Najibullah, who had replaced Karmal when Gorbachev came to power. We kept in contact with Washington through the American ambassador in Islamabad, Under Secretary of State for Political Affairs Michael Armacost, and the Afghan Desk at the State Department. Still, it wasn't until late 1986 that the Americans really started to focus on what we had been doing. By then, it was clear that Secretary of State George Shultz finally realized we were getting somewhere—and that our draft agreement, already negotiated, was not entirely to Washington's satisfaction. The Americans, for example, were upset about the obligation to cut off military supplies to the mujahideen via Pakistan as part of the package. But the administration knew it would be politically impossible to stay out of a deal that committed the Soviet Union to withdraw its troops, and that kicking up a fuss about arms for the mujahideen might be seen as a cynical attempt to have it both ways.

As the negotiations continued, so did the war on the ground. Our trips to Kabul became more dangerous with the proliferation of Stingers in the hands of poorly trained Afghan fighters. We resorted to small jets hired by the United Nations in Geneva. The planes would come in at high altitude, out of Stinger range, to await an escort into Kabul airspace by Soviet MiGs that would fly up to meet us and begin shooting flares to attract the heat-seeking missiles. Our pilot would then begin tight corkscrew turns to descend as quickly as possible, covered by the accompanying

MiGs and Soviet helicopter gunships, which would fire more flares as we got closer to the airfield.

As the American government became more involved in our negotiations, the issue of halting arms shipments to the mujahideen *and* to the Kabul government became key. The conventional wisdom in Washington was that the withdrawal of Soviet troops would trigger the collapse of the regime in Kabul and that there was no need to worry about Soviet resupplies. The agreements envisioned that the withdrawal would take a still undefined period of time, perhaps a year. During the period of withdrawal, however, the Soviets were concerned about covering their retreat north to prevent further losses; it was a huge risk, their negotiators said, to agree not to supply new weapons during the withdrawal.

At the beginning of 1988, Diego Cordovez and our team pushed for closure: new proximity talks were set that would last until a final agreement was reached. The UN negotiators moved en masse to Geneva for what would become two months of final talks. The logistics were a particular nightmare for me, since by that time I was also involved in the cease-fire negotiations for the Iran-Iraq war. It turned out to be quite a commute: I would be in Geneva until Friday afternoon, fly to New York via London, spend Saturday and Sunday on the Iran-Iraq case, fly back to Geneva Sunday night, land Monday morning, and go straight to the Palais des Nations for the Afghan negotiations.

By that point it was clear that we were going to secure the withdrawal of the Soviets; it was equally clear that the Pakistanis and the Americans had no intention whatsoever of halting arms supplies to the resistance groups. But if they failed to cut off arms supplies, the very spirit of the agreement we had asked everyone to sign would be betrayed.

Which is exactly what happened on April 14, 1988, the very day U.S. Secretary of State George Shultz, Soviet Foreign Minister Eduard Shevardnadze, and the foreign ministers of Pakistan and Afghanistan signed the five copies of the accord. A few minutes later, the United States and Pakistan exchanged a letter of their own. It expressed their understanding that the agreements they had just signed would not end the West's military support of the mujahideen. This effectively nullified an essential part of America's agreement not to interfere in Afghanistan's internal affairs. After all, if supplying an armed opposition group isn't interference in internal affairs, what is? The Russians nevertheless honored their commitment to withdraw in nine months.

In his memoir, Shultz argues that as long as the Soviets had the right to supply arms to their puppet regime in Kabul, "we must be able to supply the Afghan freedom fighters." The idea of a continuing Communist government in Kabul was so abhorrent to the Reagan administration that it was willing to break its own word, even though, as Shultz admits on the very next page of his book, the CIA predicted that the regime would quickly disintegrate without Soviet support.

As it turned out, the Najibullah government, to the surprise of many, did not collapse after the Soviets completed their withdrawal in February 1989. The seven leaders of the mujahideen in Peshawar, meanwhile, remained divided and could not shape a real political alternative to the Kabul regime. They had no plan for post-Communist Afghanistan, and neither had their paymasters in Washington or Islamabad. The superpowers had moved to the sidelines after Geneva, but their proxies kept on fighting. The West seemed somehow to believe that the war was not supposed to end and that the opposition it had propped up was supposed to fight to the last Afghan.

Our job, then, was to fill the gap, to nurture coalition politics in a way that would end the bloodshed. In the past, it would have been heresy for the UN secretary-general's office to engage in questions of government legitimacy. But the secretary-general's influence had been growing steadily, and nobody objected as we prepared a new political plan for him to review. Our idea was to try to build a new "international consensus" among the principals—the superpowers, Pakistan, Iran, and Saudi Arabia—that would force a new "national consensus" in Kabul. The point man was Benon Sevan, the secretary-general's new appointee as UN representative in Afghanistan and Pakistan.

Benon Sevan was right out of central casting, a tall, expansive Armenian from Cyprus who seemed one with the proud and combative people of Central Asia. He tried heroically to find a common platform for a national coalition government that would bring the country out of war, cajoling, threatening, insulting, and even begging leaders on both sides to come to the table. We also wanted to see whether the exiled former king of Afghanistan, Mohammed Zahir Shah, could become a catalyst for national reconciliation. My visits to Rome to meet with him had multiplied as time went on. But the elderly king thought he had only one move left, and he feared it would be the wrong one. He remained in Rome.

International consensus building was not to be, either. The five principals chose not to pursue our plan, and later the fighting evolved, it seemed to me, into a new political proxy war, this time between Iran and Saudi Arabia. With consensus seemingly impossible and with the warfare continuing, the United Nations was under growing pressure from the Pakistanis to help remove Najibullah from power. Pérez de Cuéllar and I had resisted this idea because we felt that removing an authority figure—even one as unsavory as Najibullah—would leave a vacuum that could be filled only by a more devastating civil war. We used the same logic that some claim the United States used in allowing Saddam Hussein to remain in power after Operation Desert Storm: to leave a vacuum was deemed too irresponsible. But in 1992 the United Nations had a new secretary-general, and the prospect of consigning another Communist leader to the dustbin of history intrigued Dr. Boutros Boutros-Ghali. With the Soviet Union no more, he figured the job would be easy—a decisive step early in his administration that also would earn him points in Washington. It was a devastating error of judgment, repeated later on a grand scale in Bosnia, and it marked the beginning of the United Nations' declining fortunes during the 1990s.

Sevan did manage to get Najibullah to sign a declaration indicating his readiness to leave power in March 1992. Boutros-Ghali then authorized Sevan to execute a plan in April to fly Najibullah from Kabul to New Delhi. On the day of the operation, Sevan called me in New York—I was then deeply involved in Lebanon hostage negotiations—to explain that he had made arrangements, with Pakistani help, to proceed that very night. The timetable called for Najibullah to be driving into the Kabul airport just as a UN plane from Pakistan was landing. He would then board the plane and be flown to Delhi. Benon and I had become friends over the years, but we were sharply at odds that day.

"Who will take power in Kabul?" I asked.

"The men in Peshawar will help fill the vacuum with Pakistani help," Benon replied. This was disingenuous. The Peshawar Seven, as the mujahideen groups were called, had been fighting among themselves as much as they had been fighting the Soviets.

"What is your fallback position if you can't get him [Najibullah] out?"

There was none.

"What did the Pakistanis give to prove that they could deliver a government that will control Kabul?"

Just their word, he said.

"What about Dostum?" (Abdul Rashid Dostum was an Uzbek war-lord in northwest Afghanistan who had been a longtime supporter of the Communist regime.)

"He will stay where he is," Benon said.

I insisted that Kabul would still be a political vacuum, but Benon cut me off. Your opinion doesn't matter anymore, he said: "Boutros-Ghali wants me to go ahead." Significantly, I had had no consultation with the new secretary-general on this matter.

What ensued was a tragedy for everyone involved.

Benon tried to guarantee the deal on his own recognizance, figuring that each party would live up to the commitments they had made to him, despite the shifting alliances among the Afghans. Najibullah was the first to deliver what he promised. That night he was driven toward the airport in his own car. He passed through two checkpoints. But close to the air-port, where Sevan's UN plane was supposed to land, he encountered a third checkpoint. The car was stopped, and Najibullah was asked the password. He gave the wrong one and immediately realized he was trapped by people who were not from his own Pashtu tribe. His driver executed a screeching U-turn, doubled back at high speed, and made for the UN compound, the only place that could guarantee his safety. Under cover of darkness, he made it.

Meanwhile, Sevan's plane was approaching the Kabul airport, flying into a trap. The control tower did not clear it for landing. As the pilot made another pass, shots were fired and the plane was hit. The pilot decided to land, to avoid being shot down. He also was under Sevan's or-ders, and Sevan was not a man to be deterred by a few bursts of auto-matic-weapons fire. In his mind, he had an agreement to satisfy, although he could not know at that moment that it had come apart. He found out soon enough: upon landing, his plane was surrounded by partisans he didn't expect. Dostum had not stayed put in the northwest. Instead, his Uzbeks had swooped down to prevent Najibullah's escape, and they had no intention of allowing the groups from Peshawar to take over the country free of charge. They had seized the airport.

Najibullah's people had already abandoned their posts, leaving the vacuum we had predicted. Uzbeks are feared and respected throughout Central Asia. Rough warriors, they are often referred to as the Prussians of Central Asia. They held Sevan for three hours before he talked his way out and was allowed to fly back to Pakistan empty-handed, leaving Najibullah in the UN compound in Kabul.

What happened afterward was ugly. The Peshawar Seven took over the government and almost immediately began to fight among themselves, bringing even more destruction and death to Afghanistan. The new civil war continued for four more years; thousands of Afghans were killed, maimed, and widowed. Najibullah, sheltered by the United Nations during this period, was finally seized and hanged in the public square by the vengeful young Talibans who captured the city in September 1996 and imposed on it a harsh fundamentalist rule—and a rough peace.

Could I have done more to oppose the misguided decisions that left the political vacuum in Kabul? To this day, I believe we were responsible for much of what ensued in that tragic place. Our failure was one of the reasons I resigned from the United Nations. Accountability required no less. The pain of that mistake, however, will remain with me always.

CHAPTER 3

Peacemaking

The Secretary-General Becomes a Player

THE COLD WAR FAVORED KAFKA AND ORWELL—absurdity trumping reason, big lies drowning out simple truths. At the United Nations, diplomats spoke in riddles so as not to offend the five permanent members of the Security Council or the nonaligned movement among Third World countries. Ideology had replaced religion, and it was every bit as dogmatic and antithetical to the continuous compromises inherent in civil societies. The mind-set of peace might embrace diversity, but the mind-set of war—hot or cold—perceived diversity as a threat. Exclusion was the order of the day, and it was an affront to the principles of universal inclusion upon which the United Nations had been founded. But that was the way the world worked, and for more than three decades, it had rendered the organization impotent.

Our challenge, working for Pérez de Cuéllar, was to get beyond all that and reinvent the office of secretary-general. By 1988, Afghanistan was a first notch in the belt and the end of the Iran-Iraq war was a second, clear signals that the secretary-general had become a real player in international affairs without using the instruments of a state, which are mainly money and weapons. He had done so because he had built genuine credibility supported by two pillars: he was prepared to propose his own ideas and take diplomatic initiatives based on what he believed to be right, and he was perceived to be without the vested interests or hidden agendas that undermine the effectiveness of states in such matters.

But establishing an independent political role for the secretary-general was not a matter of simple decree or bureaucratic reassignment. It involved a cultural shift of no small magnitude at the United Nations itself, a reexamination of what the institution of the secretary-general would be all about. It also meant going beyond "peacekeeping" and getting into "peacemaking."

Neither word appears in the UN Charter signed in San Francisco in 1945. Peacekeeping, the use of UN military personnel supplied by non-involved member countries to separate belligerents during negotiations or the implementation of cease-fire agreements, first happened almost by accident not long after World War II. UN peacekeepers were used first in 1949 in Kashmir, along the India-Pakistan border, and in the Palestine region after the first Arab-Israeli war; they were also used seven years later in Suez, after a cease-fire ended the second Arab-Israeli war. Over the years, peacekeeping had become an accepted part of the United Nations' mission, and the United Nations' Blue Helmets had become familiar figures in hot spots around the world.

Peacemaking, or efforts by the secretary-general to negotiate an agreement to end conflicts between opposing factions, was not a word that tripped easily off the tongues of UN bureaucrats or, for that matter, of presidents and prime ministers. To the contrary, many government officials thought it blasphemous, a kind of cynical zero-sum game: if peacemaking enhanced the secretary-general's position, it necessarily followed that their states would sacrifice some measure of sovereignty. I felt that there was confusion between the concepts of sovereignty and power. Many seemed to consider them synonymous; in fact, sovereignty can be relinquished in order to secure more power. A trade agreement implies giving up some sovereignty, but it can enhance the legitimacy of government and thus its power if it produces better living standards for the population. I tried to explain that the secretary-general could never infringe upon the power of a state because a state's legitimacy comes from its people, and its people alone. Peacemaking was simply a function that would make the secretary-general more useful to UN member governments. An active, peacemaking secretary-general could take political risks that individual governments might find impossible to take at a particular time. Besides, there was precedent, though not in a judicial sense. The organization's first peacemaker had been Dr. Ralph Bunche, still revered at the United Nations for his 1949 work in ending the first Arab-Israeli war.

But the Cold War had chilled the United Nations and the secretary-general as major negotiating forces. And with the arrival of Ronald Reagan in the White House, Pérez de Cuéllar realized when he became secretary-general in 1982 that there was little room to maneuver between the two superpowers. Either we could accept the status quo and muddle along, or we could go for broke and change the equation: we could try to add the word "peacemaker" to the secretary-general's portfolio of responsibilities, make the United Nations more useful, and perhaps save it from the oblivion of the League of Nations. If we could pull it off, our successes would improve the United Nations' reputation—and, like the hot investment banking firms of the 1980s, we would be able to trade on that success to attract new "clients."

The UN bureaucracy viewed the idea of peacemaking as a new concept instead of one with an honorable history. It soon became known among its opponents as "Picco's concept," after the thirty-four-year-old, untested Italian upstart who seemed too eager for his own bureaucratic empire. But I had the support of Pérez de Cuéllar, who was willing to break eggs. In practical terms, we brought inside his office the political management of the major negotiations under way, leaving the under secretaries and many of those working in the political offices very unhappy. My modus operandi was to work with a very small group of people and, in some cases, in great secrecy. This added to the bureaucratic discomfort. But there was no time for committee decisions, and certainly I had no appetite for consultations with people unfamiliar with the personal and political risks involved. In the process, we bypassed some higher-ups completely or gave them only limited information on the state of negotiations. To this day, I regret having hurt some of my senior colleagues during those years, but I was convinced then and still believe that we had no choice but to take that road—to take big risks if we wanted big rewards. That old catchall excuse for inaction, "The time is not ripe," simply wouldn't do anymore. In retrospect, if we had lived by that dictum, the Afghan agreements, the end of the Iran-Iraq war, and the liberation of the hostages from Lebanon could never have been achieved.

It was apparent to me at the time that peacemaking could not be agreed upon as a concept and then implemented; it had to be the other way around. If we could work on our peacemaking activities and produce results, it would obviously be easier to sell the concept as a permanent part of the secretary-general's brief. We set out to do just that with our Cyprus, Iran-Iraq, and Afghanistan negotiations. It also was apparent to me that peacemaking was linked to the credibility of the secretary-general—as a person, not as an institution. Peacemaking needed personal, intellectual, political, and ethical credibility. Deeds more than words were its currency. Credibility, I came to realize, had little to do with impartiality but rather with a personal commitment to search for a solution based on the principles of the UN Charter. How could I have been impartial in front of the kidnappers of innocent hostages? Credibility was the ability to deliver what you promised.

Conceiving a new peacemaking function for the secretary-general was one thing; giving it a legislative basis was something else entirely. But we knew that official recognition of some kind was necessary if we wanted it to be accepted as a new institutional role. For starters, I began to introduce the word into speeches that were written for Pérez de Cuéllar—and even that seemingly small thing caused fingers to wag. I got "peacemaking" into some administrative reports that went out under his signature. Still, no intergovernmental body at the United Nations had ever used the word in any of its resolutions. We needed to remedy that, and we did—but not for many years.

Meantime, action would have to do. In 1989, well after we had embarked on our peacemaking enterprise, the secretary-general secured the authority to open his own political offices in the field; the idea was to provide better support for his diplomatic initiatives. In time, we would set them up in Afghanistan, Pakistan, Iran, and Iraq. These were to be distinct from the UN Information Centers. They were meant to transact political business and collect political information, and they had the implicit backing of the Security Council.

The job of arguing for the money to set up these offices fell to me. So it was that I came before the UN's Advisory Committee on Budgetary Questions in the company of Kofi Annan, then the organization's budget director and now its secretary-general. In his eagerness to help me, Annan made a startling comment: "Well, in other words, ladies and gentlemen, what Mr. Picco is trying to set up is intelligence offices in this area." I thought his description would doom my request, which had been inflated in the expectation that it would be reduced, but to my amazement, there wasn't a peep. Later, when I returned for resources to continue the offices, I received an even warmer welcome.

The offices had special standing. I succeeded in negotiating full diplomatic status for our office in Teheran as if it were an embassy, something no UN office had ever enjoyed in any part of the world. So in Baghdad, Teheran, and Kabul we established what could be called peacemaking offices. In the end, the offices were closed by Boutros-Ghali despite the protests of both the Iraqi and Iranian governments. Marrack Goulding, who succeeded Brian Urquhart as under secretary with responsibility for the Middle East, said that the real reason they had been closed was that they were known as "the Picco offices," which made the new secretary-general "uncomfortable" with them.

When Ambassador Samir Shihabi of Saudi Arabia was elected president of the General Assembly in 1991, it was a window of opportunity for me and my desire to get the word "peacemaking" into an official UN resolution. Ambassador Shihabi had been a good friend and supporter. He had always believed in me and my work. Samir understood the predicament and agreed to help. We needed a third plotter and found one in Nitya Pibolsoubggram, the Thai ambassador to the United Nations and another friend, who was then serving as chairman of the Special Political Committee. The plan was to slip the word "peacemaking" into a draft resolution the committee was debating. It did not matter where such a word appeared; the objective was simply to include it in a document on which the membership of the United Nations would vote. The deed was done with an incidental reference to "peacemaking" in the draft of a long resolution dealing with "peacekeeping"—the latter effectively becoming midwife to the former. Later, Samir made sure the resolution would sail through the General Assembly unchallenged. In early December 1991, fewer than twenty days before Pérez de Cuéllar left the United Nations at the end of his second term as secretary-general, the peacemaking work he had done was finally recognized by name.

But there was more to come. On January 30, 1992, during the first meeting of Security Council heads of state, perhaps the most solemn occasion in the history of that body, a declaration was adopted defining the new roles and functions of the United Nations and the secretary-general in the future. Among those major functions, peacemaking appeared in its own right in capital letters. The draft, originally prepared by the British, became one of the most important UN documents of the 1990s. My battle for peacemaking was over.

Cyprus was the first important test of our peacemaking efforts. The United Nations had first become involved in Cyprus in 1964, when peacekeeping troops were dispatched to restore calm after Turkish Cypriots reacted violently to constitutional changes engineered by Archbishop Makarios III, the Greek Cypriot leader. Ten years later, the island was physically divided after the Turkish Army intervened following a Greek Cypriot coup. Pérez de Cuéllar and Cyprus had a long mutual history dating back to 1974, when he had been president of the UN Security Council, and 1975, when Secretary-General Kurt Waldheim had named him special representative for the island. When he became secretary-general in 1982, everyone expected him to take a direct hand in helping to find a solution to the crisis. By that time, I had worked on the Cyprus case, on and off the island, for seven years. As I took up my new duties in his private office, it was clear that if experience, knowledge, and commitment meant anything, we were better positioned than anyone else to find a way through the fog of suspicion and animosity separating Greek and Turkish Cypriots. We could see the big picture. Cyprus would probably remain somewhat divided geographically, but its constitutional structure needed to reflect a unitary state. The hard part would be finding a formula to achieve this without one side or the other considering itself a loser.

The gap between the two sides was then, and is now, enormous. For Turkish Cypriots, the "motherland" is sixty seconds away by jet fighter and is a big political and economic supporter. For Greek Cypriots, the motherland is five hundred miles away and less well off economically. Greece is a member of the European Union; Turkey is not and resents its exclusion. But Turkey has more clout in international affairs as the southern bulwark of NATO during the Cold War and the frontline state neighboring Iraq and Iran today, and having a military "entente" with Israel.

Negotiations, when they finally began, would take place on two tracks. The principal officials in the Office of Special Political Affairs were conducting their regular discussions, overseeing the UN force in Cyprus, issuing political guidelines, and generally doing business as usual. Separately, the secretary-general's private office worked to develop new ideas and proposals that, we hoped, might point to a solution to the overall problem. We kept one set of files that we shared in meetings with the entire team. But access to files on the confidential plans, trips, and meetings I held with the Greek Cypriots and the Turkish government was strictly limited to Pérez de Cuéllar and my assistant, Judith Karam. The Office of Special Political Affairs realized something was amiss, and Brian Urquhart, who ran the office, took it up with the secretary-general. He didn't get much satisfaction.

We were, in fact, taking an unconventional approach. Standard diplomacy called for negotiations with representatives of the two communities on the island, with their national benefactors in the background. But Turkey was much closer to the emotional fault line in Cyprus than Greece was. So in 1984, we conceived a very undiplomatic plan to strike a deal—but not with Rauf Denktash, the leader of the Turkish Cypriots. Instead, we went after the president of Turkey, General Kenan Evren. Denktash had always played domestic politics in Ankara to his favor. However, with a general now holding the presidency, we thought we could bypass Denktash and go to the Turkish capital. Our objective was to strike a deal directly with Ankara, then "convince" Denktash to accept it. We hoped we could use an intermediary, Turkish General Ertugrul Saltik, to negotiate with Evren. I had met him years earlier and knew he had been part of the military coup that had brought the army to power in 1980. He had since been placed in charge of the Turkish Army in the Aegean, was rumored to be the next chief of staff, and was even said to be a possible successor to Evren some day. If anyone could get the word to Evren and speak with authority for the military junta, it was Saltik. We arranged a meeting between him and Pérez de Cuéllar.

Saltik listened to our suggestions but said he needed time to consult his government, which we understood to mean President Evren. For a variety of reasons, however, communication through Saltik proved to be too slow. We needed another channel. Fortunately, I found one. Tugay Uluçevik, a Turkish diplomat I had befriended when I was posted in Cyprus, had risen in the Foreign Ministry over the years and was much more involved now at the decision-making level. He was also the son of an important general in the Turkish Army who before his death had been a close friend of Evren. With Pérez de Cuéllar's permission, I began a series of negotiations with him in the autumn of 1984; he would fly to

New York from Ankara, and we would talk in the privacy of my home over the weekends. The contents of our discussions were relayed directly to the president. Simultaneously, I was maintaining a secret dialogue with Ambassador Andreas Mavrommatis of Cyprus, mostly in Geneva. Once the groundwork was laid, the idea was to convene a summit meeting between the leaders of the Greek and Turkish Cypriot communities to discuss all the other details and, we hoped, reach an agreement.

By the end of November, General Evren had accepted the proposal. It called for a geographical division of Cyprus along these percentages: a bit more than 29 percent for the Turks, a bit less than 71 percent for the Greeks. The Turks would agree not to lay claim to the presidency, but there were many constitutional protections of their interests. The formula became known as "the 29 percent–plus."

From December onward, I met several times with Mavrommatis without ever getting a clear-cut indication that Greek Cypriot President Spyros Kyprianou would accept the deal. Still, we were reasonably optimistic—and in any event, now that Evren had bought in, we had to move quickly or risk a leak that would almost surely bomb everything. A meeting was convened on January 17, 1985. In his memoir, *Pilgrimage for Peace,* Pérez de Cuéllar noted, "I had reached the conclusion that enough progress had been made to justify the convening of a high-level meeting of the two sides." That conclusion was based largely on my conversations with Mavrommatis. I was wrong.

The two Cypriot leaders finally sat face-to-face in the presence of the secretary-general, in what was referred to as the Security Council Consultation Room in New York. Things didn't go well; in fact, they didn't go at all. Kyprianou did not clearly indicate that he was accepting the plan, which put Denktash in the comfortable position of not having to respond. Denktash was obviously upset that the operation had been planned without his knowledge and was delighted that Kyprianou had effectively refused to play.

In one of the first breaks during the meeting, Denktash asked me to join him alone in a small room that adjoins the Security Council Hall and serves as the secretary-general's office when he attends Council meetings. He closed the door and let me have it with both barrels: "You tried to go around me, Picco, and you almost succeeded, but the person that will make me sign an agreement on Cyprus is not born yet." We had known each other for many years, and he had defended the Turkish

Cypriot community with determination and courage. Denktash never budged from his vision of an independent state, despite the cost to his people. His ability to work the levers of Turkish domestic politics made him extremely popular and impossible for the Turkish Cypriot opposition to unseat or the government in Ankara to undermine. He believed that eventually the world would recognize him; he once reminded me that even East Germany had been recognized after twenty years. But twenty years after the Turkish invasion he was still there, and his people still had no recognized passports.

Cyprus was a failure, and I was partly to blame. I told Pérez de Cuéllar that perhaps it would be best if he took me off the case, which would also provide him with some political cover from those critical of our handling of the Cyprus affair. He agreed. I had miscalculated, and I had to pay the price. It was time to move on to other things.

CHAPTER 4

The Soviet Union and Iran

Unwitting Midwives for a New United Nations

FOR MOST PEOPLE, THE FALL OF THE BERLIN WALL in 1989 defined the end of the Cold War. But at the United Nations, we had been reaping the benefits of the new era for three years. The Soviets considered the United Nations a tool of the West, or so went the rhetoric, and Nikita Khrushchev had even suggested once that the organization have three secretaries-general—one from the East and the Warsaw Pact, one from the West and NATO, and one from the Third World. But by 1986, Mikhail Gorbachev had signaled that he not only intended to cooperate with one secretary-general but also to support greater authority for him. With Soviet cooperation, Pérez de Cuéllar even tried to organize a peace conference on the Middle East—long considered off-limits to the United Nations—using the Security Council's five permanent members (the United States, USSR, Britain, France, and China) as the initial vehicle. In the end, it didn't fly; there would be no Ralph Bunche of the mid-1980s.

Still, we couldn't help but feel that events were moving in our favor. I was working on Afghanistan and the Iran-Iraq war. My colleagues in Pérez de Cuéllar's private office were focused on other international trouble spots, such as Namibia, Western Sahara, and El Salvador. We were the secretary-general's commandos, working in small teams or alone, avoiding publicity that would only embarrass our clients and harden their positions. We were not in the business of upstaging governments on the front page of *The New York Times*. Our diplomacy was based on the Charter's principles of self-determination and nonaggression, and our objective was to come up with win-win solutions, except in cases where nations had blatantly violated international law. Mahatma Gandhi said that an eye for an eye leaves everyone blind. It's a brilliant formulation, an almost perfect combination of morality and realpolitik. It's how we wanted to play the game.

Pérez de Cuéllar's first meeting with Gorbachev in March 1985, on the occasion of his predecessor's funeral, had gone well. But it would be more than two years before they would meet in Moscow again in an official capacity. That trip, in June 1987, was worth the wait.

We had visited Moscow many times over the years to discuss Afghanistan-related issues with the Soviets, particularly Foreign Minister Andrei Gromyko, and we were put up in familiar surroundings—a villa in the Lenin Hills near Moscow University. Many of the villas in this particular neighborhood were actually the homes of past Communist leaders and were similar in appearance and surrounded by small parks; they were now used to house visiting dignitaries and host official receptions. Ours, for example, had been Khrushchev's residence in the 1950s. My room, usually the same on every visit, was one flight above the ground floor and was decorated with heavy furniture and curtains, dark carpets, and other furnishings that suggested a merchant family from czarist days. The secretary-general was on the same floor, occupying a suite with an adjoining reception room. The rooms were quite large and equipped with telephones, which we assumed were bugged.

The ground floor included the kitchen, reception rooms, two sitting rooms, and a couple of television sets. I spoke no Russian, so watching TV was hardly an edifying experience; even so, there were enough spectacle and beauty in some of the fare—poetry recitals, for example—that I sometimes enjoyed watching anyway. I also went jogging, uphill at the beginning of the run, downhill at the end, usually about forty minutes round-trip. It was pleasant exercise: the Lenin Hills provide a beautiful panoramic view of Moscow that includes one of the five wedding-cake skyscrapers built by Stalin in the 1930s. The huge, identical buildings were meant as a visible challenge to American urban architecture—a signal that in Stalin's Russia, size mattered.

By then the Russians were used to us. During my first visit, I had surprised them by leaving the compound early in the morning to run, but since the entire area was controlled by Soviet security forces, there were no problems. At the top of the hill, there was a small church. One morning, I entered the church and saw two old women lit by some candles, the only illumination in the place. It struck me as a scene out of old Mother Russia, hard to square with its location just walking distance from a compound built for the Communist elite. When I returned from my runs, I would have breakfast with the Soviet officials who were to accompany us during the day. These were not Continental breakfasts but tremendous affairs consisting of a variety of meats, fish, cheeses, tarts, breads and cookies, fruit juices, milk, coffee, and tea.

When Pérez de Cuéllar and I met with Gorbachev, he was accompanied by his foreign minister, Eduard Shevardnadze, and his gatekeeper, Anatoly Chernayev, a party man who never spoke. It was an intimate meeting by Soviet standards—in fact, by any standard of diplomacy. And in a welcome departure from any previous meeting between a UN secretary-general and a Soviet leader, we actually had an agenda that had been detailed in advance. (In the past, Soviet leaders had not considered the UN secretary-general important enough for substantive discussions and would meet with him only as a matter of protocol.) I felt twice blessed: the agenda was focused on my special areas—the Iran-Iraq war, Afghanistan, and the Middle East—and I was about to meet a world leader who had already become a legend.

The venue also represented a fundamental change in attitude. Gromyko had preferred to meet in the magnificent Kremlin rooms evoking the power of imperial Russia. Meetings with him, however, had been predictable and boring; it's very hard to muster enthusiasm for the work when all you hear is rote reading of prepared texts. Gromyko wouldn't stick his neck out, not even a millimeter.

Gorbachev, in contrast, had chosen a modest room. He had his briefing papers open before him when we arrived. He greeted us, then closed the files and pushed them aside. "Let's get down to business," he said. "You are here to discuss three subjects, but first I want to tell you something about my vision of the world as we see it from here."

Our meeting lasted three and a half hours. Gorbachev began with a half-hour presentation of his views of the United Nations and of the state of international affairs. In previous conversations with Soviet leaders, the emphasis had always been on the Soviet Union itself, that huge country spanning eleven time zones and evoking the classic images of fear, power, revolution, and military might. Now the new man in the Kremlin was evoking a much wider world—a community of nations he wanted his country to join.

"We are a player in this world, one of many," he told us. "The UN until now has not been seen as very useful, and at times as an enemy. I will change that, because the UN will become part of our foreign policy. We have no intention of having enemies but rather of working with others." The Soviet Union, he insisted, wanted to strengthen the role of the secretary-general.

The vision for a new United Nations had come first from Pérez de Cuéllar himself. Western leaders had largely ignored the United Nations or sniffed imperiously at its claims to relevance in what was, after all, a bipolar world. Now the leader of a superpower was giving that vision legitimacy. If he were on board, the relationship between East and West was bound to change—and part of the change would take place through the United Nations because Gorbachev wanted it that way. He knew that after decades of Kremlin demonizing of enemies beyond the Soviet Union's borders, it would be easier for the Soviet people to swallow less aggressive relations with the rest of the world if change came through the United Nations rather than through traditional diplomacy in Washington, London, Paris, and Bonn. "I have to convince a nation to change," he said. Lip service would give way to genuine support for the United Nations and, under its umbrella, to cooperation with Western member nations.

On the specifics, he made clear what was to come. He had decided to withdraw from Afghanistan within the framework of the UN negotiations. He had no love for Iran and its Islamic revolution and said it was the United Nations' proper role, working with the major powers, to end its war with Iraq, a country with strong military and economic ties to Moscow. (Less than two months later, the Soviets would join the West in calling for a cease-fire.)

When the meeting was over, he took Pérez de Cuéllar by the arm in a gesture of friendship and escorted him out of the room—something highly unusual for a Soviet leader. Pérez de Cuéllar was also to see other signs of change in the leadership. Shevardnadze, for instance, invited the secretary-general to a genuinely informal dinner at his home that featured Georgian music, cognac, vodka, and artists—and no politics. But it was Mikhail Gorbachev who was the agent of change, and the world would soon be a much different place because of forces he set into motion.

Pérez de Cuéllar and I met with Gorbachev for the last time in January 1990. The Berlin Wall had fallen, and the Soviet leader was mindful of the tidal forces sweeping East that had brought it down. For seventy years, he said, the Soviet people—indeed, all the people in the Soviet Union's vast continental empire—had been fed with promises that had never been kept. "I also have given promises to my people, and I need two more years to start fulfilling them," he told us, "but I do not believe I have two more years." He was right: in August 1991, Mikhail S. Gorbachev was out.

The Iran-Iraq war was the first major conflict since World War II in which the two superpowers found themselves on the same side. Moscow had long-standing military ties to Iraq, and, perhaps more important, it was deeply concerned about an Islamic revolution taking place in a country on its southern border, particularly one that had just outlawed the Communist Party. The United States, of course, was tilting heavily toward Iraq after the debacle at its embassy in Teheran. By the end of 1982, only two years into a war that would not end until 1988, only China among the permanent members of the UN Security Council—the "Perm Five"—was on the fence. The other four had sided with Iraq. It would have been difficult to imagine the stars more favorably aligned for an activist UN secretary-general, and Pérez de Cuéllar wasn't going to miss the opportunity. His public demeanor—that of a courtly, bespectacled statesman who seemed to choose his words with great care—may have suggested the image of a reluctant diplomat. But it wasn't the complete picture. What was hidden from sight was a mind that embraced innovation and a heart that accepted risk and private—though not public—confrontation if that was the price of peacemaking.

By early 1987, he was calling on the Security Council to reach a meeting of the minds on the conflict. For six years, they had worked together, trying to come up with a formula in sync with what they thought the two belligerents wanted. Now, Pérez de Cuéllar told them, the time had come to tell the two sides what the international community wanted and to give the decision some teeth. The Iran-Iraq war was so far outside the usual reference points framed by the Cold War that it had no real precedent—and that made it easier for Pérez de Cuéllar and his team to conduct innovative diplomacy. Indeed, we hoped to parlay the success in grouping the Perm Five together on the Iran-Iraq war into a similar initiative for the Palestinian-Israeli conflict. The second part of the equation, it turned out, was not to be. The innovation was to group the five permanent members, something that had never occurred before.

Resolution 598, calling for an Iran-Iraq cease-fire and stipulating what would be required of the warring countries, was adopted by the UN Security Council on July 20, 1987. As we will see, some remarkable events occurred in the thirteen months before Iran and Iraq finally agreed to furl their flags and call it quits on the battlefield, and I was privileged to be at the center of them. But Resolution 598 was critical, and while it was the fifteen-member Council that did the voting, the document really belonged to Pérez de Cuéllar. It was a mark of how far he had come in reshaping the office of UN secretary-general and where he wanted to go. His office had become a credible force in the affairs of nations.

A symbolic measure of the new reality took place barely two months after the Security Council vote on 598. The secretary-general had taken to hosting the foreign ministers of the Perm Five at a private luncheon in his conference room every fall, early in the new session of the UN General Assembly. This wasn't so easy, given the room's modest dimensions—roughly fifteen by twenty feet. Nonetheless, on September 25, 1987, Pérez de Cuéllar squeezed five foreign ministers, five ambassadors, three interpreters (for the Russian, Chinese, and French ministers), and nine members of the Secretariat around a single table. It was quite a sight: here were some of the most powerful men in the world, squeezed in so tightly at table that they seemed to move like robots able only to move their arms from the elbow up. When I was a child, my training in table manners included wrapping a napkin around my middle and holding it in place throughout the meal by pressing it against my sides with both elbows. If I relaxed one elbow, the napkin would fall and I would be reprimanded. This time it didn't matter. I was a note taker and didn't have much time to eat.

The principal subject at this "unity lunch," as it was called, was how to maintain a solid front and end the Iran-Iraq war. A discussion of sanctions against Iran if it persisted in its refusal to accept the Security Council's resolution demonstrated both the possibilities and the pitfalls of the new era. The Soviet Union, China, and France claimed that sanctions were premature, but the Five were in concert on the key point: they wanted the secretary-general to continue to negotiate with the two countries, and they were prepared to give him a very long leash. In effect, Pérez de Cuéllar was on his own.

U.S. Secretary of State George Shultz was the dominant figure. Years earlier, Jeane Kirkpatrick, as American ambassador, had been openly contemptuous of the United Nations; her successor, General Vernon Walters, had supported the United Nations and become a major player in its activities. Now here was the man in charge of U.S. foreign policy—backed fully by Soviet Foreign Minister Eduard Shevardnadze—telling us to move ahead and not bother him with details and requests for further guidance. "This lunch has been very useful, and it would be a good idea to repeat it on a regular basis," Shultz said. "Furthermore, the secretary-general should not hesitate to call the five foreign ministers together as and when the need arises." The United Nations, Shultz was saying, was important enough for the secretary-general to convene the Perm Five on his own initiative. After years of disregard and insults directed at the United Nations by the superpowers, the unity lunch was a great victory for Pérez de Cuéllar, confirming the secretary-general's larger political role. It was time to seize the moment, and we did.

CHAPTER 5

A Different Kind of Diplomat

T HE LONG WAR BETWEEN IRAN AND IRAQ started in 1980, and it would be eight years before the bloody conflict came to an end. By 1988, I was the head of the task force assigned to negotiate the cease-fire agreement. The United Nations' role as a peacemaker in the Iran-Iraq war was a defining moment for the organization—and the most important achievement of my time serving the United Nations.

It was a conflict outside the East-West pattern of the Cold War. Eventually, both East and West supported the Iraqi side in every imaginable way: militarily, politically, economically. Baghdad received similar assistance from neighboring Arab countries. The reason for the unprecedented alignment behind Iraq was the near-universal desire to contain the Iranian revolution and the spread of political Islam to other parts of the region. But the legal justification for the war was something else: Saddam Hussein's denunciation of the Treaty of Algiers, signed in 1975 by the shah of Iran and Saddam himself. That treaty had established the border between the two countries along the Thalweg Line—right down the center of the Shatt-al-Arab navigable waterway.

Saddam's timing was astute: he aimed to take advantage of a young, unsecured revolutionary regime in Teheran and perhaps even to provoke its collapse. Ayatollah Ruhollah Khomeini had taken over Iran only eighteen months before Iraqi mechanized divisions entered Iranian territory. The revolution was still in chaos: in September 1980, Iran was as much at war with itself as it was with Iraq as clerics and leftist forces struggled for primacy. It would take another year before the country regained some semblance of stability, but not before a campaign of murder, assassination, and internal bombing by the leftist muhajideen Khalq, which had a different kind of revolution in mind. The bombing victims included Mohammed Behesti, secretary-general of the Islamic Revolutionary Party; the prime minister, Ali Raja'i; four cabinet ministers; and eighty others.

In the first few months of the war, Iraqi forces would conquer and occupy more than four thousand square miles of Iranian land. At the same time, the "Mobile Units of the Wrath of God," a strong street militia, were roaming the streets of towns and cities all over Iran to fight the opponents of the Ayatollah Khomeini. As 1981 began to unfold and lengthen, the Khomeini regime was beginning to consolidate its power. By the end of the year, the leader of the muhajideen, Musad Rajavi, and former president Bani Sadr had fled to Paris. And in 1982, the Tudeh (Communist) Party had been eliminated. But if the early chaos had given Iraq an opening to press the military advantage, Khomeini's renewed strength may have had the opposite effect. By the end of 1981, Saddam's forces occupied no more than two hundred square miles of Iran.

It took five days for the international community to react to the war raging between the two countries. No member of the Security Council wanted to raise the issue, preferring to believe that the conflict posed little or no threat to peace and security. Secretary-General Waldheim finally took the initiative and called a meeting of the Council on September 28, 1980. The response was in character for the times: a resolution was adopted calling for a cease-fire, but it crucially failed to demand a withdrawal of Iraqi troops to their borders. Soon enough, the world would begin to realize that this was not going to be a short war.

Eventually, this would become my war—but not for a while. Olof Palme, the former prime minister of Sweden, became Secretary-General Waldheim's envoy for the war, and Pérez de Cuéllar retained him when he took over at the United Nations in 1982. Palme's initial efforts were promising. He established personal contact with Behesti, a major figure of the revolution and a unique asset: when Palme visited him, they could converse in German, cutting their aides out of the conversation—a highly unusual step for a leader of an infant revolution. Indeed, one-on-one meetings with foreigners are considered blasphemous by most revolutionaries and authoritarian regimes. But the connection was not to last: Behesti was killed in the bomb blast in June 1981. But Palme's work continued, later focusing on freeing the many ships trapped by the war in the Shatt-al-Arab.

My first trip to Iran, in 1983, was with Diego Cordovez and had to do with another war, the one in Afghanistan. Teheran had taken a strong anti-Soviet position on the conflict, backing some of the Afghan Shiites and others in their struggle against the Communist regime. It was a textbook case for the Islamic revolution, with East and West fighting a proxy war at the expense of the local population. Teheran accordingly refused to take part in negotiations; it did agree to be kept informed, which is why we were there.

When we arrived, we were taken to the former Hilton Hotel, now the Esteghlal (Independence), in the hilly northern part of town, which had always been a fashionable district. The rooms still bore the signs of the revolution: Bullet holes pocked the walls and the balcony glass, and the carpeting was frayed and worn, as if trampled by army boots. Just inside the entrance, a huge American flag had been laid over the foyer floor, then covered in transparent plastic, making it impossible to go into the hotel without walking over the Stars and Stripes. New management had replaced some of the longtime employees, though several still remained from the old days, trying their best to carry on with some dignity despite their frayed uniforms, missing buttons, and wrinkled appearance. Verses from the Koran covered walls in the corridors.

Nobody in Teheran joked or even smiled. Humor appeared to have been banned by the revolution, or at least by Iran's state of war. Something else was missing, and after a couple of days that first time, it dawned on me: there were no colors. The streets were full of men and women wearing black, dark brown, or dark blue—no reds or yellows or greens. And music—not a note to be heard, another concession to the revolution's strictures. I'm a bit tone-deaf, but music has always been a part of my daily life and its absence was jarring. Even my morning runs proved to be a trial in Teheran's hot, muggy weather since revolutionary modesty demanded trousers and long sleeves, not the shorts and T-shirts I would have preferred.

Our trip was an exploratory visit, with not much at stake in political terms—an opportunity to learn as much as we could about a country that had undergone a significant transformation. Our education came in some unusual ways. We asked, for example, to see the Treasure of the Shah, not knowing exactly how our hosts would respond. They agreed with no reluctance at all. The Treasure was kept in a small room in the basement of one of the palaces in central Teheran, behind three bolted metal doors. A different group of guards belonging to different command forces held the keys for each door. No single institution controlled total access. This arrangement, I later learned, reflected the workings of postrevolutionary society—different centers of power that might or might not coincide with the political authorities' agendas. Individuals and even government officials felt an allegiance to their own religious centers, making for overlapping jurisdictions and a kind of de facto system of checks and balances.

It was the shah's treasure room that formed the most indelible memory of that visit, and not just because of what it contained: buckets of rubies, emeralds, and diamonds, and draperies woven entirely from thousands of natural Persian Gulf pearls instead of silk. What impressed me was that everything appeared untouched and was displayed to us proudly as the national treasure of Iran and its people. Even though the Islamic revolution had overthrown the shah, the new regime still had national pride in his wealth and his achievements. In retrospect, it made sense: the Iranians, after all, were fighting a war against Iraq to retain a border agreement signed by the shah himself.

On that first trip I met several people whose lives would intersect with mine over the years ahead. Ardebili Kazempour was a deputy foreign minister in his mid-thirties, educated in America and always with some kind of deal in mind. Javad Larajani, another deputy in the Foreign Ministry also educated in the West, was a mathematician turned diplomat turned politician. I began to find it easy to speak openly with these Iranian diplomats who had been educated in the West and who had an intellectual agility that derived from their training in mathematics and semantics. There seemed no need for the mediating language of our profession: they knew what I was saying, and I understood their difficulty in making decisions in a revolutionary climate. They were navigating between sophistry and semantics, which made dealing with them at once a pleasure and a challenge. They would not deal with the Security Council because they thought its members were biased against them. But they could expect little else from the members of the Council after violating the norms of international behavior by holding members of the U.S. Embassy hostage for more than a year.

Between 1982 and 1985, Olof Palme devised a number of plans that took into account the aspirations to end the war in full, as well as less ambitious steps such as limiting the effects of the conflict on merchant navigation in the Persian Gulf. For the most part, these plans and ideas were a product of the fertile mind of former Pakistani diplomat Iqbal Riza, then a UN Secretariat staff member working with Palme. Riza was a sophisticated connoisseur of the culture, religion, and history of Iran and other countries in the region. He also brought fine political instincts and high moral standards to his work, which included three major initiatives that probably helped save thousands of lives.

One involved prisoners of war. Like a vast Homeric struggle, the military balance in the Iran-Iraq war shifted back and forth during its eight years of bloodshed. From 1982 to 1984, it had tilted in Iran's favor: Iraq was reeling, perhaps even willing to sue for peace, and Teheran was declaring its readiness to enter Baghdad. Iranian forces were already in Iraqi territory, and Iran held many prisoners of war. (The number would exceed forty thousand by war's end.) Baghdad was complaining that its captured soldiers were being subjected to political indoctrination; those who refused to go along were mistreated, the Iraqis said. Iran was behaving with all the callous arrogance of a victor—and between 1983 and 1985, its authorities banned the International Committee of the Red Cross from visiting Iraqi POWs. The UN secretary-general, through Iqbal Riza, stepped in to fill the vacuum. Under the UN flag, Riza visited several POW camps and almost certainly prevented the situation from deteriorating any further.

He also intervened in the "war of the cities." As the intensity of the war grew, the two sides had begun to launch missile attacks at each other's capitals. The military consequences of these attacks weren't terribly significant, but the missiles killed civilians and had a serious psychological impact on the population, especially in Teheran. Riza managed to negotiate a missile cease-fire, and in June 1984, Pérez de Cuéllar was able to announce a truce in the war of the cities.

Most important, the secretary-general put the prestige of his office on the line to call attention to the use of weapons that were outside the laws of war. The Geneva Convention of 1925 had banned the use of chemical weapons, a response to their use in World War I, and no country had yet violated that proscription, not even Nazi Germany, which had found other inhuman methods for killing on a massive scale. But in 1983, reports from the battlefield suggested that the Iraqis were on the run and had decided to use whatever means were available to repel the

Iranian "invasion." Saddam Hussein, it was said, had used chemical weapons on the Iranians and even on his own people—on Iraqi Kurds, who were considered disloyal to the regime in Baghdad. But with the West and the Soviet Union politically united against Iran, if not enthusiastically pro-Iraqi, the Security Council was silent until Pérez de Cuéllar brought up the issue. It was his office, with Riza as its moral voice, that organized and sent investigative teams to the battlefront and that would issue reports on chemical weapons once or twice each year for the remainder of the war. The use of poison gas stopped, at least temporarily.

The three diplomatic initiatives of Iqbal Riza, undertaken at Pérez de Cuéllar's behest, appeared to be at odds with the Security Council's timidity in dealing with the war. Teheran now saw the secretary-general as a presence separate and apart from the Security Council, a presence more understanding of the Iranian predicament. The Iranians had first encountered a UN secretary-general when Kurt Waldheim had arrived in 1981 with a brief from Washington to win the freedom of the U.S. Embassy hostages. It had been a dramatic visit, but Waldheim had still been perceived as doing America's bidding. Pérez de Cuéllar, however, had taken up the case of chemical weapons when nobody else seemed to care because the victims were Iranian. Iqbal Riza and the secretary-general had helped secure a truce in the war of the cities. Indeed, in a world of nations they saw as almost uniformly hostile to their interests, the Iranians considered Pérez de Cuéllar the one official anywhere who was willing to listen to their position. At that point, I began to be more directly involved in working on ways to end the Iran-Iraq war.

In March 1985, Pérez de Cuéllar visited the Gulf on a trip designed to sound out the belligerents on a comprehensive plan to end the war. Despite Iran's growing belief in the secretary-general's credibility, we knew its leaders would not happily pull up a chair to a peace table. At the time, Iran seemed to be winning the war and using it to strengthen the revolution. And for Teheran, peace was beside the point; what it really wanted was "justice"—in this case, an admission by Iraq that it had wrongly started the war. In the Zoroastrian philosophy of ancient Persia that had preceded Islam, justice had always been more important than peace; even in the revolutionary Iran of the mid-1980s, the principle had staying power.

The Iranians, in short, were reluctant to set an agenda in advance, since it would include discussing the end of the war. The secretary-general, of course, could not agree to visit Teheran if it meant that talk about ending the war was off-limits. So we left without a stop in Iran locked up, hoping we could sort out the details when we got to the region. The first stop was Saudi Arabia.

Saddam Hussein had forged military, financial, and political alliances with various Western countries at various times, and he had a long-standing relationship with the Soviet Union, which supplied him with arms and intelligence information. But Baghdad also had two deep-pockets benefactors in the region—Kuwait and especially Saudi Arabia. In the context of the war, the Saudis, the principal guardians of the holy mosques in Mecca and Medina, saw the Iraqis as defenders of their country. The mullahs in Iran were challenging Saudi Arabia for the moral and political leadership of the region; Saddam may have been secular, but for the Saudis, he was the enemy of their enemy. The kingdom, by some accounts, provided Iraq with $60 billion during the war; Kuwait, it was believed, chipped in another $18 billion. Saddam would repay them both a few years later by invading one and threatening the other.

The VIP Pavilion at Riyadh airport seems an apt expression of the kingdom—wealthy beyond imagination and hospitable without limit. It is about the size of a football field, its cathedral-high ceiling shaped like a huge tent, its many corners and niches fitted with sofas, armchairs, and coffee tables. The Arabic coffee, served in tiny cups with no handles, is not black but transparent, the essence of coffee from cardamom. Simply raising an empty cup quickly brings a waiter to refill it. The low sofas require some training in proper etiquette. It is deemed improper in the Arab world, for instance, to sit in a way that displays the bottom of the shoes, which is considered an offense to one's host. Thus it's understandable why Arab robes, or thobes, are very long and flowing; underneath, one may assume a comfortable position without insult.

We carried with us Iqbal Riza's detailed plan, developed from one drawn up for Olof Palme, which set out a series of steps, each one designed to build confidence and lead to the end of the war by a certain date. We were trying to discover if either side was really willing to end the war. Iran had already declared itself, saying that the fighting could end only after the aggressor had been determined and blame had been fixed—publicly. Prince Saud al-Faisal, the Saudi foreign minister, reported that the Iraqis were prepared to discuss the question or turn it over to a committee. We at the United Nations had begun to discuss among ourselves subtle ways to finesse it. Did responsibility for the war, for example, mean responsibility for starting it or continuing it? An inquiry, stated in this way, would probably confirm that Iraq had started the war and that Iran had simply continued it. Indeed, the Saudis suggested that Iraq could be found responsible for starting the war and Iran for prolonging it. "The two countries do not seem to share the same responsibility for the continuation of the war," the prince said.

Saud al-Faisal, literally the most princely of princes, possessed an appealing mix of qualities; he was at turns the British gentleman who never utters a confrontational word and the Bedouin whose gracious behavior, compassion, hospitality, and personal dignity stem from a deep belief that all are equal before Allah. He was religious but not bigoted, proud but not arrogant; he conveyed a sense of authority rather than power. In his delicate way, he was saying that he was prepared to back a peace settlement, but not at the price being demanded by Ayatollah Khomeini— the removal of Saddam, whom the ayatollah did not consider a true Muslim. Saudi Arabia, said the prince, harbored no hard feelings against Iran, but its reasons for underwriting Saddam were clear: the Saudis had much more to lose from an Iraqi defeat than any other country in the region. In fact, the prince implied, they had so much at stake that they had become principals, not mere observers. When Pérez de Cuéllar offered the United Nations as a useful forum for both sides to save face, the prince responded, "Impartiality is not useful at this point. It may imply that the two countries are on the same footing." There was no real interlocutor in Iran who could guarantee anything. In Iran, he warned, any agreement could be overturned in the streets, which made the country impossible to deal with. Furthermore, the prince said, "the authorities in Teheran are afraid of a visit by the secretary-general. Such a visit would indicate to public opinion that the government was refusing peace. Public opinion is very important in Iran because virtually every family has been personally touched directly by the war."

In Qatar, a tiny oil-rich sheikdom where a hotel haircut cost $80 in 1985, we got word that the Iranian government was prepared to receive the secretary-general. The invitation was signed by the "authorities" in Iran, not by a single minister, which was a good sign. Reading from a text, the Iranian chargé added, "The secretary-general is a guardian of peace and should thus notify the Arab countries of his duty. We hope that during your visit to Iran you will acquaint yourself with the real facts, bearing in mind the responsibility assigned to you. We hope that your efforts will result in the restoration of the rights and security of the region. Your Excellency will clearly observe in Iran the bloodshed we have been victim to, and having said that we know that you will act with a better understanding in light of the responsibilities assigned to you. You will also observe that our people will rely on themselves when an international organization maintains continuous silence in front of aggression. The best way and the lasting way for acting to pursue an international achievement is the restoration of our rights."

As we interpreted it, they were not limiting the agenda.

We flew to Teheran aboard the plane of Sheikh Khalifa bin Hamad al-Thani, the emir of Qatar. It was a wide-bodied British jet, superbly appointed as a flying boardroom. The chairs were huge and thickly padded, upholstered in the Qatari national color, a dark Bordeaux, and were arranged around a heavy rosewood conference table.

This was Pérez de Cuéllar's first visit to Teheran, and we were put up at a hotel instead of a state guest house—an inauspicious signal of our status. Our first meeting, with Foreign Minister Ali Akhbar Velayati, reinforced the point. Velayati was a pediatrician by profession, a devoted family man and an ascetic Muslim who rose each day at 4:30 A.M. to say his prayers and study medical journals before going to his "day job." He was the public face of the Iranian revolution in the chanceries and capitals of the world, and his ties to Ayatollah Khomeini were strong. He was unfailingly courteous, soft-spoken, and well mannered, but his words on this occasion contained fire—a tirade against the Iraqi regime that accused Saddam of violating international laws left and right. "When agreements are signed, agreements are kept," he said in a pointed allusion to Saddam's repudiation of the 1975 Algiers agreement with Iran over the Shatt-al-Arab. We had expected this, and we would hear it time and time again in other discussions and negotiations.

We then met with Ali Khamanei, who had become president of Iran in 1981. A former student of Khomeini, he was a tall, thin man who always dressed impeccably in black and seemed anxious to project an image of supreme dignity, power, authority, and fear—important attributes to Shiites, who had been forced into hiding and considered heretics for centuries. Khamanei had lost the use of his right hand in

1981 during the bomb blast that had killed Prime Minister Raja'i. Our meeting was just as formal and dour as our host.

His first remark to Pérez de Cuéllar, a Peruvian, stressed the importance to Teheran of the arrival of a secretary-general from a Third World country. We realized the importance of our efforts thus far when he complained that although the United Nations was generally untrustworthy, exceptions included the secretary-general's decisions to investigate the use of chemical weapons and halt the bombing of civilians. Even so, attacks on civilian targets were crimes against humanity that had to be punished regardless of the outcome of the war; similarly, attacks on merchant shipping and the use of chemical weapons would have to be dealt with on their own and not be made part of any grand bargain to end the war. To start a war, to be an aggressor, was also a crime deserving punishment by itself. So much for our plan to trade off the wartime sins of both sides and tie them up in a tidy peace package.

"The Iraqi officials believed in the logic of force," Khamanei said. "They began the war because they wanted to abort the Iranian revolution. But a revolution cannot be aborted by a war. It can only be fed by it. Iraq did not take this into account when it began its aggression, but what is very serious is that the UN did not condemn this aggression. The secretary-general alone has shown himself to be serious in this regard. If the UN did not condemn this aggression, would it not have failed in its duty to the Charter?" We had been expecting this intransigence, but to receive a lecture about the UN Charter from a leading figure of the Iranian revolution was something of a surprise—and certainly a first for a secretary-general. Ardebili Kazempour, whom I had first met two years earlier, summarized the message in three words when he approached me after the meeting: "condemnation and reparations" were the conditions for Iran to end the war.

Pérez de Cuéllar had also gone to Teheran to meet for the first time with Hashemi Rafsanjani, the power broker in Iran as speaker of the Majlis, or Parliament, who later became president in 1989. The two men couldn't have been more different. The secretary-general was a product of European culture, a descendant of the Spanish elite, who had a taste for classical music and art; he was, in his own words, a "diplomat ad nauseam." Rafsanjani was the son of a merchant family that had made its fortune in pistachios, but he had been a devotee of Imam Khomeini since his student days in Qom in 1962 and the link between Iran and the ayatollah after Khomeini had been sent into exile in 1964. He had not himself been an ayatollah then, but he had been among the five men chosen personally by Khomeini to help him put the new regime together after the imam returned to Iran in 1979.

At their meeting, Rafsanjani wore a brown robe and a white turban, thus stating that he was not a descendant of the Prophet. His Mongol features made it impossible for him to grow a beard, a disadvantage in a country where a beard is a symbol of devotion and power. Yet one had the clear impression that despite the lack of a high religious title and, for that matter, a beard, he still had the power to make things happen. When he met us, he was smiling and spoke jovially, with none of the deliberately forbidding distance and formality of Khamanei. The atmosphere was friendly, and we knew our interlocutor was someone who felt secure enough and strong enough to hold his own in a meeting with a foreigner as distinguished as the secretary-general of the United Nations.

Pérez de Cuéllar first went into a private session with Rafsanjani. I was with the secretary-general as a note taker, and Rafsanjani was attended by Foreign Minister Velayati; Javad Larajani, whom I had met in 1983; and a translator. In fact, Cyrus Nasseri was a lot more than a mere translator. A diplomat who later became ambassador to Geneva, he had been educated in the United States and was one of the young "California boys" surrounding the speaker of the Majlis. Some in Washington suspected him of being one of the students who had taken over the U.S. Embassy in 1979. Over the years we had become friends, and whenever I raised the embassy question with him he always denied it categorically.

The two leaders began their meeting with some verbal sparring. Rafsanjani said that revolutions make the work of the United Nations more difficult, since they create new conditions. To this the secretary-general replied that the United Nations did not oppose revolutions if they signified a process of change for the better. "A revolutionary personality at the helm of the United Nations would help," Rafsanjani jabbed back. The secretary-general quickly had to regain his composure. "If revolutions solely meant development and justice, then I would be in favor of them every day," he replied.

Rafsanjani elaborated on the idea of the "imposed war," code to indicate that Iraq had started the war and that the world did not currently want it to come to an end. Then, picking up on a familiar theme we had just heard, he faced the secretary-general: "Iran cannot trust those who come as mediators and show no justice, those who want to pass judgment but do not accept the elementary reality that Iraq was the aggressor." Of all the dignitaries speaking out on the Iran-Iraq war, he added, only Pérez de Cuéllar had spoken the truth thus far.

The two men moved on to chemical weapons, with Rafsanjani acknowledging that they had terrified the Iranian troops. He then made a disclosure: "We possess more advanced facilities to produce chemical weapons, but we do not want to use them. We would not even do so if Iraq continued to use them." Velayati interrupted Rafsanjani to say that the Iranians did not even want to produce poison gas. But Rafsanjani just repeated that they did not want to use chemical weapons, leaving open the possibility that his country might have manufactured them. There was an important political distinction: although the ban on the use of chemical weapons went back to 1925, a more comprehensive ban on production had been agreed to only in the early 1980s.

Rafsanjani went on to insist that Iran would never be subdued by military might. He underlined his point by referring to a TV news clip that showed a bomb falling on Iranians at prayer in a mosque; after the explosion they had continued with their prayers. Iran had no claim on Iraqi territory, but Rafsanjani refused to buy our package without first trying to unwrap it: "The aggressor and the victim," he said, "cannot be treated equally." He wanted to proceed step-by-step, but he was also prepared to say that Iran wanted to end the war. I jotted down a proposed text and passed it to Larajani, who was sitting beside me. It included a public commitment by Iran to end the war. I pressed him several times after the meeting, stressing that they should put their pen where Rafsanjani's words were. Finally, after I had made myself a thorough nuisance, Larajani said, "What do you want me to do with this? Sign it? Fine, I will do it. Remember, I am also a professor of semantics. The interpretation of this text can be what it seems to say today and also the opposite of it tomorrow." There was no signature.

The encounter with Rafsanjani did not seem to have led anywhere, at least not this time. The Teheran government was prepared to discuss the violation of international laws by Iraq, including the convention forbidding the use of chemical weapons, the mistreatment of POWs, and the targeting of third-party civilian vessels. The eight-point plan, which included a step-by-step approach to ending the hostilities, had been put forward. The Iranians did not reject it outright, but, in their minds, it re-

mained incomplete because it did not designate Iraq as the party responsible for starting the war or discuss the issue of reparations. Still, the visit
had launched a working relationship between Pérez de Cuéllar and Rafsanjani that would yield dividends—both in helping to end the Iran-Iraq
war and in securing the release of the hostages in Lebanon. But these
things would come later. In 1985, nobody in Iran could afford to speak
of ending the war.

We flew back to Qatar, and Pérez de Cuéllar thanked the emir for his hospitality with a personal briefing on our trip to Teheran. Then it was on to
Baghdad. There were no smiles among our hosts at Baghdad airport nor,
for that matter, during our entire visit.

We were to be hosted at a guest house and meet first with Foreign
Minister Tariq Aziz, a Christian whom we knew well. This was both a
warm-up for the main event and a recognition of Pérez de Cuéllar's
standing: an official guest of lower rank would probably have to wait in
his hotel until summoned for his audience with the president. Saddam
Hussein was then, and still is, a fanatic about security, so the exact time
and place of any meeting with him are never revealed, even to the most
exalted visitors, until very close to the event. Even then, everything is ap-
proximate and always subject to change, with the guest learning the
venue for a meeting only while en route in the official motorcade. All this
does not reflect a concern for his guest's security or the niceties of protocol. What worries President Saddam Hussein is his own safety: assistants, secretaries, drivers, and miscellaneous staff could easily pass on
information about his whereabouts to "the enemy."

We were told only at 5:45 P.M. the day we arrived, April 8, that a
meeting with Saddam was scheduled for 7:25 P.M., which gave us little
time for our preparatory visit with Tariq Aziz. We traveled by car to the
Presidential Palace—actually, a Presidential Palace, since there are many of
them scattered throughout the country. To allay security concerns, we advised every member of the secretary-general's party to forgo a briefcase
and take only a notepad.

Once we entered the presidential compound, we drove through
what appeared to be several miles of empty streets before arriving at our
destination, a newly constructed building with honor guards standing

along the long corridor that led to the reception room where we would meet Saddam Hussein. There was no exchange of words, no noise of any kind. A protocol officer escorted us to a waiting room, where we stood for a few minutes before again heading down the corridor to the reception room. I was carrying a leather folder, a pen, and a pad. As we walked along the corridor, I deliberately dropped my notepad so the security men would see that there was nothing dangerous in my folder. Predictably, they rushed to pick it up before handing it back to me.

The president of Iraq stood relatively close to the door to receive his guests, greeting each one with formal courtesy and polite small talk. How was the trip? Are you comfortable in your accommodations? The formal salon was rectangular, measuring perhaps sixty by twenty-five feet. The seating was arranged with hierarchical precision. An Iraqi flag on a staff adorned a small desk behind the president's chair where his personal security guard would take up his station.

An interpreter sat in a small chair behind Saddam Hussein, a superb professional who translated questions back and forth in English, French, and Arabic almost as fast as his master's natural rate of speech. The conversation flowed as if the president were reading a speech, which he most definitely was not, and the interpreter spoke under Saddam's voice, carrying the most subtle of his modulations and emotions. I come from a veritable Tower of Babel, where interpretation in the United Nations' working languages is a daily occurrence, but I have rarely seen such a bravura performance. Unfortunately, the content did not quite match the eloquent presentation.

Saddam Hussein expressed full confidence in the United Nations, its secretary-general, and the Security Council's resolutions, all of which had been in his favor. Iraq wanted peace, he insisted, but peace was not possible because Iran was infected by the fatal disease of expansion. Neither the Iraqi people nor the international community could ever accept Iraq being swallowed by Iran to become an appendage of an empire under religious cover—which struck me as an acknowledgment by Saddam that defeat on the battlefield was not considered to be out of the question. He then accused Iran of interfering with Kuwait, attacking Bahrain, and, of course, trying to topple his regime "on the basis of divine will."

"I would expect that the secretary-general would not put pressure on Iraq to jeopardize its sovereignty," he declared, which meant he would not entertain a request for a cease-fire. He even raked over old slights, re-calling the telegram he had sent Ayatollah Khomeini to congratulate him on the success of his revolution. "The reply I received was very stiff," Saddam complained to us. "He used a form of address that in Islam is used only for infidels."

He then went on to say that when Bani Sadr had been president of Iran, he had sent three ambassadors to Teheran to ask the Iranian regime not to interfere with the Iraqi government. "Bani Sadr himself rejected those messengers and replied that the Iranians were prepared to reach Baghdad with their army." This was a new accusation against Bani Sadr, apparently Saddam's rather blunt attempt to justify further Baghdad's de-cision to strike first. He followed up by detailing all the Iranian border in-cursions and maritime attacks during the fortnight preceding the invasion of Iran.

"If you want to speak of who started the war, Secretary-General," he said, "these are my facts."

The origin of these skirmishes was by now lost in the fog of war; they could just as well have been provoked by Saddam Hussein to justify his mass attack of September 22, 1980. He stuck by his accusation that Iran had been the aggressor and the one to start the war, and now that he had regained what he had lost in the fighting, he was prepared to end the conflict. He was so concerned about a possible takeover of the southern part of Iraq that he was even prepared to accept an investigation of sorts into who was responsible for the war. He called for the withdrawal of both armies to the original borders, thus conceding the very point that had pushed him into the war in the first place. But Saddam Hussein, like Rafsanjani, did not accept the eight-point plan, which he felt was against his interests because it did not call, first and foremost, for an end to the fighting.

Saddam Hussein certainly did not look like a man who was losing, nor did his country. Although Baghdad was a capital at war in 1985, it was a bustling city with no signs of suffering. Iraq had a large middle class in those days, and petrodollars were still making it possible for ev-erybody to buy goods and services. The bazaar was crowded, and the gold market was bustling. We noticed little war-related damage. Security was extensive and absolute, and Saddam Hussein seemed to be in total control. There was a sense that once the president had made a decision and issued an order, the entire country would salute and march to it down to the last soldier. The chain of command was efficient and fast. If an order were by some chance not carried out, the reason would be not a weak link in the chain of command but rather a conscious decision to delay it. This was completely opposite to the way things worked in Iran—or, to be precise, the way they did not. In Iran, a high-level decision would be discussed later, and even a subordinate official could slow it down. Decision making was really a political tug-of-war.

Iraq and Iran also demonstrate differences in the way countries negotiate. In general, countries with a monolithic and very authoritarian structure maintain the same position in negotiations, immutable for a long period of time. Then, one day, they advocate a different position with the same bottom-line vehemence, insisting all the while that nothing has changed at all. The other side rarely sees it coming, but the change is incorporated into the entire apparatus of government within twenty-four hours as new instructions and orders flow down from the top of the pyramid. This was the Iraqi style, an echo, I thought, of the Turks from my Cyprus days and, for that matter, the pre-Gorbachev Soviet Union.

The Iranians seem to be the polar opposite (and they remind me, to some extent, of the Pakistanis and Greeks). When you start negotiating with them, you are led to believe they are reasonable, flexible, understanding, and ready to adjust their position. The problem is that the verbal dexterity they display is a mask to hide reality, which is a reluctance to change position and sometimes even a willingness to revisit what everyone thought was settled ground. They may be intellectually stimulating, but they're a bear to pin down.

Tariq Aziz did not speak during our meeting with Saddam—no surprise there—but met with the secretary-general the next morning to follow up. It turned out that Iraq was interested only in a full solution and was amenable to a number of ways of reaching it. Both sides could go before the Security Council (where Iraq was favored over Iran); the secretary-general could organize proximity talks; or there could be simultaneous negotiations to work out a complete solution in public and a step-by-step agreement in private. Iraq could not accept a partial solution.

The Iraqi foreign minister believed that if the Iranians wanted to settle, they would do it through the United Nations, and Iran felt likewise because the secretary-general had based his position on international law as opposed to the interest of nations. I found this an illuminating way of seeing the secretary-general's advantage over any state and even over the Security Council, which is after all the sum of many national interests. In short, the secretary-general had a particular value, compared with intergovernmental bodies or individual states, especially when both sides seemed to be groping for a middleman to unlock them from intractable positions.

Iqbal Riza and I had to comb through every single word of our notes from Teheran and Baghdad, compare them with the eight-point peace program, and see if it could be modified into a slightly different formula that we could sell as something new. The fact was that for the first time, Iraq had agreed—informally, to be sure—to an investigation into the causes of the war. If the investigation were to couple responsibility for the beginning of the war with responsibility for its continuation, both sides would come out on an equal footing. The task of the secretary-general was to take what people said at face value and try to work on it. That, and calling their bluffs, were two instruments we could use in our efforts. But Iran still wanted a sequential approach and Iraq wanted a comprehensive, "simultaneous" one.

At first blush, our initial trip to the Gulf seemed to yield little progress. What it did draw was a fair amount of skepticism within a UN bureaucracy not terribly enthralled with the new peacemaking role that the secretary-general was trying to create. But bureaucrats who hide behind their desks are often the first to launch missiles against change. It is one of the conundrums of life that those who know the most about something are often afraid of making decisions while those who may be less knowledgeable end up making the choices and taking the risks. That was certainly the case at the United Nations. I admired how much some of my colleagues knew about the Middle East, Lebanon, the Arabs, Islam, and Iran, and I wished I had known more. But their refusal to show any initiative was upsetting. Many of us in the secretary-general's office, including Iqbal Riza and myself, tried to see fresh opportunities in every situation. Others, including some of those with knowledge superior to my own, were mentally lazy, lacked ideas and political courage, and feared breaking precedent. In the end, our perseverance would prevail.

Late 1985 and 1986 were transition years in the Gulf. The war was spreading, with new attacks on civilian targets and merchant shipping. By the end of 1986, 180 merchant ships had been attacked and 100 seamen had been killed. "It is remarkable," the International Chamber of Shipping said that year, "that the death toll has not been greater, given the sophisticated modern weapons used in the attacks." Iranian troops were on Iraqi territory, taking over the Fao peninsula. The Iraqis had resumed the use of chemical weapons, but the Iranians had unleashed two major offensives with waves of new troops, perhaps the last round of fresh recruits. Iran wanted, in the words of Khomeini, to march into Baghdad and obtain the justice that the international community refused to deliver.

It would be the disruption in the flow of oil out of the Persian Gulf that would finally concentrate the minds, if not the hearts, of the global community on the Iran-Iraq war. Oil, shipping, and political-risk insurance rates started to take center stage. Meantime, the great supporters of Iraq in the Arab world, particularly Saudi Arabia, were beginning to wonder whether Iran could actually be defeated. By the late summer of 1986, Prince Saud al-Faisal, the Saudi foreign minister, asked Pérez de Cuéllar whether the Security Council perhaps should take a more balanced position on the conflict in an effort to get Iran to join negotiations to end it. At that point, though, we were still no closer to a solution. Moreover, the Iran-contra affair was now a political fact of life. As 1986 wore on, one word seemed to sum up almost everything having to do with the Gulf: pandemonium.

CHAPTER 6

The Iran-Iraq War

Securing the Peace

T HE BELIEF THAT IRAN COULD NOT BE BEATEN on the battlefield had grown stronger when it became clear that even chemical weapons could not stop its advances. In the fall of 1986, it moved Tariq Aziz, Saddam Hussein's foreign minister, to become a global road warrior, presenting Iraq everywhere he went as the one country fighting the good fight on behalf of a world threatened by fundamentalist Iran. When he met with Pérez de Cuéllar during this period, he talked about the possibility of Iraq's being split into two countries—one of them an Islamic republic in the south—if it did not receive further assistance from the West and other nations. "That is what the West has to realize, why Iraq needs to be helped," he told the secretary-general. "And if it means that we have to use all—and I mean all—kinds of weapons, we shall use them, no matter what the convention or what anybody says. We are fighting a war for you as well."

The concern was real and shared by many in the world. However, the Iraqi Shia—the majority of the population, even though Sunni Muslims were in charge—never indicated during the long war that they would side with the Iranian Army against their own countrymen. But there was little doubt that deep rifts in the family of Islam were manifest in the war. Iran's human waves were aimed at Basra, a major city in southern Iraq with a large Shiite population, and many of the offensives were nick-named "Karbala," after the town in Iraq where Imam Hussein, one of the major Shiite figures, had been killed. Hussein had been the son of Ali and Fatima, who was the daughter of the prophet Mohammed, and he had been expected to succeed the Prophet as the new leader of the Islamic world. The Shia believe that only descendants of the prophet Mohammed can govern the Muslim world; the Sunnis do not. The one group, the Shia, are determinists; the other, the Sunnis, accept a more secular view of society. Shi'ia means "partisan" in Arabic, and the partisans of Ali and Hussein—harassed by the Sunnis and others—went underground and developed their own form of Islam, living largely out of sight for centuries. They emerged, finally, with a keen sense of victimization, an acceptance of individual sacrifice, and a belief that justice is a more important concept than peace. Iran felt that Shiism had been victimized once again, this time by Iraqi aggression, and its Karbala attacks—separate and apart from their tactical value—had great symbolic importance.

Pérez de Cuéllar's position as a potential peacemaker, meanwhile, was improving. Moscow's new foreign policy under Gorbachev had vested more authority in the secretary-general's office, and the revelations of the Iran-contra affair had dramatically weakened Washington's credibility in the Middle East. Arab nations had believed the United States was behind Iraq, in deed and in spirit if not in open declaration, and the games played by Oliver North that had sent weapons to Iran were seen as a betrayal. In Pérez de Cuéllar's office, we thought that a single initiative by the secretary-general could amount to a political trifecta: we might rescue Washington from the humiliation of Iran-contra, test the new Soviet foreign policy, and unify the Security Council's Perm Five on a single political platform for the first time in UN history. It was a deceptively simple idea. The Five had never met in formal caucus because of the Cold War's imperatives. Pérez de Cuéllar aimed to change that and bring the Five together as one, at least on the issue of ending the Iran-Iraq war. Instead of asking the parties to the conflict what they would accept, the Five would come up with a unified position, signaling to the rest of the world that their collective position and will were behind an end to hostilities.

It's possible the idea first came from Sir Crispin Tickell, the British ambassador to the United Nations, who had arranged a dinner meeting of the Five at his residence in October 1986 to discuss the war. But it was Pérez de Cuéllar who gave it life when he called for a "meeting of the minds," which is how the effort became known in the months ahead. On January 16, 1987, the secretary-general met with the Perm Five and the president of the Security Council, who represented the rest of the body. It was the first time such a limited group had met together on any basis.

They were presented with the skeleton of what would become, six months later, the text of Resolution 598. For diplomacy's sake, the same meeting was repeated with the entire fifteen members of the Council a week later. The meeting took place in the conference room of Pérez de Cuéllar's office, leaving it up to historians and legal experts to define whether or not it could be considered an informal meeting of the Council. The secretary-general was on the way to becoming a significant political player.

Over the early months of 1987, the Perm Five ambassadors met every two weeks in New York, but their political counselors met even more frequently—and on some occasions I would join them. Within two months, the enterprise had gone public, and with it rumors that while the minds might be meeting, they were having trouble agreeing on anything. In fact, they *were* struggling with a critical question: What would happen if a resolution were adopted but not implemented by one of the warring parties? Would the Five be prepared to intervene militarily and adopt strict sanctions against the recalcitrant nation? Washington and London were answering yes, because they fully expected Iraq to accept the resolution and Iran to reject it. Moscow and Beijing leaned the other way.

Given the differing viewpoints, Pérez de Cuéllar had begun to worry that the entire approach might collapse, and he asked me to do what I could to keep the meetings alive. My solution wasn't diplomatic: I literally begged the Five to continue meeting, even if it were just to have coffee and even if they just agreed to disagree, so that the perception of unity would be maintained. They did, but five months after the call for a meeting of minds, the Perm Five had still not developed a common position. The war was not an abstraction. From January through May 1987, nearly fifty ships in the Gulf had been hit, including the USS *Stark*, an American frigate hit by an Iraqi Exocet missile in what could only be considered friendly fire. Kuwaiti ships had been reflagged: now American and Soviet colors flew on their decks in an operation designed to protect the flow of oil out of Gulf ports.

By June, Iran was still pressing its advantage on the battlefield, and an increasingly concerned Arab League formally informed the secretary-general that Iraq was prepared to accept an investigation of the start and continuation of the conflict. This was an open concession to Teheran, which had always insisted that the war had been started by Saddam Hussein with an act of aggression on September 22, 1980. The war would not end unless Iran's position became the world's position. On June 30, 1987, Washington finally conceded the obvious—that it would be all but impossible for Iraq to win the war short of an unimaginable bloodbath— with a White House statement calling for "an earliest possible negotiated end, leaving no victor and no vanquished." Having finessed the thorny question of military support and sanctions in the event one of the war- ring parties balked, the Perm Five meeting of minds had reached an agreement on what should come next.

Three weeks later, on July 20, 1987, the Security Council passed Res- olution 598, setting the endgame in motion. The resolution called for an immediate cease-fire and withdrawal of forces to "the internationally recognized boundaries," a UN observer team to verify the cease-fire and withdrawal, and prompt release and repatriation of POWs. Critically, it also called for the secretary-general "to explore, in consultation with Iran and Iraq, the question of entrusting an impartial body with inquiring into responsibility for the conflict and to report to the Security Council as soon as possible." As the Arab League had promised, Iraq immediately accepted the resolution. Iran did not—but it did not reject it either. We had a problem: It was fine for the Perm Five to find common ground, and it was fine for the full Security Council to pass Resolution 598. But it was all hot air if Iran refused to accept it.

The answer to this dilemma, we felt, was to start preparing what would become known as the "implementation plan." If a detailed plan to implement the resolution were drawn up and the two sides in fact im- plemented it, then any debate on whether Iran accepted Resolution 598 would be academic. What Pérez de Cuéllar did next was unprecedented in UN history: he took the "liberty" of writing down fourteen pages of what the resolution actually meant in operative terms—in effect, rewrit- ing a resolution of the UN Security Council so that it could be imple- mented sooner rather than later. Whether this exceeded his authority is an open question, but it was plainly the shortest route to the end of this long, bloody war and, in the twelve months of negotiations on the plan to follow, a way for the Perm Five to save face. Indeed, the Five would support, encourage, and defer to Pérez de Cuéllar over this period in a political ballet that redefined the relationship between the secretary- general and the Security Council. It was no longer a zero-sum game: the power of the former could increase the power of the latter, and vice versa.

We went through a series of acrobatics to bring Iran to the table, but it did not surprise me that the special envoy sent to consult with the secretary-general was none other than Javad Larajani, the master semanticist himself. Any negotiator who wants to ignore the text of a resolution and stall usually tries to trace a dispute back to the beginning of time. Larajani went through the "indispensable ingredients of the peace process." He said he was not really concerned about the "scripture of the resolution" but rather its philosophy. Then he declaimed, "The time of authoritative prophecies is past, and there can be no new Koran." He said that Iran was not rejecting the resolution outright because it contained some "positive elements" but at the same time insisted that Iran and Ayatollah Khomeini were not going to accept any resolution adopted by the major powers, especially the United States.

The Iranians wanted a cease-fire to be implemented, but not before a committee or some UN team was established to determine who was responsible for starting the war. The Iraqis, on the other hand, wanted a "sequential" implementation of the resolution, starting with a cease-fire as its first step. It was fairly easy for our implementation plan to accommodate these demands and allow them to start at the same time. We could certainly be flexible under the circumstances. The plan itself had never become an official document of the United Nations, yet the Security Council members referred to it in their official correspondence with the secretary-general. A nonexistent document, in effect, was the backbone of ongoing diplomatic negotiations.

As members of the Security Council tried to come up with a common position on an arms embargo in the event one side in the war didn't go along, Iran was beginning to move. In February 1988, Teheran indicated to Pérez de Cuéllar that its acceptance of his implementation plan was "tantamount" to its acceptance of Resolution 598. "Tantamount" was the word first chosen by Iran's ambassador to the United Nations, Mohammed Jafar Mahallati—"Amir" to his friends. The son and grandson of ayatollahs, Mahallati had been pushing for peace for some time but had avoided being purged, perhaps because his grandfather had been a teacher of the Ayatollah Khomeini. In the end, even that wouldn't be enough: Mahallati eventually lost his position and, a few years later, left Iran, although he never abandoned his country and his people.

Despite the signal to Pérez de Cuéllar and the efforts of people like Mahallati, there was still no political basis in Teheran to end the war.

Human-wave attacks by Iranian soldiers, who believed that martyrdom in battle brought direct ascent into Heaven, had captured 350 square miles of Iraqi territory. But the rising toll argued for a truce. The supply of young men on the streets of Teheran was finite, and Iran was running out of human cannon fodder. Meanwhile, the U.S. Navy had stabilized the situation in the Gulf itself, neutralizing Iran's navy, and missile attacks aimed at cities were slowing as supplies ran low.

Iran's occupation of the Fao peninsula also came to an end in April 1988—the Iraqis claiming they had removed the occupiers, the Iranians claiming they had left because they would not remain on land that was not theirs. A more plausible explanation, according to Western intelligence officials, was that Iraq simply gassed the Pasdarans, or Iran's Revolutionary Guards, then burned potentially damaging evidence.

Slowly and steadily in early 1988, the Iran-Iraq war was beginning to exhaust itself even as Baghdad was gaining the upper hand on the battlefield—a fact that engendered a certain ambivalence among the Perm Five. They had, after all, backed Iraq as the line in the sand against Iranian fundamentalism, and now their support was paying off just as a deal ending the war seemed in prospect. What to do? Individual states might want to press for victory, but that might prove risky in the court of international public opinion. Our goal was to end the fighting—without victor or vanquished if possible. At that point, Pérez de Cuéllar's implementation plan was keeping everyone afloat, and everyone knew it. The answer to the question of what to do, then, was almost preordained: let the secretary-general handle it. One by one in the late spring of 1988, the Perm Five ambassadors told Pérez de Cuéllar to "do what you think is right."

We kept negotiations alive by discussing the secretary-general's implementation plan and tried to bridge the gap between Iran and Iraq one inch at a time. Resolution 598 was an official Security Council document, of course, but the implementation plan was a creative work in progress—a set of proposals on how to put Resolution 598 into action that took poetic license with the resolution's language. "Pérez de Cuéllar was using his authority as Secretary General to modify the rules of the game for Security Council negotiations," wrote American diplomat Cameron Hume in his book *The United Nations: Iran and Iraq, How Peacemaking Changed.*

We devised a process that would pivot on what we called "D-day"—the day hostilities would end. D-day plus so many days would mark the exchange of prisoners; plus so many more days, the establishment of the impartial body; plus another several more, the start of negotiations on the border; and so on. We dissected each item and positioned every specific move on a schedule, from the entry of UN monitors into the region to the involvement of the International Red Cross in the exchange of prisoners. This amounted to rewriting the resolution piecemeal, but since it was happening in informal consultations and being presented in writing to the Council, it went down more easily.

To calm Iraq's fears that a cease-fire would simply be used by Iran as an excuse to regroup and resume fighting later on, Pérez de Cuéllar came up with a slight improvement of the resolution's language by calling the end to hostilities an "irreversible first step"—a small semantic wrinkle, perhaps, but it helped at the time. We were meeting almost daily with Middle East and Arab ambassadors, foreign ministers, or representatives of the Perm Five, and we knew we had to improvise, to come up with new elements regularly, if we wanted to maintain the diplomatic initiative.

On May 8, I drafted a memorandum for Pérez de Cuéllar entitled "A Political Agenda for the Secretary General on Regional Issues." As always, my fundamental goal was to help create a new and broader peacemaking role for the office of the secretary-general. The memo included one comment on the Iran-Iraq war that turned out to be far more important than my long-range objectives. "With regard to the war," I wrote, "it is interesting to note that the Saudi Defense Minister had, only a few weeks ago, stated that for all intents and purposes, the war may well come to an end in 1988 for want of necessary materials and will to go on longer." The comment had appeared in an American newspaper editorial in mid-February—apparently the result of his meeting with the paper's editorial board or perhaps even a single editorial writer. But it got virtually no coverage beyond that, which was intriguing: as I read it, Prince Sultan was sending an unmistakable signal that Saddam's principal bankers were not prepared to underwrite his battlefield adventures forever. This could prove useful down the road, I thought, and I tucked the prince's words away for possible use another time.

At the end of May, Ali Akhbar Velayati, the Iranian foreign minister, came to New York from Teheran, and in early June, Tariq Aziz followed from Baghdad. Velayati was still unable to give us a formal acceptance of Resolution 598, so he occupied his time and ours by elaborating on the already tiresome distinction between the secretary-general, whom he respected, and the Security Council, of which he was suspicious. This was the exact opposite of what we heard from Tariq Aziz, who made the secretary-general a partisan villain and the Security Council a hero. The accusations of partisanship were not all that disturbing; we knew they came with the territory. People accuse the United Nations and other mediators of partisanship even when they are not biased because it is an easy way to put pressure on the middleman and find out what he is made of. Any intermediary who tries to relieve the psychological pressure by yielding rather than standing up to it should find another job. Relaxing your guard begins an inevitable process: you lose credibility, you lose the issue, you lose control.

On July 3, 1988, a frightening incident occurred, tragically proving how war weary everyone involved had become. The USS *Vincennes*, a heavy cruiser on patrol in the Gulf, shot down an Iranian civilian Airbus in the mistaken belief that it was a military plane crossing a go–no-go line. It had been flying west across the Gulf from Bandar Abbas to Dubai when it crashed, killing all 284 passengers. Rather than breaking off all contact, however, the Iranians used the incident to repair relations. When Pérez de Cuéllar met the Iranians in Geneva on July 7, Javad Larajani pointed out that this was the first time Iran had ever voiced a complaint to the Security Council. He said that "this may actually be the occasion to melt the ice between Teheran and the Security Council, which also means the United States." Larajani claimed that what Iran wanted from the Council was a resolution that would view Iran in a sympathetic light. He never once used the word "condemnation." It helped that the United States sponsored the resolution that formally expressed regret for the incident, and that the Reagan administration quickly agreed to the concept of paying compensation to the families of the victims—although it was at odds with the Iranians, who wanted the money to go through the government first.

Pérez de Cuéllar was not really a party to the *Vincennes* negotiations, so I decided to take some time off to attend a foreign policy seminar sponsored by an American foundation. The seminar was taking place off the coast of Yugoslavia on the beautiful island of Brioni, once the summer residence and hunting preserve of the late President Tito. I arrived on July

17. The next morning, a call came from the secretary-general's office, demanding that I return at once. At half past midnight on July 18, Ambassador Mohammed Mahallati of Iran had called the secretary-general at his Sutton Place residence to alert him to a letter that had been sent only a few hours earlier by the president of Iran, Ali Khamanei, conveying Iran's acceptance of Resolution 598—the move we had been seeking for a year. Within a few hours, Mahallati had requested that Pérez de Cuéllar declare a cease-fire then and there; if this were not done immediately, he added, the United Nations would be responsible for any further bloodshed that occurred on the battlefield. I took the first boat back to shore, a fast hydrofoil across the Adriatic to Venice, then planes to Rome and New York. By the morning of July 20, I was back at my desk.

We could now start the last leg of the negotiations to implement Resolution 598 and end the war. As the final, nonstop negotiations began, my secretary wrote my lucky number on my office door: 8/8/88. I was born in 1948 on the eighth of October, the eighth month of the year during Roman times. I was also delivered by a Dr. Quarantotto, which means "forty-eight" in Italian. My secretary had gambled that since I was conducting the negotiations, they would end successfully on August 8, the only day in the Western calendar with that combination of numbers. Amazingly enough, she turned out be right.

Why was Iran suddenly suing for peace? Cameron Hume, the American diplomat who followed the war at the United Nations and later wrote an account of the peacemaking efforts, enumerated the factors that, in his view, may have pushed Iran to settle: "the inability of the Iranian military to overcome losses suffered during the failed attack on Basra at the end of 1986; the Iraqi advantage in the tanker war, especially after the U.S. entry into the Gulf; the demoralizing impact of Iraqi attacks on civilian targets during the war of the cities; the fear in the Iranian army that Iraq would again use chemical weapons; the destruction of the Iranian navy; the recent defeats of the Iranian army at Fao Shamlacheh, Majnoun and Delhoran; and the nearly ten-to-one advantage that Iraq now had in battle tanks."

By the time Khamanei had accepted the resolution, I believe that the Iranian leadership had not only been told that it was losing the war, but also that Iraq might occupy a large part of the country. According to U.S. officials, who briefed me at the U.S. Mission just across First Avenue facing the United Nations, the Iraqi Army was poised to penetrate hundreds of kilometers into Iran. The Americans had posted maps to show the likely route of Iraq's thrust into Iran.

There are moments when UN officials have to confront the interests of member states that might not conform to the morals and ideals represented by the United Nations itself. This was one of those moments. Whatever the legitimate interests of the West and East in blocking Iran, and whatever the fears of the conservative regimes in the Middle East, if we did not seize this moment to stop the war, what were we doing there? I had no reason to doubt the U.S. intelligence assessment that an Iraqi invasion of Iran was imminent. But if faced with such a potentially mortal blow, what would the revolutionary regime do? Cornered, the Iranians would strike back wildly with the only weapon they had left—a wave of terror against the Western nations supporting Saddam. Peace was the only option.

Khamanei's letter of acceptance was concise. Ali Akhbar Velayati, the foreign minister since 1981, had to have known that a letter of such importance was above his pay grade and could be signed only by the highest authority, or at least by the president of the republic. But the true significance of the letter was that it was signed during the life of the imam; two days later, Khomeini spoke of the letter as a poisoned chalice. The central command of the Iranian Army issued its own letter as a domestic political counterweight. It began with the vocative "O Iranian people!" once again rallying the Iranians to arms even though the fighting would soon be over. It was not that the military necessarily wanted to continue the war; rather, it wanted protective cover against a public admission that it could no longer keep up the fight.

Diplomatic events confirmed our suspicion that Iran feared a major invasion by Iraq. The very day of the military appeal, Pérez de Cuéllar disclosed that he would unilaterally announce the date for the cease-fire, D-day, immediately freezing both sides in place if they heeded his call. That would be followed by negotiations on all other aspects leading toward a peace agreement. The Iranians declared they were ready to accept the date; to underscore their eagerness to end the war, Mahallati came to Pérez de Cuéllar, warning him that "the blood of every civilian Iranian killed from now on will be on the conscience of the UN." But Iraq let it be known that there could be no date for a cease-fire without first conducting full-fledged negotiations. The two countries had done complete 180-degree turns, reflecting their altered states on the battlefield. Now it was Iran that wished for a sequential implementation, cease-fire first, and Iraq that insisted on an overall approach, namely negotiations first.

The secretary-general had the authority to name the cease-fire date on his own but no power to make it stick aside from moral suasion. If one side decided to call his bluff and refuse, he and the Security Council would lose everything. The question was whether to put pressure on Iraq before or after the announcement of the date. A tug-of-war began, with Iran asking what was delaying the cease-fire and Iraq holding out for direct negotiation before the fighting could stop.

Pérez de Cuéllar did not let the two sides take the initiative; instead, he announced his plans to send a military team to Iran and Iraq to work out how the United Nations would supervise a cease-fire. So, without naming a date, he imparted a sense of imminence, putting pressure on both sides and raising public expectations. Iran, of course, immediately accepted the UN team, while the Iraqis dragged their feet, arguing as good diplomats that another clarification was needed. Iran, the Iraqis claimed, would only use the cease-fire to buy time to rebuild its military capacity and renew the war—and, Baghdad said, everyone knew it.

The military team, under the leadership of General Martin Vadset of Norway, the commander of the UN Truce Supervision Organization (UNTSO) in Jerusalem—charged with the supervision of the truce that had ended the first Arab-Israeli war in 1948—was assembled in Geneva for briefings by legal and other UN officials. This took several days, during which Pérez de Cuéllar had to obtain permission for the team to visit Iraq as well. Iraq's reluctance to be drawn into a process that would lead to the end of the war was now apparent. For several weeks, U.S. officials had indicated to us that while Iraq had accepted the fact that it could not march all the way to Teheran, it still intended—as one American official put it—"to teach Iran a sound lesson before all this comes to an end." When the Iraqis had been at a military disadvantage, they had regularly accused the secretary-general of not pushing hard enough for a cease-fire. Now Baghdad perceived Pérez de Cuéllar's attempts to end the war as patently anti-Iraqi. Iran's acceptance of Resolution 598 had put the Iraqis into an awkward position: they could not be seen as refusing to make peace, but they also had no intention of stopping the war.

Ambassador Ismat Kittani, a Kurd who had served as a UN official in the 1970s and had many good friends in UN circles, was Iraq's permanent representative in New York at the time. It fell to him in the days after

Iran's quick acceptance to calibrate his government's message—that of a country that was not against peace but not completely in favor of a cease-fire either. Kittani met with Pérez de Cuéllar four times in twenty-four hours, not counting the time he spent with me privately. He delivered a long message from Baghdad insisting that Iraq would talk directly to Iran only about a cease-fire; this, of course, was not mentioned in or even envisioned by the UN resolution that Baghdad had already accepted. If we had enforced this new demand on Teheran, the entire diplomatic operation probably would have collapsed, which may well have been what Saddam Hussein wanted.

We talked business with Kittani in offices, hallways, and elevators—and even in elevators, a note taker was required. Everything was recorded to guarantee an accurate account, because in the aftermath of heated discussion, memories are often unreliable. We were thinking, talking, and reacting all at once, and afterward, we needed to review the positions of all sides to measure progress. We had a team returning from the front with the results of its investigation of the use of chemical weapons, a UN group visiting prisoners of war in lieu of the Red Cross, and the new Vadset mission, which was on its way although currently stuck in Geneva. (General Vadset was to study the terrain and logistics for the deployment of a UN force to monitor the eventual cease-fire.) Time was very short, the war continued, and people were wondering why, since both sides had accepted the resolution, nothing on the ground had changed. Diplomatic efforts can be sustained for only so long before they fizzle out or blow up. We needed some kind of document that could be initialed by both sides, so we were reviewing our implementation plan as the possible basis of a peace treaty.

We managed to keep the latest Iraqi demand secret from the Iranians for twenty-four hours, until the evening of July 21, even though there had been a closed meeting of the Security Council that afternoon to bring its members up to speed. Mahallati, who throughout the day had been asking to see the secretary-general, was finally scheduled for 7:30 P.M. The Iranian ambassador asked first about the Security Council meeting. Pérez de Cuéllar read aloud a text that appeared almost routine in the way it was drafted. He quoted, in a fairly unexciting manner, the contents of the two letters he had received from the two foreign ministers and added, "Some Council members were interested in my discussing with the two foreign ministers the various aspects of the resolution."

The crux of the matter was that Iraq wanted direct negotiations with Iran; but Iran, having already accepted the resolution, was not prepared to sit down with a regime it accused of aggression. An invitation for both foreign ministers to come to New York could have been seen as a trap to force Iran into conducting direct negotiations with Iraq. Pérez de Cuéllar knew, however, that he had to get both sides to New York; since the Iranians were prepared to talk to him to clarify matters, he agreed to meet with Foreign Minister Velayati on that basis. The Iranians said yes—so long as it did not mean sitting down with the Iraqis. We figured that Velayati's acceptance, once confirmed, would be enough to draw Iraqi Foreign Minister Tariq Aziz to New York in the hope that the two would end up speaking directly. We were right: Aziz said he would be there as soon as his Iranian counterpart had arrived.

They both flew into New York on July 25—Velayati during the day, Aziz in the evening. Velayati, who had arrived with a party of eight, said he was authorized to agree to a cease-fire as soon as possible. We engaged him in a detailed discussion over three days on every aspect of the implementation plan, which would lead to an accord that would end the war; he agreed to it in every detail. At that point, we also told him of the Iraqis' request for direct talks. Velayati was not prepared to accept direct talks with the Iraqis, certainly not before hostilities ended. Negotiations on the entire peace agreement could begin, he said, but only through the intermediary of the UN secretary-general.

Tariq Aziz saw Pérez de Cuéllar for the first time on July 27, making it abundantly clear that he had come to New York only to meet with Velayati and that he had no mandate to discuss any issues of substance with the secretary-general. The session was not confrontational; but Tariq Aziz was in no hurry for a cease-fire, arguing that the world had already waited a year for Iran to accept Resolution 598 and that there was thus no urgent need for Iraq to agree to an immediate cease-fire. By that time the Iraqi Army had advanced some seventy to eighty kilometers into Iranian territory, and Tariq Aziz was plainly setting the stage for a long-haul series of negotiations and perhaps even for a breakdown in the process itself.

By July 29, the Iranians and the United Nations had resolved virtually all issues under discussion, and Velayati, after four meetings with us, was growing increasingly anxious to hear when and under what terms the Iraqis would accept a cease-fire. After three-plus days of meeting at separate tables, it was time to see Tariq Aziz again. At 6 P.M., we met with him for the second time. After a few opening remarks, Pérez de Cuéllar passed across the table the same text for the implementation plan that he had already given to Velayati. Tariq Aziz was expected to lean forward and take the text in his hands. Instead, he seemed glued to his chair, forcing the secretary-general to drop the paper a foot and a half from the blotter in front of him. He made no move to touch it. "In our last meeting I stated my position very clearly, as my instructions were strict," he said. "I am not prepared to discuss any substantive proposals with your Excellency. I proposed a face-to-face meeting with the other side. When we start those meetings, we shall be prepared to discuss substance. In coming here today I was expecting to receive some clarification from you on this question. I apologize, therefore, but I cannot receive this paper."

It was an awkward moment for Pérez de Cuéllar both personally and professionally. The secretary-general rose from his chair, stretched across the table, and grabbed the text back, popping it into its folder. "You can leave if you want," he said with some firmness. There was an ominous silence as we waited to see what Tariq Aziz would do. By telling Tariq Aziz he could walk out at any time, Pérez de Cuéllar had refused the snub and the implied accusation of partiality, a gamble that required real guts. I had never seen him so upset.

Tariq Aziz finally broke the silence with a familiar recitation of Iraqi policies, but he also gave us a clear indication of the limits of his mandate. "I am not the head of state but rather the foreign minister, who, as envoy of my government, tries to assess the situation and to report it as it is," he said. "The decisions are usually made in one's capital." He would wait in his residence, he added, until he could talk face-to-face with Foreign Minister Velayati: "He will not get a cease-fire unless he sits with me," Tariq Aziz said. "If there is to be a cease-fire, he will not get it from Washington. He has to make peace with Baghdad." He was right about Washington but wrong about Baghdad.

When things grow complicated, a document of fourteen pages is a definite handicap. Three lines are more useful, so on July 30, I prepared a paragraph for the secretary-general proposing that Iran and Iraq discuss implementing the cease-fire in talks with him. Their agreement would then be made public, and they could sit down together to discuss a comprehensive settlement shortly after a cease-fire. In other words, we were suggesting agreement on a date for a cease-fire and a date for direct talks, both here and now. Tempers were so high that I decided to use a surrogate to get the message to the Iraqis. On July 31 at 4 P.M., I handed the draft statement to the second in command at the Egyptian Mission and asked him to secure an Iraqi reaction within forty-eight hours. The following day, the Egyptian ambassador called me to say that the Iraqis had refused to accept the three-line paper. However, it remained the key to solving the problem, because the objective had now been reduced to fixing a date for the fighting to end and negotiations between the two sides to begin.

The Iraqis were using the leverage of their advancing army to reject the cease-fire, although few knew of their possible thrust into Iran. On August 1, I devised an even simpler paper outlining the procedure. First, in separate talks with Pérez de Cuéllar, both sides would agree on how the cease-fire should be implemented. Second, the secretary-general would invite the two foreign ministers along with the members of the Security Council to his office, during which time he would announce that an agreement had been reached on a formula for the implementation. Third, he would publish the text of the agreement, including in it a set D-day, the date for the cease-fire.

That same day, with the newspapers reporting that peace was at hand, I received a visit from a U.S. diplomat, a great Arabist and political counselor at the U.S. Mission to the UN. He was also a personal friend who was deeply involved in the diplomacy of ending the war, and he brought me an astonishing message from Washington—from none other than George Shultz, the U.S. secretary of state. The message: Perhaps it would be better to reconsider what we were doing and call off our negotiations since they seemed to be going nowhere. "We do not think it can be done at this stage, and Washington believes that in October, the secretary of state and the Soviet foreign minister will put their heads together and will be able to end the war," he said.

Stunned, I tried to digest the meaning of the message and its implications, both politically and for me personally. It appeared, at first blush, that the two superpowers did not believe an agreement was possible at this stage. But the fact that a few more months of war might mean an even larger Iraqi invasion of Iran, particularly in the western regions of the country, which included some prized oil fields, haunted me. I remembered then that at the U.S. Mission I had been shown maps detailing the military situation, and it crossed my mind that perhaps somebody was counting on a dramatic military incursion to inflict a lethal blow to the Khomeini regime. Iraq had miscalculated before, in 1980, when it had hoped for the same result. Now there was no doubt in my mind that if an operation such as that were undertaken, the Teheran regime might react by fighting guerrilla wars throughout the Gulf and spreading terrorism around the world. Huge civilian losses, both in the region and outside it, were quite likely, I thought. This was not what the role of a UN official was about. It would have been against everything I believed in to acquiesce, yet it was a message from Washington, which had accepted and even encouraged the secretary-general's expanded role as peacemaker.

I was alone in New York because my family had left for Italy on vacation, so Pérez de Cuéllar asked me to join him at his home at the end of the day. Only he and his wife were there. I related the message I had received from Shultz via my friend the U.S. diplomat. We stood at the edge of the lawn that runs toward the East River with its busy Fifty-ninth Street bridge, an icon of New York. Pérez de Cuéllar then asked me a fatherly question: "Gianni, how old are you?"

"Thirty-nine," I answered.

"I am sixty-eight. I think you should consider very seriously what you have been told and what you want to do in life. If you wish to remain in this business, you may have to ponder very carefully what you were told. I am sixty-eight and at the end of my career. I am ready to support you in whatever suggestion you will give me. If you wish to abort the negotiations, I will cover you. If you wish to go ahead, remember that we have only a very few days, at the most a week. They will not give us more than that. Go home, sleep on it, and tomorrow you will tell me. Think about your life, but if you wish to go ahead, we have only one week."

Pérez de Cuéllar had realized that a decision to proceed would require guts from both of us, and he obviously had decided to give me part of the choice of what to do next.

His wife, Marcela, had joined us on the doorstep. "I'm sure you will make the right decision," she said.

I went home and tried to calculate how many civilians would die during three more months of war, assuming Shultz and Soviet Foreign

Minister Eduard Shevardnadze actually succeeded in ending the war in October. There were no guarantees. If we had a window to end the war now, could we knowingly let it pass? Forecasting the duration of wars is a hazardous business. When World War II started in 1939, Hitler calculated that it would last only six weeks.

The following morning, *The New York Times* headlined that the United Nations would soon declare a cease-fire between Iran and Iraq. The story was wrong: we weren't there yet. I also told Pérez de Cuéllar that we had no choice but to go ahead with our negotiations. In that case, he reiterated, "remember, we may not have more than a week to make it happen." This, after all, was what the United Nations was all about: ending wars, not prolonging them. I called my friend at the U.S. Mission so he could relay my reply: "I am prepared to accept the message given by the secretary of state on condition that you assure me that the war will indeed end in October and that, in the meanwhile, there will be no civilian casualties."

"You're refusing," he said.

"No, I'm accepting."

I was not prepared to give up what I viewed as a mandate to me from the United Nations and a duty to myself. I do not want to be misunderstood. In Cyprus, I had experienced enormous personal gratification by helping families gather their harvest, obtain water, and send their children to school, and again in Afghanistan by making contributions that helped end the foreign occupation of the country. But this was the first time since the days of Ralph Bunche, forty years earlier, that the United Nations would actually be playing a major role in ending a massive conflict.

With a new clock ticking, we had to come up with something new. Prince Bandar bin Sultan, the Saudi ambassador to Washington, had come to New York to follow the negotiations—in effect, looking after his country's financial investment in Saddam Hussein. Having failed with the Egyptians, we approached Bandar with my short paper, in the hope he could convince Tariq Aziz to accept its contents. Velayati had already agreed, and Bandar clearly liked what he saw.

The next day, *The New York Times* published another exclusive, obviously not leaked by us, under the headline CEASE-FIRE PLAN BY UN LEADER REJECTED BY IRAQ. The press was being used to send messages, while we were trying to keep the Security Council informed and use it to pressure Iraq to end the war. The Perm Five formally backed Pérez de Cuéllar. Their endorsement was then delivered by Sir Crispin Tickell, Britain's UN ambassador, to Tariq Aziz, reassuring him that a cease-fire would be only a first step. The message also gave full support to our paper. Meantime, we were juggling everything: we had to keep the military team ready, keep the discussions on chemical weapons going, shuttle the Iranian and Iraqi foreign ministers in and out separately, and keep the Perm Five up to date.

A UN official in Baghdad cabled me that the only way to break the deadlock would be to appeal directly to Saddam. That seemed too vague and risky an alternative, despite the fact that Prince Bandar had also failed to convince the Iraqis in New York to accede to my short paper.

On the morning of Saturday, August 6, I was at home, just getting ready to go to the office, when I received a call from Ambassador Kittani of Iraq, with whom I had remained in regular contact. He was calling from a car on the way to the airport. Tariq Aziz was with him, walking out on the negotiations without even so much as a good-bye to the secretary-general. Saddam Hussein had summoned his foreign minister home.

Tariq Aziz then said that the Iraqi president had announced he would agree to a cease-fire if Iran would consequently open direct negotiations on all the issues in the UN resolutions—in other words, my short paper. But there was a sting in the tail, an unacceptable condition: Iraq, Saddam said, must regain the use of the Shatt-al-Arab in accordance with "our inalienable rights." It was not clear what those rights were. Indeed, the status of the boundaries of Iraq was the precise reason Saddam Hussein had gone to war. Iraq had gone to war to gain complete control over the Shatt-al-Arab. In effect, Saddam was saying he wanted to achieve Iraq's war goal in exchange for a cease-fire.

In its way, it was another fine move by a consummate tactician. Even though he was calling Tariq Aziz back to Baghdad, Saddam nevertheless wanted to demonstrate his desire for peace. Tariq Aziz also hinted to me from his car that he might return in a few weeks. A few weeks of war, I thought. Saddam's ploy was to withdraw his foreign minister, signal his acceptance of the secretary-general's position, then wait to hear from Iran whether a settlement would include what must have been his minimum demand: Iraqi control of the Shatt-al-Arab. The Iraqi president was showing negotiating flexibility while he kept the war going by withdrawing his envoy from the negotiating table.

Pérez de Cuéllar understood that withdrawing the negotiator was a way of short-circuiting him. Without an Iraqi in the room, it appeared that no negotiations could be pursued. As he had anticipated, we had been given no extra time. But we found another way. Velayati met with the secretary-general and heard Saddam's latest message. His own escape route home was blocked by his instructions not to return to Teheran without a cease-fire agreement. He told Pérez de Cuéllar, "I will reply to you, and it is up to you to give our answer to Saddam." I tried to feel out Kittani, who had always served as a reliable go-between when his foreign minister was in town. Now he told me that he could not talk to me and, almost in sorrow, indicated his inability to do anything at all. Without Tariq Aziz there, he could not afford to be seen negotiating with me. "I can no longer do with you what I did until now," he said. I was without an interlocutor.

My lines through Egypt and Kuwait were also not working. With the clock ticking, I finally urged Pérez de Cuéllar to play the card I had been saving for last. Since the Iraqis had left the table, we decided to substitute the next best thing—their Saudi bankers. Prince Bandar was still in New York, and it was his father the defense minister, Prince Sultan, who had indicated his government's donor fatigue and its desire to end the war in 1988. We contacted Prince Bandar, who then contacted the Saudi foreign minister, the subtle and elegant Prince Saud al-Faisal, in London; he joined us later that day in New York. The idea of involving Saudi Arabia as a surrogate negotiator for Iraq was a long shot, given the country's traditional shyness about publicity for its diplomacy, but there was no other way. The House of Saud did not let us down.

By Saturday night the two Saudi princes were in New York, and we made our first joint contact. We had no idea at that point if we even had enough time to try our Saudi option. We called on Kittani just after noon on Sunday, August 7, to report that the Iranians had accepted Saddam's idea for a cease-fire plus direct talks under the auspices of Pérez de Cuéllar, with the date for such talks to be set by the secretary-general. While there was no commitment by the Iranians on the question of the Shatt-al-Arab, every item could be discussed during those talks. Kittani would not accept the word of the secretary-general verbally; he needed an official document. Pérez de Cuéllar said he would write a letter outlining the elements of Iran's answer. He added that on Monday he planned to announce that the cease-fire would begin on August 19, with peace talks commencing on August 22. Kittani called back shortly to say that his government wanted a letter from Iran, not from us. That was easy enough. Velayati wrote a letter to the secretary-general affirming Iran's agreement to the procedure. Then the Iraqis pulled another one: Kittani informed us at 3:30 P.M. that Velayati's written assurance would not do and that he would need an official letter from the highest authorities in Teheran. Kittani made it clear to me that we could not declare a cease-fire before we had a formal acceptance from Baghdad. He was almost panicking about it. He felt such a move would force Saddam to say no to peace in public.

We knew that Iran would accept the dates we suggested, but Saddam seemed to be raising the ante every couple of hours. We changed tactics. All we needed now was a piece of paper confirming both sides' agreement to a cease-fire and a meeting for further peace talks. We did not have that piece of paper when we prepared to brief the Security Council informally early on Sunday evening. But we sensed that we were tantalizingly close, so Pérez de Cuéllar stuck his neck out and told the Council that he intended to announce the cease-fire the next day, August 8, at 11 A.M. He then suggested the same thing to the press. The boss was aware of the risk he was taking. "This cease-fire is certainly having a forceps birth," Pérez de Cuéllar said as he entered his private office off the Security Council chamber. That drew a quick response from Paul Kavanagh, an Irishman serving in his private office: "If it goes much further," he cracked, "it will have to be a cesarean."

At around 7 P.M. Sunday, we went off to meet the Saudi princes at their apartment in the Waldorf Towers. The sticking point was Baghdad's behavior. Even if we could physically get the letter from Teheran delivered overnight, we figured that Saddam would come up with something new Monday morning. We had to convince the Saudis that the best we could get from the Iranians was the letter from Velayati, and we needed them to deliver the Iraqi president posthaste. The conversation centered on raising the ante at our end: King Fahd would have to intervene, either directly with Saddam or with the prestige of his crown. The two princes, Prince Saud al-Faisal and Prince Bandar bin Sultan, agreed to do what they could; in the tradition of the House of Saud, one never says one can do something until one has done it. Our conversation lasted two hours and included Ambassador Samir Shihabi, the permanent representative to the

United Nations, who had served with great honor in the Saudi diplomatic service for forty years and who would become president of the General Assembly two years later.

We had brought with us a short letter I had drafted for the secretary-general, indicating the agreement of both sides. The letter was based on my short-form draft of August 3 and actually became the document that ended the Iran-Iraq war. The purpose of this document was to avoid waiting for a reply from Saddam to our formulation by simply stating the facts and counting on his nonreaction. It was addressed to both governments and gave no indication that the secretary-general required a reply. It read as follows:

> Excellency,
>
> In pursuance of the official contacts I had with the Islamic Republic of Iran and Iraq, I should like to inform you that both governments have agreed that direct talks between the Foreign Ministers shall be held under my auspices immediately after the establishment of the cease-fire, in order to reach a common understanding of the other provisions of the Security Council, Resolution 598 and the procedures and timings for their implementation.
>
> > Yours sincerely,
> > Javier Pérez de Cuéllar

Velayati had already covered all possible points with Pérez de Cuéllar, so we did not even discuss the letter with him. The princes then agreed to consult with King Fahd, to work throughout the night given the time difference, and to meet with us again at ten the following morning. We had gambled that we would have the Iraqis' agreement and had convened a meeting of the Security Council for eleven. Our scheduling didn't hold: the Saudis were still working the case through the late morning.

Finally, the two princes arrived at the office of the secretary-general at 12:15 P.M., accompanied by Shihabi and Iraqi Ambassador Kittani. When we sat down, it was not yet clear whether they had secured the agreement from Baghdad. In fact, it appeared they had not; Princes Faisal and Bandar began to confer privately in Arabic and then requested some modifications to the draft of the secretary-general's letter. It was our turn, and Pérez de Cuéllar and I conferred in Spanish on the requested change.

The secretary-general knew that I had a fairly clear sense of how far we could go in asking Iran for changes. I told him we could not risk going back to Velayati with significant changes; if we did, we would only play into the hands of those who wanted to delay a cease-fire. Pérez de Cuéllar replied, only half in jest, "Unfortunately, I cannot accept that change because Mr. Picco tells me we cannot. Please do not ask me to do what I cannot do." Prince Faisal and King Fahd spoke again in a flurry of phone calls, and still the princes could not say anything final.

The Security Council was waiting restlessly downstairs, but we still did not have the final word from Saddam. The princes told us that no communication from him had been received. But then, at 1:05 P.M., the phone rang. It was King Fahd of Saudi Arabia. With his foreign minister, Prince Saud al-Faisal, serving as interpreter, the king said, "I would like to be the first to congratulate you, Mr. Secretary-General. You have just brought the Iran-Iraq war to an end."

Pérez de Cuéllar said he was very pleased, but could he also hear the same good news from the leadership in Baghdad? The king quickly added that we would be receiving a call from Baghdad shortly to confirm what he had just said. Less than a minute after he hung up, the phone rang again, only this time Tariq Aziz was on the line. It was 1:15 P.M. Prince Saud al-Faisal took the call and put it on speakerphone. "I am in the office of the president, and he has just agreed to the formulation you have just discussed," said the Iraqi foreign minister. Apparently, Saddam wanted to shift the cease-fire date from August 19 to August 20, which I believe was just to make a point. That was one day's difference from what we had agreed to with Velayati, but I took it upon myself to encourage the secretary-general to say that the new date was fine. After the letter had been read back to Tariq Aziz in Arabic, Pérez de Cuéllar insisted on hearing him agree to it in English.

We walked out and accompanied the Saudi officials to the elevator. Although their role had been crucial, they had remained true to the style of the kingdom's foreign policy and to the nature of the House of Saud, having never once spoken about it publicly. We later called Velayati, who arrived at 1:40 P.M. and quickly accepted the one-day postponement of the cease-fire. Pérez de Cuéllar reminded him that he had secured the cease-fire, the reason Velayati had come to New York. He could therefore leave on the date he wanted. I then prepared the text for the secretary-general to read to the Security Council.

Downstairs, the Council and the press had been waiting for the secretary-general since morning, but first Pérez de Cuéllar wanted a sandwich and a glass of red wine. We sat with two other colleagues at a table next to his office overlooking New York City. We had only a half hour before we had to report to the Security Council. As we sat at the table, the secretary-general announced that he was promoting me on the spot to the rank of director, the highest in the international civil service, just as a general would promote one of his officers on the battlefield. He said, "Gianni has just delivered to me the end of the Iran-Iraq war." It was August 8, 1988—or 8/8/88, the mystical number on my office door.

Against all the rules, I had already arranged a small celebration for my chief. I had my assistant, Judith Karam, strategically placed in the Council's visitors' gallery. Her task was to keep her eye on me as I stood behind the secretary-general's chair, so that when I nodded she would break into applause, prompting others to following suit.

So, at three o'clock on the afternoon of August 8, 1988, the secretary-general and I went down to the Security Council, and in an open session, Pérez de Cuéllar formally announced the end of eight years of brutal and costly war. Judy began the applause on cue, much to the surprise of the diplomats in the Council, where public displays of positive emotion are rare indeed and the sound of two hands coming together is unheard of. After all he had endured, after all we had been through, Pérez de Cuéllar deserved that small homage.

Part Two

The author (front) on his first trip to Lebanon.

CHAPTER 7

A Quid pro Quo
with Iran

I STILL VIVIDLY RECALL MY FEELINGS that hot August night when I walked home from the United Nations sometime after 9 P.M. The world had changed, at least in my eyes, and the fifteen years of my career had suddenly taken on new meaning. They now seemed worthwhile. Only a few hours earlier, the fighting between Iran and Iraq had come to an end, an accomplishment that had sealed a new role for the UN secretary-general just six months after the Geneva agreement on Afghanistan. To satisfy political objectives, some had wanted the war to continue for several months longer; instead, tens of thousands of lives on both sides would now be spared. The political and moral dimension of the Iran-Iraq cease-fire was a milestone that changed my professional life forever. It was then, and remains, the most important moment of my diplomatic career.

Perhaps my euphoria at this time was both premature and unprofessional, because we still faced the task of establishing the formal peace negotiations between Iran and Iraq, and ultimately a formal peace agreement between the two countries was never reached. But the fighting, at least, was over. The Iraqi people had also suffered a very high number of casualties during the war. After all, it was a country of 17 million against one of some 50 million people. By pressing to end the war then I believe we did the right thing. I also hoped that Iran felt it "owed us one" for helping to end the conflict and prevent an Iraqi thrust into its oil districts. Perhaps now I could begin work on the Western hostages in Lebanon with the Iranian government's support.

Actually, I had been raising the hostage issue with Iranian officials in an informal manner for some time. The ideological connection between the Iranian revolution and the Lebanese groups who claimed responsibility for the kidnappings was no secret. Still, for years, Iranian officials had told me that the government had no connection with the operations of "those groups." Later, however, they simply would tell me that "the time was not ripe" to bring this up with the government in Teheran.

There was a very specific reason why the UN secretary-general was so deeply interested in pursuing the release of the hostages in Lebanon. Apart from his humanitarian concern for the individuals held captive in blatant violation of international law, two UN officials had also been victims in the kidnapping spree of the 1980s. Moreover, the issue of the hostages contained two elements ideally suited for Pérez de Cuéllar in his new role as secretary-general. First, he could put to practical use his newfound credibility acquired with the Iranian government during the cease-fire negotiations with Iraq, a credibility that no other institution in the West had achieved. Second, while he had no political mandate for this work from the Security Council or the General Assembly, which made it even easier, we doubted that any country would publicly oppose his humanitarian efforts. Indeed, political credibility and the freedom to maneuver would be key elements as we went forward. We needed a product, and by that I mean a very solid proposal that would lead to a solution of the hostage problem. The desire to solve it was simply not enough.

I was not involved in the early rescue efforts to free Alec Collett, an official of the UN Relief and Works Agency (UNRWA), which ministers to Palestinian refugees. He had been seized in 1985 by a group calling itself the Revolutionary Organization of Socialist Muslims. Two videotapes of Collett were delivered not long after his kidnapping. In the first, mailed from Switzerland, he claimed that he was being well treated and was receiving the necessary medication for his diabetic condition. In the second, dropped off at a foreign news bureau, he appealed to Prime Minister Margaret Thatcher to release the Palestinians convicted of seriously wounding the Israeli ambassador to Britain in a 1982 assassination attempt that had been the ostensible reason for Israel's invasion of Lebanon. Experts who examined the tapes thought they indicated that Collett was being held by Abu Nidal, the notorious Palestinian who had organized the massacre of Israeli athletes at the 1972 Munich Olympic Games.

Despite the best efforts of Samir Sanbar, the courageous chief of the UN Information Office in Beirut during the height of the Lebanese civil war, we had never been able to obtain any reliable information about Collett's condition or whereabouts, or whether he was even alive. It must be said, however, that we had always suspected that Collett's disappearance, unlike that of most of the others, was not connected to groups linked to Hizbollah, or Party of God—the offspring, established in Lebanon in 1982, of a militant Shiite movement that had broken with more traditional elements. In 1986, a tape that purported to show the hanging of Alec Collett was made public by the kidnappers. However, given the poor quality of the video, experts could not confirm Collett's death.

A second UN kidnapping occurred on February 17, 1988. U.S. Marine Lieutenant Colonel William Higgins was taken hostage while on duty with the UN Interim Force in Lebanon (UNIFIL). Pérez de Cuéllar immediately mobilized the entire UN machinery in Lebanon to deal with the Higgins case, and Under Secretary for Special Political Affairs Marrack Goulding made several trips to Lebanon about it. The secretary-general later sent letters to the president of Syria and the foreign minister of Iran, while approaches were made to Chairman Yasser Arafat of the Palestine Liberation Organization, the Algerian government, and various Lebanese dignitaries of all religions. Despite all the efforts, the United Nations was not getting anywhere. The officials involved dealt with these cases as if they were simply "Middle East matters." But the fact was that all of the kidnappings in Lebanon that had taken place in the 1980s—perhaps with the exception of the Collett case—had little to do in operational and political terms with the traditional players in the region.

I started to pursue Higgins's case somewhere in the midst of our negotiations on the Iran-Iraq cease-fire during the summer of 1988. On July 29, little more than a week before we reached the cease-fire agreement, the Security Council adopted a resolution specifically calling for Higgins's release after reports of his death surfaced and called upon all member states to use their influence to help. There was no reference made to a possible role for the secretary-general because nobody believed he could be a player on the hostage issue. In October, the American television network CBS reported that Higgins had indeed been killed, which prompted Pérez de Cuéllar to contact Velayati again. The Iranian foreign minister again claimed that he did not know which group had abducted Higgins. UNIFIL then tried to build a coherent mosaic out of the bits and pieces of information it had. It didn't amount to much. Higgins and Collett had been added to a growing list: as 1988 drew to a close, there were at least seventeen Western hostages in captivity. Six more would be taken in the early months of 1989.

The more I thought about it, the more I thought it was simply common sense to begin talks about the hostages with the Iranians. Given what we had just done in ending the war, when would there be a better time? So instead of trying to unravel the bundle that was Beirut by picking up a thread that led deeper into Lebanon, we picked up the thread in Iran instead. We had already learned a valuable lesson from the experience of Terry Waite, the British emissary of the archbishop of Canterbury, who had himself been kidnapped, thus joining the plight of the very hostages he had been trying to liberate. As we now know, he had been used in the Iran-contra weapons scheme by U.S. Lieutenant Colonel Oliver North in order to liberate two American hostages, Reverend Lawrence Jenco and David Jacobson, in 1985–86. The highly controversial and bizarre affair had involved the trading of the hostages for a shipment of Hawk missile spare parts to be dispatched to Iran via Israel. Separately, another American hostage, Benjamin Weir, had been released as a consequence of two further consignments of ninety-six TOW missiles sent to Teheran by the Reagan administration.

In later years, when asked for the difference in my approach to securing the release of the hostages to that of Terry Waite, I responded, "He went to Beirut from the West and I went to Beirut from the East." In those days, the East began in Teheran.

The families and colleagues of many of the hostages had started to wage their own campaigns. Early on, the president of the Associated Press, Louis Boccardi, had assigned Larry Heinzerling, a second-generation AP man with considerable reporting experience in dangerous places, to explore avenues for gaining the release of the AP's Beirut bureau chief, Terry Anderson, who had been kidnapped in broad daylight in March 1985. The AP's unpublicized campaign complemented the public campaign of Peggy Say, Anderson's sister. They had all come to confer with us and ask for help. Other governments, notably Pakistan, Germany, and Switzerland, were also trying to help via international and political channels. The International Committee of the Red Cross was actively providing any assistance it could to all parties involved. The ICRC was acutely concerned about all the hostages, especially since some of its own officials had been abducted for short periods of time.

By the autumn of 1988, governments with citizens in captivity still had no idea whether their people were alive or dead. Newspaper stories from Lebanon, quoting so-called diplomatic sources or people with few morals, would contrive bits of information about the fate of this or that hostage. It was a cruel game for the families. My first order of business, then, would be to try to verify who was alive and who was dead—or so I thought. It wouldn't turn out that way.

My regular assignments at this point included the negotiations between Iran and Iraq that followed the cease-fire, tracking developments in the Middle East and working on the Afghan civil war. By the end of 1988, I still had not received a full-fledged assignment to pursue the hostage releases, but I did receive a green light from the secretary-general to sound out the Iranians on their possible assistance. My first contact was Cyrus Nasseri, the Iranian ambassador to the United Nations in Geneva.

Iran was by no means a monolithic country. Nasseri had been working closely with Hashemi Rafsanjani, speaker of the Parliament, who became president in 1989. We had first gotten to know each other in 1984 during the first meeting between Pérez de Cuéllar and Rafsanjani in Teheran. Educated in America, Nasseri knew that the most influential Iranian personality in Lebanon at that time was not Rafsanjani but Ali Akhbar Mohtashemi, former interior minister and Iranian ambassador to Damascus until 1986. Mohtashemi had played a pivotal role in the creation of Hizbollah in 1982 and had promoted a much more radical line to the Lebanese groups than the position of the official Iranian leadership in Teheran.

This was not a traditional diplomatic negotiation, and it could not be dealt with by sitting in a comfortable chair in some old palace in Europe. Nasseri and I met over a long dinner at his Geneva residence on December 14. Much to my surprise, Nasseri said he would raise the hostage issue with Teheran. I also recounted the secretary-general's requests to Velayati for news about Lieutenant Colonel Higgins. Nasseri told me that Iran had no news, but he recommended that Washington make a gesture to encourage the hostage holders to reciprocate. I replied that those who were holding the hostages should also make a symbolic gesture, especially since Christmas was approaching, and Iran could encourage them to do so. The groups holding the hostages, I suggested, could permit an observer to visit the captives and verify their good health. He said that he would soon be leaving for Teheran and would let me know. However, no reply ever came from Teheran. Nasseri later told me that the time had not been right and that approval would have been extremely difficult to attain. He asked me when the next big festival on the Christian calendar was. I told him it was Easter. He then responded as if he believed something could be done by then, but once again nothing was.

Even so, by 1989, it was clear that the hostage problem was not a "traditional" Middle East issue and that better knowledge of Iranian involvement would be critical. Nabil Berri, the traditional political leader of the Lebanese Shiite community and a man well known to many UN officials, was not the right channel. The key was to enter the Shiite Islamic world of Hizbollah and its subdivisions. Lebanese Shiite clerics who had studied in Najaf, Iraq, together with Iranian clerical figures such as Ayatollah Khomeini, had attained political prominence following the Israeli invasion of Lebanon in 1982. The militant Shiite fighters had been credited with various attacks on the Western multinational force in 1983 and 1984 and had claimed responsibility for the kidnappings. These new developments were unfamiliar to Mideast-based UN officials, who were more knowledgeable about the traditional actors in the region.

On January 20, 1989, George Bush was sworn in as the forty-first president of the United States. A former ambassador to the United Nations and director of the Central Intelligence Agency, Bush was far more experienced in world affairs than his predecessor. Moreover, he had gathered around him a very sophisticated foreign policy team. In his inaugural speech, he spoke directly to the hostage issue and allusively to Iran: "There are, today, Americans who are held against their will in foreign lands, and Americans who are unaccounted for. Assistance can be shown here and will be long remembered. Goodwill begets goodwill. Good faith can be a spiral that endlessly moves on."

"Goodwill begets goodwill": that was the key sentence that would officially trigger Pérez de Cuéllar's operation to free the hostages in Beirut. Those code words soon became the basis of everything I did until the last of the hostages was released and I resigned from the United Nations in June 1992. They had been drafted by someone in the Bush administration, probably Brent Scowcroft, the self-effacing air force general who ran the new president's National Security Council. But in my mind and the minds of many of my closest colleagues, it was a public promise by the leader of the West's most powerful nation that could not be made without being kept. The Bush administration would not make formal contact with the secretary-general until August 1989, but the president's words that day in January were enough to strengthen our determination to proceed.

I lived much of 1989 carrying several dossiers, which meant that my travel schedule resembled that of an overworked airline pilot. From mid-January through early February, for instance, I traveled to fifteen different cities: from New York to Vienna on January 18; to Amman, Jordan, on the 19th; to Cairo on the 21st; to London on the 22d, then to Frankfurt on the 23d; to Teheran on the 24th, Dezfūl on the Iranian-Iraqi border on the 25th, Basra, Iraq, on the 27th, and Baghdad on the 28th; to Frankfurt on the 30th; to Jerusalem on the 31st; to Damascus on February 1 and back to Amman on the 2d; to Cairo on the 3d; to Tunis on the evening of the 3d; and back to New York on the 5th. These trips were taken under the pretext of the United Nations' efforts, led by Jan Eliasson, to forge a permanent peace of the Iran-Iraq cease-fire, but they also served as a way for my colleague Jean-Claude Aimé and me to maintain our contacts in Middle Eastern countries. I took other trips with Benon Sevan, my colleague on the Afghanistan brief, that were aimed at settling the civil war in that country. Many of these trips required not only two different passports—Israeli and Arab visas could not appear on the same document—but also separate tickets issued for the same reason.

In some of these meetings in the Middle East, my interlocutors, particularly if they were Palestinian, appeared to imply that they had some knowledge of the hostage dealings. I kept track of every bit of information, of course, but when nothing came of it, I began to sense that very few Middle Eastern governments could really help us much. Moreover, I was learning that government officials typically pretend to possess information, especially when it involves intelligence or covert operations, even when they do not. Still, I was too new to the game to rule anything out. I was learning to waltz with shadows.

The substantive advantage of dealing with several issues at the same time was that I could use elements of one issue as leverage for another. When I approached Iran, for example, I suggested that its assistance in freeing the Western hostages in Beirut might create a more favorable climate in the West toward the government in Teheran and change the balance of Western support for Iraq in the peace negotiations between the two countries.

In February 1989, an unexpected development further poisoned the political climate between Iran and the West and made approaches to Teheran even more difficult. Indian-born author Salman Rushdie was accused of blasphemy by Iranian clerics for his new book, The Satanic Verses, and a fatwa, an Islamic directive, was immediately issued by Imam Khomeini calling for his death. But I refused to be deterred by events that could be neither anticipated nor controlled. On April 23, 1989, I briefed Pérez de Cuéllar on my first small hostage proposal to Cyrus Nasseri. It amounted to two one-act plays. First, an "impartial" observer, such as a member of the secretary-general's office, would go to Lebanon to determine the health status of the hostages. Second, a high-level political meeting in a neutral country would be arranged between a member of the office of the secretary-general and a spokesman for the Lebanese groups holding the hostages. We obviously hoped that both proposals would be accepted, but we knew we had a better chance of getting something if the other side had two suggestions on the table.

Later that day, Pérez de Cuéllar met with Iranian Foreign Minister Velayati, who said he would consider our proposals. As he was about to leave, however, Velayati dropped a bombshell: "Some Lebanese sources," he said, had told him that Lieutenant Colonel Higgins had been killed around the time (July 1988) of the shooting down of the Iranian Airbus by the USS Vincennes.

By mid-May, Ambassador Nasseri officially communicated to me that our request for a show of goodwill by the Lebanese groups was not on and that he had "no influence on those people." I was not going to take no for an answer. By late May, I was in Teheran again for discussions on Afghanistan—Iran was supporting one of the tribes involved in the civil war—and was able to meet alone with Velayati. I reminded him that he owed Pérez de Cuéllar an answer to our request that Iran play an influential role in solving the hostage problem. His response was anything but circumspect. The foreign minister had indeed made contact with the "Lebanese people," as we had begun to refer to them, thus preserving a kind of wink-and-nod anonymity and the appearance of distance between Teheran and the Lebanese. The Lebanese apparently were considering a secret meeting with me in Europe, but there was still no response to my request to visit the hostages and verify their health conditions. The following day, May 30, Velayati informed me that the venue of the meeting had been determined: it would be Damascus, not Europe, and no date had been set. Of course, this now raised the question of how and when the Syrians should be informed, Velayati explained, but that was not my problem. As I was leaving his office, I was asked to pose for some mug shots—perhaps, I hoped, for circulation among certain people who would need to know what I looked like before meeting me.

By mid-1989, the only success we could report was that we had seriously engaged the government of Iran in the Lebanese hostage matter. During the course of that year, I met alone with Velayati about a half-dozen times, and more than twice that with Nasseri and other Iranian officials in New York, Europe, and the Middle East.

I never mentioned the subject of the hostages in New York outside the most tightly restricted circles; success, if we were to have it, required complete secrecy within the United Nations itself—virtually an oxymoron. Even within the secretary-general's office we never discussed the case in ways that might reveal my involvement. Everything I did on the hostage issue was marked for the files, "No Distribution. Original 1— Sec. Gen., G.P. Copy." It went into the "pink folder," inviolable to everyone except me and my assistant, Judith Karam. When I would tell Judy, "Put this in the pink folder," she knew what I meant. The two of us defended the file as if it meant my life, which is precisely what it would mean later in Beirut.

A Minnesotan of Swedish stock, Judith Karam had been a secretary with top-security clearance in U.S. embassies in Indochina during the Vietnam War. She then married a Lebanese Maronite Christian, a professor of economics in New York, and left government service to raise her children. She returned to work in the early 1980s, joining the United Nations as a secretary to American Under Secretary William Buffum. When she took the UN examinations for a promotion from General Service to Professional Level, she placed first, but at the time there was no opening for her in our office. She went on to serve a brief stint in the Protocol Department before joining our office as my assistant. Judith was the first American woman to be received by President Rafsanjani during the war as a member of the UN team, and after I left the United Nations in 1992, she became the UN desk officer for Iraq and Yemen and was the first woman to lead a UN mission, to the border of Iraq and Kuwait after Desert Storm.

In all political institutions, be they international organizations or governments, officials like to feel that they are always in the loop and sometimes unwittingly reveal information because they do not understand its implications. The hostage saga was an extremely unusual operation in the secretary-general's office. As negotiations began to unfold, it became very clear to me that any indiscretion could threaten the hostages' lives as well as my own. I wanted to avoid all unnecessary risks, so the entire affair became the exclusive province of Pérez de Cuéllar and myself. As expected, this caused bureaucratic clashes with other UN officials, especially within the secretary-general's office. To this day, I regret that, during those years, it was necessary to deceive the secretary-general's *chef de cabinet*, Virendra Dayal, who had no knowledge of the details of my operations—or even my whereabouts.

Dayal often complained to Pérez de Cuéllar, who would listen but give only vague responses. Then in frustration he would go to Judith and command her, "Tell me where Picco is!"

"I don't know," she would reply.

"Judith, I am your superior, I can fire you! You have to tell me!"

"I can't tell you what I don't know. Mr. Picco is very secretive. He doesn't tell us where he goes."

"You must know! You must have made his reservations!"

That was meant as a particularly telling thrust, which Judith parried with ease.

"Oh, Mr. Picco makes many reservations, and then at the airport he changes them all the time."

This was true. I would make three reservations at a time to cover my tracks. But Judy actually knew where I was every single hour. I would phone her from the most unlikely places and inform her of any change in my schedule by using a simple code—Wednesday meant Tuesday, Friday meant Thursday, and so forth. We also nicknamed people and subjects: the southerners meant the Israelis, the northerners meant the Lebanese, the turbans meant the Iranians, and so forth.

With Dayal, I felt I had no choice but to maintain my secrecy. Early on in the game, my Syrian intelligence contacts had advised me to be extremely prudent in my discussions with him; as far as Damascus was concerned, he had already jeopardized my operation once before by referring to one of my earlier trips as if it had been of no influence in the sequence of events that was to follow. My suspicion was that Dayal, an Indian national, tended to share information with diplomats of various countries in order to strengthen his position as somebody "in the know." He probably was right to do this because his bureaucratic position required that he know all the secretary-general's activities. Was the Syrian official right or wrong in his advice to me? I do not know. But I didn't have the luxury of giving Dayal the benefit of the doubt.

On June 3, 1989, Ayatollah Khomeini died in Teheran and our hopes for a more pragmatic government in Iran began to rise. On July 4, American Independence Day, Velayati declared in Geneva that he was ready to start whenever I was. The Lebanese had already picked Damascus as the site for our meeting. Velayati asked me to suggest two dates, one before the Iranian presidential elections and one after. I gave him my business card with two dates written on the back, July 16 and August 12. Velayati took the card and put it in his pocket, signaling that he would answer later.

Three weeks later, this delicate diplomatic construction collapsed. On July 28, with no date yet set for Damascus, Israeli commandos kidnapped Sheikh Abdul Karim Obeid from his house and took him to an Israeli prison. The Israelis hoped that Obeid, a leading Shiite cleric in southern Lebanon of some prominence within Hizbollah, could be used in trade for Ron Arad, an Israeli airman shot down over Lebanon in 1986 and still missing. The worldwide publicity was enormous.

Ali Akbar Hashemi Rafsanjani was elected president of Iran in July 1989, a good sign from our point of view, but the heightened tensions on the Lebanese-Israeli border were such that I never received a reply on a date for the Damascus meeting. The day after the kidnapping of Sheikh

Obeid, the Lebanese groups released a video showing Lieutenant Colonel Higgins being hanged. It took eight days for Pérez de Cuéllar to officially announce that Higgins had indeed been killed. But the question of when still lingered: Did the tape reflect a death that had just occurred or one that had taken place a year earlier, as we suspected?

By the end of July 1989, various Lebanese groups allegedly responsible for the detention of the Western hostages had begun to issue statements threatening to kill them in retaliation for the Israeli kidnapping of Sheikh Obeid; Iranian newspapers, meantime, were linking the killing of Higgins to the kidnapping of Obeid. We seemed to be starting off on the wrong foot, or so I thought. It turned out I was wrong.

Hope was reborn soon enough. On August 8, Sheikh Mohammed Hussein Fadlallah, the spiritual leader of the South Lebanese Shiites, declared publicly that Hizbollah was ready to free the hostages. On August 16, a long article in *The Wall Street Journal* described one Imad Moughniya, a name virtually unknown in the West, even though he was probably the most important man in control of Lebanon's hostages. Meanwhile, IRNA, the official Iranian news agency, was reporting that Iran was ready to help free the Western hostages in Lebanon but that its influence on their captors was merely spiritual.

On August 17, Rafsanjani told the foreign minister of Pakistan that he was prepared to assist in efforts aimed at obtaining the release of the hostages in exchange for some demonstration by Washington that it was no longer hostile toward Teheran. The new president, far more pragmatic and less ideological than his predecessors, had begun to see the end of the war with Iraq as a time to stabilize the revolution and return Iran to a position on the international stage.

From my point of view, Rafsanjani was doing more than trying to shift policy; he was also bringing to power a group of people whom I knew personally—in many cases, the same officials who had negotiated the cease-fire with Iraq. They, too, had tired of the long war and were ready to return to a more normal life. One was Cyrus Nasseri, the recently appointed ambassador to the United Nations in Geneva and proud father of a newborn daughter, who seemed to have replaced the revolution as the prime object of his affections. Another was Javad Zarif, who had been closely involved in ending the war and would become deputy foreign minister in 1992 at the tender age of thirty-three. Self-contained and wise beyond his years, Zarif had been selected by no less than the

Ayatollah Khomeini as Iran's ambassador to the United Nations in New York. His education abroad had made him totally fluent in English, but it had also separated him from his mother for some years. When the ayatollah wanted to take her son away again and plant him ten thousand miles away in New York, she finally put her foot down. She was in her late fifties and wanted him close to home, ayatollah or no ayatollah. So much for the supposed powerlessness of Iranian women! Velayati told us frankly and in English, "His mother doesn't want him to go." Zarif's help would prove invaluable to us as we pressed for the release of the hostages.

Things were looking up on another front as well: at last the Americans were engaging. In early August 1989, President Bush contacted Pérez de Cuéllar and asked him to receive Brent Scowcroft, his national security adviser, with an eye toward communicating with Rafsanjani. The White House had come to us because it realized we had direct access to the Iranian leadership and would be received on a one-on-one basis by the new Iranian president. It was another indication of the secretary-general's enhanced profile in international affairs.

At the beginning of August, Pérez de Cuéllar decamped to the Hamptons on the south shore of Long Island for ten days' vacation as he did every year. Messages and officials were shuttled back and forth every day. Plans were made for Scowcroft's visit. Scowcroft explained that Bush was prepared to embark on a series of reciprocal gestures that would ease relations and free the hostages. The basis of the policy was, of course, the passage about mutual goodwill beamed to Iran during Bush's inaugural address at the start of the year. Scowcroft's message was simple: both he and the president wanted a message delivered directly to Rafsanjani, with no intermediaries. They also wanted to hear his reaction to it. The secretary-general and the national security adviser played a bit with the wording; then Pérez de Cuéllar told Scowcroft that he would "work on the message and have Picco deliver it to the president of Iran."

My boss then called me in to discuss the message.

We agreed that it would be better to cast the message not as having come directly from Bush but rather as coming from Pérez de Cuéllar, explaining Bush's thinking. This might seem like a distinction without a difference, but relations between Washington and Teheran were so strained that if Rafsanjani were forced at some point to admit to radical factions in Iran that he had accepted a message from the American president, it would gravely embarrass him. We felt that we needed to protect Rafsanjani as the new man in Iran. Nasseri once said to me, "What Iran needs is a Gorbachev. I just hope we don't have to wait seventy years for one."

It was courageous of Bush to take the first step in trying to find a real solution to the hostage problem, a welcome change from his predecessor. I often joked that American politicians fell into two categories, those with passports and those without them—the latter often relying on secondhand information and stereotypes of foreign cultures. From our point of view, Ronald Reagan had been a man without a passport. Bush, in contrast, had lived and worked abroad. He had represented the United States in China and at the United Nations, had run the CIA, and had worked in the commercial world. I think we developed a very good rapport with him because he was a man with a passport.

My meeting with President Rafsanjani was set for August 25, about a fortnight after Scowcroft's visit. In my diary, I noted that this was the first time I had arrived in Teheran alone and without a visa. Everything seemed to be very well organized. Even the hotel appeared to be a bit cleaner than usual. A year after the end of the war, most of the graffiti had been removed from the walls, including the once ubiquitous slogan "Down with America." I noticed that some Iranians were even walking around wearing ties. The next morning, I met with the UN people in Teheran, and at around 5 P.M., Javad Zarif called to say there would be a slight delay because of a parliamentary vote to confirm the appointments to the new cabinet.

The following day I was granted an audience with Rafsanjani late in the afternoon, so I used the daytime for meetings dealing with other subjects such as Afghanistan. This would allow me to raise other issues if it became necessary to change the subject during my meeting with Rafsanjani. Zarif collected me for the trip to the Presidential Palace, where we waited a mere ten minutes. Everything around us was completely silent, in strange contrast to the Iranian government buildings, which were usually filled with people in constant motion. When I entered his office, Rafsanjani was sitting at his desk. My first impression was a sense of overpowering whiteness, accentuated by the afternoon light flooding the room through huge windows. The many sofas were white. Rafsanjani's turban was also white, indicating that he was not a descendant of the Prophet, as was his tunic, worn beneath a light brown mantle.

I sat down facing the president, offered him my best wishes on his birthday, which happened to be that day, and began to read the carefully crafted message from Pérez de Cuéllar: "I would like to comment to you on U.S.-Iran relations. I know George Bush very well. I have known him on a close basis since 1971 and I feel certain that I know how he thinks. I know that he would like to see improved U.S.-Iranian relations. Indeed, he has spoken to me on the subject and I call to your attention the statement he made in his inaugural address: 'Goodwill begets goodwill.' I do know for a certainty, in my own mind, that President Bush has sought the release of the American hostages . . . he would react swiftly by taking action on Iranian monetary assets blocked by the United States and other appropriate gestures. . . .

"You have called in public for the reverse of this sequence of actions. You should know that, in light of the political realities surrounding the Iran-contra affair, it would be impossible for President Bush to proceed in other than the sequence suggested. I am in a position to assure your Excellency that taking an initiative on the hostages would inevitably elicit a positive response on the part of the United States. Should you find it appropriate, my discreet good offices could be utilized in this matter for the benefit of all concerned. I am therefore interested for humanitarian reasons to pursue a dialogue with your Excellency on this matter and I would value highly the possibility of discussing it with you personally. The Belgrade Non-Aligned Summit meeting in September will, I hope, provide me the opportunity to discuss with you this and other important issues to the solution of which the Islamic Republic of Iran and the Secretary General can jointly contribute."

Zarif, the only other person present, was translating. I could see that Rafsanjani, motionless, was following the text very closely. He replied quickly, expressing regret at hearing such a message. He said that he regretted even having received it and that he had done so only because it had come from his friend the secretary-general of the United Nations, and certainly not because of its content. I can only imagine what his response would have been had we not interposed ourselves as intermediaries and left Bush as an open target!

I took careful notes on his comments: "We have had no relations for some time with those holding the hostages. They are not the traditional Hizbollah. When we were asked by Mr. [Robert] McFarlane [Reagan's national security adviser during the Iran-contra affair], we did try to contact them. After the promises were not carried out, those groups became alienated. We cannot establish one-way relations. These people are not easy to find. They do not have an address. It is difficult to get in touch with them. In the last few days, when the Lebanese situation has been highlighted [by the seizure of Sheikh Obeid], they told us that they were not ready to talk to us until Obeid was freed. As a first step, Sheikh Obeid must be freed. Also, the U.S. has frozen our assets without any legal basis. At the same time, it expects us to get involved in something of no interest to us. Like Mr. Bush, we also have internal concerns. They should not wait for anything to release our assets. For us to help the U.S. we need signals, one of them being that they must halt their unreasonable animosity towards us. Why should the American people be so illogical as to accept the freezing of our assets without reason? Bush can unfreeze the assets, and if they cannot do that, they should also know that we too have Iranian hostages in Lebanon. Bush could help us by pressuring the Maronite community, which is holding our hostages. The release of our hostages would be seen as an incentive for us. I accept this message only out of respect for the Secretary General. Otherwise, I would not have received it. In a situation of no relevance to us, there is no reason for me to accept the message. But I did. Please convey my greetings to the Secretary General."

We ended the meeting because there was clearly nothing more to say. When I got into the car, Zarif told me that I should never have brought the message because it implicated Iran directly in the hostage operations, a connection it had always denied. Still, I was pleased that Rafsanjani had even received the message and commented on it. But I was saddened by what Zarif said because I thought the whole episode might count against him professionally—or worse.

By raising the existence of Iranian hostages in Lebanon and requesting that the United States take the first goodwill step, Rafsanjani had helped to educate me in the complications I would face down the road. The Iranian president never made it to Belgrade for the summit meeting; instead, Pérez de Cuéllar met with Velayati. Surprisingly, the foreign minister indicated that the process of freeing the hostages could begin if the United States released 10 percent of the assets it had frozen after the seizure of the U.S. Embassy in Teheran in 1979. A few weeks later in New York, he dropped the other shoe: Washington also needed to make good on Reagan's promise to pay compensation for the victims of the Iranian Airbus shot down in 1988 by the *Vincennes*. There was still a long way to go.

CHAPTER 8

A Dangerous Game
with Many Players

ONCE THE WHITE HOUSE HAD LAUNCHED ITS NEW INITIATIVE with the secretary-general's office, Bush and Scowcroft maintained continuous contact with us, although they never interfered with the political or planning aspects of our hostage operations. Equally important, Scowcroft never gave me the impression that he underestimated the sophistication or the ability of the Iranian government, its top officials, or the Lebanese groups. The professionalism of Bush and Scowcroft stood in vivid contrast to the cockeyed Iran-contra hostage operations of Oliver North under Ronald Reagan two years earlier. North appeared to have had only a superficial knowledge of the political realities of the Persian Gulf, not to mention of the players involved. He had failed to recognize the complexity of the political relations that had emerged in the region following the Iranian revolution.

When briefed about my visit with Rafsanjani, Scowcroft expressed surprise that it had taken place without any witnesses present, which was unusual for such a high-level meeting. A few days later in New York, President Bush came to the United Nations to speak before the General Assembly. He indicated to Pérez de Cuéllar that he had received the message concerning the release of 10 percent of the frozen Iranian assets and hinted that he would respond one way or the other before the secretary-general met with Velayati at the end of September. But Pérez de Cuéllar heard from James Baker instead. On September 19, 1990, the U.S. secretary of state informed the UN secretary-general that Washington would not be responding to the message from the Iranian president; to do so, Baker explained, would show too much eagerness on the part of the United States to deal with the Iranian government.

We were caught in the classic turf battle between the State Department and the White House's National Security Council. In the months ahead, Baker and Thomas Pickering, the U.S. ambassador to the United Nations, would confirm our early suspicions that the White House wanted to move faster in communicating with Iran than State did. Why? We later learned that Baker had doubts about our ability to pull it off. In fact, we didn't have a track record on the hostage issue, so it wasn't until late summer of 1991 that Baker finally came around.

Tom Pickering was one of the best American ambassadors I ever had to deal with. He had a superb mind and a powerful delivery and was a sharp political thinker. Three weeks later, he tried to modify Jim Baker's position. On October 10, he indicated to the secretary-general that "the line is now open between the secretary-general and the U.S. government on this issue."

Pickering stressed that Washington's guiding principle was that the hostages must be freed purely on humanitarian grounds, never as the result of any deal. He quickly added, however, that Washington was examining the question of compensation for the Iranian Airbus victims. Eventually, Washington would agree to compensate the families of the victims but not the government of Iran, as Velayati had requested. He also reminded us that American lawyers were in touch with their Iranian counterparts in The Hague on the issue of the Iranian assets blocked in retaliation for the seizure of the U.S. Embassy in Teheran. Essentially, he was saying that the United States wanted the hostages released but did not want to be seen dealing openly with the Iranians. The conversation with us continued so far in this direction that Pérez de Cuéllar finally said, "Wait a minute, Tom, it was Washington that asked to start these messages, not me. So decide if you want to deal with it or not." Pickering conceded the point. The Bush administration had absolutely no desire to be caught striking an unsavory bargain for the hostages, as Oliver North had, with a government it deemed an outlaw regime. So there we were: Pickering was telling us that Washington would, under no circumstances, negotiate the liberation of the hostages; at the same time, he was reminding us about the possibility of unfreezing the Iranian assets and paying compensation for the victims of the Iranian Airbus downing. It seemed, at first, like a typical example of constructive ambiguity.

Still, Pickering was laying claim to a sound and even moral policy of refusing to reward an illegal action. It was clear to me early on that we, as UN officials, could never strike a deal in which money would be paid for the release of the hostages or, worse yet, in which we bartered the captives for convicted criminals held in other countries. In other words, since day one, I had made it clear to everybody that we would deal only regarding people "detained without due process," and not regarding anybody else. These principles, which were inviolable to me, were not upheld by some of the countries with citizens detained in Lebanon. I faced a challenge on this issue with respect to the two German hostages in Lebanon and came down on the side of the law; sadly, Boutros Boutros-Ghali, by then UN secretary-general, did not.

Even as we were talking with Pickering, we also knew that the Americans were using other channels beside the secretary-general's office. Washington, for example, had asked the Associated Press to send Larry Heinzerling, AP's man assigned to the Terry Anderson case, to Germany with a State Department lawyer for a conversation with a German intermediary who would then speak to the Iranians. The AP's advantage was that it could buffer the U.S. government against criticism that it was trafficking with the Iran.

We understood why the Americans wanted to try all possible routes to the hostages: these were, after all, mainly their nationals at risk. At one point, I was aware that three governments—those of Pakistan, New Zealand, and Syria—and two private organizations were trying to help Washington spring the hostages. The problem, however, was that the various channels could compete with one another unknowingly and be manipulated by the other side. It happened many times in 1991 that I made a proposal to the hostage holders only to hear them reply that somebody else had made them a better offer. My response was always that they should take the better offer.

I did not know how many of the private channels could reach the decision makers in Iran and eventually the kidnappers in Lebanon. We thought we had the best shot because we were already connected to the former and were confident that they would lead us to the latter, although to this day no one knows how much control the Iranians had over those who actually held the hostages. The various parties involved, from Iran to Hizbollah to the Islamic Jihad and other subgroups of militant Shia in Lebanon, all confirmed that the hostages' fate was especially precarious because no single person had total control or total authority over their situation. This reality would affect the way I operated in Lebanon. I never took the simple position that a political deal, even one struck at a high level, would ensure freedom for the hostages. The fact was that their jailers or handlers could and probably would decide at the last moment whether the captives would live free or die.

On the morning of January 19, 1990, George Bush, remembering that it was Pérez de Cuéllar's birthday, called him to convey his best wishes. He relayed, with "enormous concern," information that Iran and Hizbollah were sending sophisticated weapons to Europe for the purpose of hitting American and other Western targets, and that some of the weapons had been seized by Spanish authorities. He also said that a hit squad assigned to assassinate the author Salman Rushdie, the Indian-born Muslim whose last novel had offended Ayatollah Khomeini, had already entered Britain, where Rushdie was living under police protection. The president said that he wanted to improve relations with Iran but that developments of this nature would surely destroy his chances to do so. He wanted Rafsanjani to know what he knew.

Kamal Kharrazi, later appointed foreign minister of Iran in 1997, had just been named ambassador to the United Nations in New York. He denied the charges that Iranian weapons were being sent to Europe and repeated Teheran's interest in improving relations with Washington. How? He had a list of four items: the United States could release frozen Iranian assets; it could lift the embargo on the shipment of several hundred million dollars' worth of weapons bought and paid for by the shah before his ouster in 1979; it could provide support for the Algiers agreement, which the shah and Saddam Hussein had signed in 1975 to delineate the border between the two countries; and it could urge Saddam to withdraw the Iraqi troops who had continued to occupy a piece of Iranian territory since the end of the war. Iran, Kharrazi said, would use its influence on the question of the hostages. He also invited the secretary-general to present to Iran a complete package for the solution to the hostage problem. Kharrazi's direct line to Rafsanjani was already common knowledge as he began his tenure in New York. With his shortlist, he had just served notice to the Americans and the secretary-general that he would be a serious player, not just a government mouthpiece.

The families of the hostages, meantime, were becoming prominent players in the drama as well. I certainly had no objections to their honest and determined efforts to plead for the release of their loved ones in the most public way possible. Nobody is a professional in these matters. There is no science to it, no assurances, no certainty of anything. So how can you prevent a family that is living with a tragedy twenty-four hours a day from trying to do its best? Peggy Say, sister of Terry Anderson, perhaps the best-known American hostage, was especially active. At the end of January 1990, for example, she embarked on a whirlwind tour of Europe and the Middle East, including a visit with Syrian President Hafez al-Assad and an audience with the pope. She also had a meeting with the secretary-general.

Still, there is always a potential conflict between families and government officials on the usefulness of publicity to solve problems. The victim's families were very involved in keeping the attention of the public on the hostage situation, their activities emphasizing the captives as individuals; these were not, they seemed to be saying, people to be used as pawns by governments.

The families, who often complained that their governments were not doing enough, sometimes turned to me. I tried very hard to keep family members informed about positive developments but only when I felt these reports, which often made their way into the media, would not jeopardize the operation or the lives of the hostages. I truly wanted to help these people trapped by misfortune, but my contacts with them were as frustrating as they were deeply moving because they were asking me to deliver what I was not sure I could.

Much more problematical were rogue intermediaries. For example, a former American serviceman who had become a Muslim appeared on my radar screen. He had fought with the Mujahideen in Afghanistan, whereupon he had been recruited by the Iranians to fight with Hizbollah in Lebanon. His existence had been known for some time, and he had been contacted by a hostage's family. The *Washington Times* described him as "unbalanced." Truth to tell, his information was not far off the mark, but that did not help us. Throughout the hostage operation, in fact, I would receive indications from humanitarian organizations such as the International Committee of the Red Cross (ICRC) and Human Rights Watch, among others, that individuals of dubious origin were being used as intermediaries with the groups in Lebanon. Tracking down these rumors could take time.

In the early morning of February 5, 1990, a man called the White House, said he was phoning from Teheran, and identified himself as an adviser to Rafsanjani. He was put through to Scowcroft, who was told that President Rafsanjani would like to speak directly to President Bush. Scowcroft, unable to catch the man's name, said that Bush was not available but that he might be sometime after noon, thus buying time to find out if the call was genuine. The president's national security adviser immediately telephoned Pérez de Cuéllar to ask if we could help verify the caller.

The self-proclaimed Rafsanjani adviser called back and, before his identity could be confirmed, was inadvertently put through to the president. The caller told Bush that Iran wanted good relations with the United States and was prepared to help in the release of the hostages, provided that Washington would release Iranian assets. He also said that Iran wanted the United States to make a public announcement clarifying that President Rafsanjani had taken the initiative to improve relations with the United States. Before he could answer any questions by Bush, the communication was cut off.

Bush personally followed up with a call to the secretary-general. As a gesture to Rafsanjani, he insisted that the Iranian president be alerted to the matter since it could be a potential embarrassment. Accordingly, I sent a message via Cyrus Nasseri, the Iranian ambassador to the United Nations in Geneva. We also contacted a number of government officials in Teheran, including Foreign Minister Velayati. We were able to identify a possible interpreter for Rafsanjani who could have made the phone call. But within a few days, it appeared clearer and clearer that the phone call had probably been inspired by a political enemy of Rafsanjani who wanted to embarrass the Iranian president domestically by suggesting that he had taken the initiative to speak personally to the president of the United States. It was a further indication of our anomalous situation—that there were political divisions in Iran and that not everyone might want to close the book on the hostage episode.

Nevertheless, by the end of February 1990, President Rafsanjani himself conveyed his determination to assist us in the solution of the hostage problem in Beirut. Whether President Bush's gesture of alerting him to the hoax phone call influenced his decision to move forward remains a matter of conjecture. In March, he made his cooperative position public on a number of occasions, and in early April, we saw the dividends: American hostages Robert Polhill and Frank Reed were released. The Iranian government, it seemed, had blinked first and indicated to Washington that the process—goodwill begetting goodwill—could begin.

By now the press had taken up the cause of the Western hostages. Few stories are leaked, in the Middle East or elsewhere for that matter, without some purpose. Articles in the late winter and early spring of 1990 brought to the forefront the story of Sheikh Mohammed Hussein Fadlallah, the spiritual leader of the Shia of Lebanon. In 1990, he became a very vocal supporter of a solution to the hostage problem, and his words were not to be taken lightly. Sheikh Fadlallah was a cleric with a long history dating back to the Najaf schools in Iraq, the cradle of Shiite learning frequented by many Iranian clerics during the shah's regime. By the late 1970s, he and many other Lebanese clerics had returned home as the government in Baghdad was turning the country into a secular state. Saddam adhered to the Baath Party, which was, by definition, the socialist secular party of the Arab world.

When Sheikh Fadlallah had returned to Lebanon, he and others had formed the Al Dawa movement, the core of what would become Hizbollah in 1982. On December 12, 1983, Lebanese members of Al Dawa had arranged a series of explosions in the Emirate of Kuwait during a ninety-minute operation that had killed six people, injured more than eighty, destroyed the American Embassy compound, damaged the French Embassy, and, by pure miracle, barely avoided destroying the Shuaiba Petrochemical Plant, one of the biggest in the world. The culprits, seventeen in all, had been seized and sentenced to life in prison. It was the imprisonment in Kuwait of the Dawa Seventeen, as they became known, that had unleashed the kidnappings of Westerners in Lebanon. The objective was to force their native countries to convince Kuwait to release the prisoners.

Fadlallah, meanwhile, had risen in prestige among the Shiite communities of Lebanon and had become a spiritual point of reference for the political leaders of Hizbollah. In Shia Islam, whether in Iran or

Lebanon, individuals respond to their own spiritual leaders much more than they do to any political authority. It is for this reason, perhaps, why it was—and remains—so difficult to deal with Iran. Individual ministers or political personalities do not necessarily follow the instruction of their political superiors but seek guidance from their own spiritual leader, an ayatollah or cleric, who may or may not be part of the government.

I would eventually meet Sheikh Fadlallah several months later, but in the spring of 1990, the press was eagerly following his trips to Teheran as well as his Friday sermons. His public comments were particularly important since Sheikh Fadlallah was known to have "blessed" the suicide mission of the Shiite militants against American and French military barracks in Beirut seven years earlier. Yet it was common wisdom that those on the operational side of Hizbollah would keep their spiritual leader detached from their military plans in order to protect him from possible retaliation. Regardless of the intricacies of Hizbollah's internal arrangements, what Sheikh Fadlallah said always mattered.

When, in a Friday sermon, he said that the hostage problem was close to being solved, news agencies and CNN flashed his words around the world. "This is nothing extraordinary," he added. "I noticed during my stay in Teheran a positive atmosphere. I am always urging an end to [the hostage] problem, and I raise it on every occasion." Remarkably, Sheikh Fadlallah was publicly drawing Iran into the hostage web.

But by then, even authoritative voices in Iran were arguing that, on the basis of Islamic law, there was no justification for holding hostages. The chief justice of Iran, Ayatollah Mohammed Yazdi, came out and said that Iran opposed acts of terrorism such as holding hostages because they contradicted both Islamic and humanitarian principles. The Islamic revolution, he said, did not imply violations of international law. This had a double meaning: Iran was opposed to hostage taking, and it was not responsible for what was happening in Lebanon.

Such public statements were analyzed in the West for their practical implications, but they also had much to do with the internal politicking among various clerical factions. The relationship between the Iranian clerics and the Lebanese clerics was complex and could not be sorted out through a simple analysis of the strategic interests of the two countries. It was well known, for instance, that Sheik Fadlallah, who had always had high respect for Imam Khomeini, did not consider Khomeini's anointed successor, Ayatollah Khamanei, to be on the same scholarly level as Fad-

lallah himself. In other words, one could conclude that Fadlallah had allies as well as enemies in Iran in much the same way that President Rafsanjani could count on some close friends as well as some antagonists in
Hizbollah. How this translated into operational consequences for the
hostages was yet another nightmare I would have to confront if we
wanted to secure their freedom in the months ahead.

We received an important message from Ambassador Pickering on March
5, informing us that Washington had found our channel the most
promising and would conduct its business concerning the hostages only
through us. This may or may not have been true, but it demonstrated
enough confidence for us to proceed in our work. Earlier, Pickering had
indicated that if Iran wanted to discuss hostages, a senior American official could be appointed to take over the talks; now he asked me if I was
making progress in visiting the hostages. Unfortunately, I had to report
that I had made none.

The next day I heard from a source in Teheran that others were claiming that they, too, had been singled out by Washington as the primary
channel. Three days later, Pickering called to alert me that a message was
coming from the White House to the secretary-general indicating Washington's desire to reduce tensions with Iran, but not until the hostages
were released. This was supposed to strengthen the position that the
United Nations was the only channel. Over the past several weeks,
Lebanese sources had been quoted in the West as claiming that negotiations between Washington and Teheran to resolve the hostage problem
were under way in Geneva. These "secret talks" did not exist, but the stories had achieved a life of their own. Now President Bush felt it was necessary to assure Pérez de Cuéllar that he wanted the UN secretary-general
to be the key intermediary.

The message from Pickering also reminded Teheran that Bush had
tried to warn the Iranians about the mysterious caller but had received
only intemperate retorts in return. The Iranians replied by rejecting the
hostage condition as "inappropriate" and saying that the reference to the
mystery caller was "unclear." Sure enough, the story of the mysterious
telephone call to Bush had been leaked in *The New York Times* through
Thomas Friedman, at that time a confidant of Secretary of State Jim Baker.

It looked like typical Washington infighting, with the press delivering Baker's blow against Scowcroft, squeezing him out of the negotiations. Baker followed it up by telling Pérez de Cuéllar that communications on the hostages should be conveyed personally to Bush, to Baker himself, or to Ambassador Pickering, thus painting Scowcroft out of the picture.

So there it was: on the one hand, I had to worry about the politicking in Teheran, on the other about the politicking in Washington. Eventually, Israeli politics would come into play, not to mention the political dynamic of the Islamic groups in Lebanon. No books or schools of diplomacy could teach one how to navigate these waters. This was strictly an on-the-job operation.

Six months into 1990, we had fully engaged both the Iranians and the Americans in the hostage situation. There was no more shadowboxing in Teheran about clout with Hizbollah in Lebanon and no further hand-wringing in Washington about the appropriateness of engaging the Iranians in a hostage-related negotiation. As far as I was concerned, the Iranians were discussing the matter with us and not with the Americans, and we had simply asked them to use their influence with the kidnappers. They agreed to do so at the highest level. Washington, although refusing any deal that it would regard as illegal or immoral, had begun to make us more credible in the eyes of the Iranians because of the direct relationship that existed between President Bush and Pérez de Cuéllar.

It soon became clear that Rafsanjani and Velayati wanted it known to the secretary-general and me that they deserved credit for the release of Polhill and Reed by exercising their influence with the kidnappers. Velayati also stressed that their efforts had carried a heavy domestic political cost because not everyone in Iran favored releasing hostages. They were obviously seeking something in return—but without the appearance of a deal. Their first request was for the release of Sheikh Obeid by Israel. Their second was for assistance in the peace negotiations with Iraq, specifically to receive Washington's support for the 1975 Algiers agreement, which determined the border between the two countries. We were spared a response by a larger and unexpected development: on August 1, 1990, Saddam Hussein's troops invaded Kuwait, setting up what was perhaps the supreme irony of the hostage affair.

Historically, the kidnappers in Lebanon had linked the release of hostages to the release of the Dawa Seventeen prisoners held in Kuwait. The Kuwait government, of course, considered their release out of the question; the Americans, meantime, were unwilling to pressure the Kuwaitis to relent, given the moral and legal implications of the barter proposal. For two years, I had simply been ignoring the request because I knew it had no negotiating merit.

The irony was that on the night of August 2, when Iraqi troops invaded Kuwait City, they also opened the gates of Kuwait Salidia Central Prison, allowing the Dawa Seventeen to flee. The Dawa Seventeen eventually made their way back to Lebanon. Unwittingly, the president of Iraq had untied the most difficult knot of the entire hostage saga in one fell swoop. It did not take us more than a few hours to realize that a new window of opportunity had been opened for the hostages in Beirut.

The world was now focusing on the invasion of Kuwait by a powerful neighboring regime and on the potential consequences of this violation of international law on the region. I often wonder whether we could have solved the hostage situation without this development. In a Cartesian world, the hostages in Lebanon would have been less valuable, reducing the heat a bit in a situation previously at a boil. But in the Lebanon of 1990, the opposite could also have been true. Since their lives no longer had value as human barter, the hostages had less value to their captors, who could have killed them at any moment and vanished into the backstreets of Beirut. I could not discount that possibility.

To ensure that the second scenario would not come to pass, the only thing I could do was impress upon the Iranians that the death of any of the hostages would, rightly or wrongly, be blamed by the world on their government. They therefore had a vested interest in continuing negotiations and ensuring that the groups in Lebanon did not act irrationally.

On August 15, Saddam Hussein inadvertently helped us again, this time publicly announcing that Iraq would recognize the border with Iran as agreed in the Algiers agreement of 1975. Saddam had finally conceded the major issue that had fueled his fight with Iran for eight years and cost the lives of hundreds of thousands of his people. Clearly Iraq's new enemy was much bigger than Iran.

With the world's attention focused on Iraq and Kuwait, on August 25 Velayati hinted for the first time that it might be possible for me to see the hostages when I returned to Teheran with Jan Eliasson the following week to discuss the details of the Iran-Iraq peace treaty. (Following the cease-fire, the Swedish diplomat had been appointed by Pérez de Cuéllar as his special representative to the Iran-Iraq peace talks.) Assessing the overall regional situation, Velayati foresaw that "war is almost inevitable" because the West would not permit Saddam Hussein to grab Kuwait. The Iranians feared a new war against Saddam, not only because they had just emerged from one but because they knew that this time it would be waged by the United States. Once it put troops into the Middle East, they reasoned, the United States would not only knock Saddam out of power but also gain all the justification it needed to remain and meddle in the politics of the region.

Even before the smoke cleared, Iran had received, free of charge, an unprecedented concession from Iraq in Saddam's acceptance of the border agreements he had tried to break by going to war almost a decade earlier. He had apparently yielded on the border issue with Iran in order to protect his flank in Kuwait, but that proved a strategic miscalculation on his part. When Iraqi pilots landed their aircraft in Iran during the Gulf War to safeguard them from destruction by the Allied coalition, the Iranians requisitioned them, repainting them in Iranian colors. Adding insult to injury, Iran provided the coalition forces with whatever intelligence it could.

Many in the Islamic world now perceived Saddam Hussein as a competitor with Iran for the leadership of the Islamic masses, since he was able to stand up to the West. Saddam had even called for a jihad against the West, covering himself with the mantle of a good Muslim ready to wage holy war. He tried to transform his invasion into a battle between Islam and the West. Huge pictures suddenly appeared on television screens of this utterly secular leader, who had sprung from the most important secular party in the Middle East, at prayer in the mosques. Iranians quickly recognized the danger Saddam posed to their claims of regional leadership against the West. The fact that the Dawa Seventeen were no longer on the bargaining table had given the hostages a different value for the Iranians and made Teheran feel more comfortable assisting with their release. Still, the Iranians had to proceed gingerly lest a release tarnish their stern Islamic credentials.

On September 26, 1990, when I asked for a meeting with a representative of the groups as a first step toward the hostages' release, I discovered that the kidnappers were considering moving the location of our meeting from Damascus to Lebanon. Zarif suggested that I might be able to meet Hussein Mussavi, one of the historic leaders of the Islamic Amal, an organization associated with Hizbollah since 1984 that was charged with coordinating the military units of the Party of God. But the Iranians were concerned for my safety. They were prepared to arrange a meeting with an appropriate person, but not in Lebanon. It was the first time any Iranian official had been so specific about my possible meeting.

A few days later, in a discussion with Pérez de Cuéllar, Velayati said he no longer resented Washington's refusal to reciprocate for the release of the two hostages, Polhill and Reed. He again raised the possibility of unfreezing Iranian assets and confirmed that the plan was for me to meet Mussavi. But at that point he threw a new chip onto the pile, seeking for the first time the release of Lebanese who were being held in Israel. We relayed this to Bush and Scowcroft, who received it without comment because it would involve the Israelis. Tel Aviv had not yet been consulted about the operation that was under way.

What was clearly emerging was a pattern of multiple reciprocity—except that the possible quids pro quos involved no firm commitments by anybody. It therefore seemed logical to me to start suggesting some incentives that the United Nations itself could set up to facilitate the release of the hostages—in effect, covering different bases with different options. One morally correct step, I thought, would be to set up a reconstruction and relief fund for Lebanon, the funds from which would be distributed among its various communities by the UN Development Program once the hostages had been released. Many governments had already set aside some foreign aid for the reconstruction of Lebanon. The money, however, had been frozen, awaiting better times.

Pérez de Cuéllar and I drafted a program for a special fund for Lebanon, with former Italian Prime Minister Bettino Craxi a distinct possibility to head it. Craxi had already served as a special envoy of the secretary-general on the issue of Third World debt. He enjoyed his UN position and wanted to continue in some capacity, as many people do once they become attached to the world body. The entire construct, however, was conditional—exclusively for the purpose of providing us with an extra tool should it become necessary during negotiations for the hostages. The idea, which was used and abused by me for a few months as a possible negotiating card, was to set up an economic assistance program that I knew the Italians could fund because they had money for

Lebanon in their foreign aid budget. I wanted to be sure it would be distributed fairly among all the communities in Lebanon: Christians, Sunnis, and Shia. Other potential donors were the French, Japanese, Germans, British, and Americans. I also discussed the fund with the Iranians, knowing that they would pass on their knowledge to the "groups."

The program never went anywhere. I soon learned that, contrary to common belief in the West, money was not going to solve the hostage problem. In fact, the Lebanese themselves, when the matter eventually came up, turned it down as irrelevant in the context of our discussions. Humanitarian aid from the West would not buy a single captive. I believe that the only money that eventually did change hands was Teheran's regular subsidy to Hizbollah, rumored to be about $30 million a year, which never did buy the group's total obedience. The relationship was never that simple.

It was not money or reconstruction that attracted the Lebanese who held the hostages. Their coin was pride, power, and politics. It was Hizbollah that unraveled the Lebanese-Israeli agreement put together by Secretary of State George Shultz in 1983. It was Hizbollah that successfully fought against the multinational-national force and secured its withdrawal from Beirut in 1984. And it was Hizbollah that forced the Israeli Army to withdraw in January 1985 from the Beirut suburbs all the way to the south of Lebanon. No other Lebanese group had been able to accomplish the expulsion of both the United States and Israel from its soil, wrote Magnus Ranstorp in his 1997 book, *Hizb'allah in Lebanon*.

The Kuwaiti crisis remained center stage in world affairs as preparations for war were made. But exactly because the hostage crisis was out of the public eye, I felt I could pursue it with more determination. It has always been my philosophy that the time to prepare real proposals and solutions is when nobody is looking.

Throughout 1990, we continued to receive occasional assurances from Washington that we were the only channel on the hostage case. With the same frequency, we would continue to receive indications from the same American officials that other channels were being used. It was understandable, for example, that the American authorities might use a government such as the Swiss, which had represented their interests in

Iran after diplomatic relations between Teheran and Washington had been severed in 1980. The situation was a bit muddled in Teheran as well. In the Foreign Ministry structure, the Lebanese hostage situation came under the responsibility of the deputy foreign minister for American and European affairs, Mahmoud Vaezi, who also favored the Swiss channel. (In February 1991, Pickering would admit to Pérez de Cuéllar that contacts through the Swiss channel were alive and well despite the year-long declaration of love toward us by the U.S. government.)

By late 1990, the Iranian officials I dealt with had been raising the notion that the American government might appoint an unofficial envoy, perhaps an American businessman close to the White House, who could sit directly with them and be a buffer for "official Washington." The idea went back and forth with both Tom Pickering and Brent Scowcroft. The U.S. government came back with a more formal suggestion: that Robert Kimmitt, under secretary of state for political affairs, fill the role.

This was a nonstarter in Teheran: a formal contact with such a high-level political figure, if leaked to the press, would have done great damage to the Rafsanjani team. It's unclear whether the Kimmitt suggestion was Jim Baker's way of trying to keep the hostage matter at State rather than at the White House or whether President Bush felt that the contact needed to be formal. In early 1991, Bush himself contacted the secretary-general to see if the matter had gone any further and on February 8 said that "a quiet contact would be OK for us."

Governments regularly change their minds and sometimes deceive to protect their higher interests. This is to be expected in the real world of international affairs. It also meant that Pérez de Cuéllar and I—not being nationals of any of the countries involved in the hostage problem—ran the risk of being sacrificed, politically or otherwise, for reasons unknown to us. We needed to counterprogram accordingly. I insisted, therefore, that we had to have our own cards for negotiations that would depend only on us. If we did not have at least one card, we would have to invent it and make it so appealing to those holding the hostages that they would want nothing else. This was the toughest part of being a negotiator for the UN secretary-general rather than for a national government. The secretary-general had no money or weapons to trade, yet I did not want to be at the mercy of governments that could, for politically understandable reasons, dispose of me at any time. This became even more important in the months that followed, when I realized that I was going to negotiate not only for the freedom of the hostages but for my own life as well. If anyone were going to sacrifice me, I would do the job myself.

One piece of good news emerged on another front: in September 1990, British hostage Brian Keenan was released—the result, in all likelihood, of the release by Israel of forty prisoners it had detained without due process in southern Lebanon. That left six Americans, three Brits, and two Germans still in captivity, plus a number of missing Israelis and scores of Lebanese held without due process. As the new year unfolded, the internal politicking in Iran, Washington, and Israel and within the Lebanese groups only strengthened my determination to resolve the hostage crisis in our own way. To that end, in 1991 I developed two cards I could play that depended on two people and two alone: Pérez de Cuéllar and me.

CHAPTER 9

Beirut

Anatomy of the Deal

O N THE EVENING OF JANUARY 16, 1991, Javier Pérez de Cuéllar got a telephone call from George Bush. An hour earlier, the president told the secretary-general, the order had been given to the U.S. military to launch Tomahawk cruise missile attacks on Baghdad—the first blows in the second Persian Gulf War. Bush had said that Iraq's seizure of Kuwait would not stand, and coalition forces were about to underscore the point.

The military strike cut short a diplomatic approach by the secretary-general that should never have started. The proposed solution turned on a quid pro quo: in exchange for the withdrawal of Iraqi troops from Kuwait, there would be some tangible political gains for the Palestinians. The problem was the absence of any real connection between the Palestinian cause and Saddam's invasion; the Palestinian issue simply was not a strategic consideration for Baghdad. Pérez de Cuéllar's major advisers in this matter knew a great deal about the Palestinian-Israeli confrontation but had little experience with the Gulf. They had never dealt with Saddam, and they probably did not realize that what mattered to him and to Iraq was the Gulf, including Iran, and a desire for hegemony in the Arab world.

I had been dealing with Iraq, Saddam, and the Gulf for almost ten years, and I was convinced that the latest crisis would require brinkmanship and, if necessary, war. It was the first time I knew that not everything could be negotiated. My voice was a lonely one, however, and Pérez de Cuéllar pressed ahead. In the end, Saddam himself did the moral equivalent of hooting at the naive UN proposals when he publicly rejected them on January 14, 1991, during Pérez de Cuéllar's last visit to Baghdad.

The months of failed diplomacy over the Kuwaiti crisis had weakened Pérez de Cuéllar personally and politically; the credibility of his office had been diminished, and an approach seen in some quarters as appeasement may well have cost him any chance for reelection to an unprecedented third term as secretary-general. He was my mentor and, by now, my friend as well, and it was painful to watch as my colleagues put him in such a difficult position. The episode left me even more determined to keep my hostage activities as secret—and as far away from the United Nation's bureaucratic machinery—as possible.

The entire Kuwait crisis inadvertently helped provide cover for my offscreen operations and resolved several contentious issues put on the table by the Iranians and the groups in Lebanon. The Dawa Seventeen had been set free by Iraqi troops, the Algiers agreement had unexpectedly been accepted by Baghdad, and Iraqi troops in Iranian territory had returned home. Suddenly, the negotiating table appeared less cluttered—or so I thought.

We had to seize the moment. Pérez de Cuéllar agreed to pressure the Iranians to arrange a meeting for me with a Lebanese interlocutor *valable* as soon as possible. By then, we had accepted the fact that a remote-control solution via Teheran alone would not work. We hoped, however, that an encounter with the appropriate Lebanese Shia, possibly outside Lebanon, would suffice. The request was sent to Iran in late January 1991. Shortly thereafter, on January 28, we were informed by Teheran that two Tomahawk missiles launched by a U.S. warship had fallen in Iranian territory near Dezfūl and Mahshah along the border with Iraq. Iran asked the secretary-general to relay this information to Washington and also made it clear that it would keep the matter quiet and hidden from public knowledge. It wasn't exactly "the enemy of my enemy is my friend," but it did seem that the war against Iraq allowed for the exchange of some courtesies between Teheran and Washington.

In mid-February, Ambassador Kamal Kharrazi informed us that he was trying to arrange for me to meet with Sheikh Fadlallah instead of with Hussein Mussavi. This seemed a more appropriate first step if it could be done since the Lebanese cleric had ostensibly held higher authority over his people even though he had been removed from the day-to-day operations of Hizbollah. The other reason, in the kitchen politics of the Lebanese Shiite militants, might simply have been that Hussein Mussavi was losing ground. Kharrazi made clear that he wanted the U.S.

government to be given advance knowledge of developments in the planning stages before proceeding with the meeting. It was a line he would continually take during that crucial year to make sure we would eventually "deliver" Washington—"Goodwill begets goodwill." Kharrazi also wanted to keep open the idea of a fund for the reconstruction of Lebanon. Neither of us knew then that money would carry no weight with the kidnappers nor, for that matter, with Sheikh Fadlallah.

I spent much of that month preparing for the meeting, both in substance and in logistics. Could I bring an assistant with me to take notes during my meeting with the sheikh? No, the answer came back. Some of my Iranian counterparts left the distinct impression that they expected a series of Fadlallah-Picco meetings, after which both the Western hostages in Beirut and others being detained elsewhere would be released en masse. Given their expectations, the Iranian officials were now becoming more specific about the existence of their own people held hostage in Beirut. In particular, four staff members of the Iranian Embassy in Lebanon had disappeared in 1982, during the many battles in the city over that period. According to Teheran, the four Iranians had been taken by Christian militias.

By March 1991, the war against Iraq was over and the balance of power in the region had changed more than at any time since World War II: in a matter of a few months, the United States had become a significant presence in the Gulf, both economically and militarily. The media, in both Beirut and the West, resumed their interest in the hostage case, and the rumor mills were churning. I was getting bits of information from military and civilian contacts; much of it was worthless, but everything had to be checked out. The UN Interim Force in Lebanon (UNIFIL) sent a cable reporting that "according to security sources, the release of six American hostages will take place on March 22, 1991 in a Beirut hotel. From there, the hostages will be transferred to Damascus where they will be handed over to the U.S. ambassador. The other Western hostages will be released on March 23, 1991 in the presence of the ambassadors of their respective countries." It was hard to ignore this information, especially since it came from forces that had been stationed in Lebanon since 1978, a lifetime given how much had happened over the years. A few days later, a spokesman for Hizbollah knocked down all the rumors: "We hope all local and international media will be accurate and not rely on any other source but the press office of Hizbollah. There will be no release of any Western hostages in Lebanon." The Lebanese press continued to quote various sources, with one report making the rounds saying that the Western hostages' release would be directly linked to the release of thousands of Lebanese and Palestinians held prisoner by Israel. At the same time, Hizbollah leaders like Hussein Mussavi were quoted as calling on the Americans and the Israelis to empty their jails of innocent Arab prisoners.

Six months earlier, the Iranians had raised the point that many of "their brothers" remained prisoners in Israel. Now, in March 1991, the Iranian press revived the issue, arguing that it was unfair to talk just about Westerners who were unjustly detained. Here, it seemed to me, was another possible bargaining chip for the endgame—an exchange of Western hostages for Lebanese detainees held by Israel without due process of law.

During my next trip to Teheran, on March 19, I met with Deputy Foreign Minister Vaezi to discuss details of my forthcoming visit with Sheikh Fadlallah. He had just returned from Switzerland, where he had been discussing the hostage situation with Hans Jacobi, under secretary of state for foreign affairs. "We are beginning to discuss an exchange between American hostages and prisoners of Israel," Vaezi said, adding, "The only thing I can tell you is that the 'people in Lebanon' [code for Hizbollah] know where to find two Israeli bodies." The Israelis had been searching for seven Israeli soldiers who had been missing in Lebanon since the 1980s. He indicated that they did not know about any other bodies, which made any trade increasingly difficult because the Israelis were insisting on information on all seven in exchange for the prisoners Hizbollah wanted. One body was eventually returned to Israel by the Syrians in the summer of 1991. The other six became part of my dossier and were included in the total package that I tried to put together.

Reports that negotiations with the Swiss channel were well advanced gave me pause. I told Vaezi that we would withdraw from the operation if it would help the Swiss channel conclude negotiations to release the hostages more quickly. He responded that Pérez de Cuéllar and I had been approved personally by President Rafsanjani and that there was no guarantee that the Swiss channel would work. Furthermore, Vaezi said, Iran preferred a UN umbrella to avoid the impression that this was an issue between Iran and the United States. What I had suspected was true: the Iranians were attempting to make the United Nations and the Swiss compete, hoping to get a better offer by playing one off against the other. It was a trap I made sure never to fall into again.

We told the Americans that we were, of course, aware of the Swiss channel. No big deal, they responded; we have two channels because there are two very different relationships. The Swiss channel was a general contact between the United States and Iran via the country representing American interests in Teheran in the absence of diplomatic relations; the UN channel was to deal specifically with the hostage issue through the secretary-general's office. Pérez de Cuéllar found this explanation disingenuous at best, but there was nothing much we could do about it except to proceed with our business. To that end, I met with Brent Scowcroft in Washington on April 3 to brief him on our progress with Teheran and on the people I planned to see in Beirut. He was unaware of how far the "specific channel" had advanced and surprised by the level of cooperation we had obtained from Iran.

I left New York for Teheran on April 7, a trip that turned out to be just the first leg of a longer journey. The omens seemed especially promising. April 8 was the feast of Eid al-Fitr, which ends the month of Ramadan with week-long celebrations in the Muslim world. Israel also chose April 8 to announce it was freeing a thousand Palestinians in connection with the visit of U.S. Secretary of State James Baker.

I arrived in Teheran in darkness and made my way to the Esteghlal Hotel overlooking the city from the hills. The American flag had long since been removed from the floor of the lobby. In true Middle Eastern fashion, the diplomats who received me and helped me settle in that night chatted as if I had come for a totally different reason. They talked about the number of people who had fled Iraq because of the war, many of them Christians, and how these and other refugees needed food supplies from the United Nations. Our conversation was almost anticlimactic. My meeting with Vaezi was set for the following afternoon, and I remained confident that sponsors in Teheran had made all the necessary arrangements for my trip to Damascus to meet Sheikh Fadlallah.

Vaezi had news regarding both the Swiss and UN channels. He had met with the Swiss foreign minister, he said, who had relayed a supposed Israeli offer to release 325 prisoners in exchange for all the Western hostages and three Israeli POWs. But the kidnappers in Lebanon had rejected 325 as insufficient and demanded that the Israelis release 600. Vaezi, in effect, was chiding me for accomplishing nothing while the Swiss claimed they could get back 325 prisoners from the Israelis. I never checked out his story with the Swiss, but I'm sure they were told by Vaezi that I was offering to free even more prisoners than they were.

It was our business, in any event, that I had come to conduct. "You may go to Damascus tomorrow," Vaezi told me, providing I got a visa or other document that would permit me to travel to Syria. To obtain travel documents through regular channels, however, I would need to explain the purpose of my visit, which I obviously did not want to do. Perhaps, given his country's good relations with Syria, Vaezi could intercede on my behalf, I suggested to him. He agreed, but despite his best efforts, something went wrong and I found myself having to wait. This was to become the leitmotif of my year of living dangerously: nothing would happen according to plan, absolutely nothing.

The postponement stretched into April 10, when Secretary of State Baker was due in Syria. Finally, on the morning of April 11, I met with Vaezi and received my UN laissez-passer with a Syrian visa, then flew immediately to Damascus.

The United Nations Disengagement Observer Force (UNDOF) in the Golan Heights, which patrols the border between Syria and Israel, was headquartered in Damascus following an agreement brokered in 1973 by Henry Kissinger. UNDOF officials had received a very cryptic message from the UN office in Teheran that told them little more than to meet me at the airport and provide me with all the facilities I might request. It read, "Wish to inform you that senior official from SG's office will be at your location as of April 11, 1991. May need your assistance during stay there on an emergency or urgent basis, particularly on areas of arranging travels on very short notice and providing him with your telephone numbers as known to me here. Would appreciate your confirming with return cables the number or numbers where he can be reached on a 24-hour basis." In my mind, the cable marked a turning point in our passage: the rescue operation had truly begun.

Awaiting me at the end of the airport runway were a Syrian colonel, two officials from the Iranian Embassy in Damascus, and Steiner Bjornsson, the administrative officer of UNDOF. It was an awkward moment. The Iranians did not know why the Syrian colonel was present and were confused when they and the colonel simultaneously began moving toward me. The colonel may have believed that the Iranian diplomats were meeting someone else. Being relatively new to the game myself, I was unsure whom to greet first and decided to see who approached me. The person who sized up the moment was the savvy Bjornsson, an Icelander who had served the United Nations in many countries and seen his fair share of awkward situations. He moved forward in tandem with the Syrian colonel, and I then proceeded to greet the two Iranian officials.

The welcoming party was clearly not what the Iranians had expected. My first stop that evening was supposed to be the Iranian Embassy, where Ambassador Mohammed Hassan Akhtari, a cleric who would become pivotal in our hostage plans, was in charge of the arrangements. But the arrival of the Syrian colonel apparently forced a change of plans. One of the Iranians made a quick telephone call, then informed me that my meeting with his ambassador had been postponed to the following day.

Much to the surprise of the Iranians, the Syrian, Colonel Darwish Fawzil, who turned out to be very cooperative on every trip I made to Damascus that year, immediately invited me to dinner for that very evening. I could not be discourteous to my host, but I was hoping to get my meeting with Ambassador Akhtari rescheduled for that night. It wasn't simply a matter of urgency. In the Middle East, real business, particularly politics, is often transacted at night; indeed, virtually all my hostage negotiations would take place after 10 P.M., which is considered early in Beirut and other capitals of the region. But it wasn't to be; dinner with Fawzil was. I had no idea how much he knew about my mission, which lent a certain surreal quality to our conversation. I took the position that he knew a lot and that I therefore didn't need to say much. It was safer to be cryptic; if he didn't understand, I doubted he would have said so for fear of revealing how little he knew.

The morning after my arrival, I presented myself at the Iranian Embassy, which was located only about one hundred feet from the local UN headquarters. This proximity afforded convenience all around, not only for me but for Syrian intelligence, which could observe my movements with minimum effort. I was escorted to the ambassador's office. Ambassador Akhtari, a large and suave bearded man who refused to be hurried by events, arrived within a few minutes. A cleric wearing a white turban,

with a justified sense of importance, he was sitting in a chair that had belonged to the legendary Ali Akhbar Mohtashemi. Mohtashemi was the
former interior minister who had established Hizbollah in Lebanon and
opened the door for the Iranian Revolutionary Guards to establish a base
in the Bekaa Valley. To me, Mohtashemi was the Trotsky of the Iranian revolution, the ideologue who believed in exporting the revolution.

Akhtari did not at first exude a great revolutionary spirit, but he took
care to make it clear that he had been mandated by President Rafsanjani
to assist me in my activities in Damascus and Lebanon. Tea and cookies
were served as he told me, in Farsi through an interpreter, that he was less
than charmed with the fact that the Syrians had known about my visit. He
said that this would "complicate matters." "Complicate" became a eu-
phemism he and his Iranian colleagues employed more frequently as
time went on. When Ambassador Akhtari said there was a "complication," it meant we had to change plans.

The arrival of the Syrian colonel also posed a complication since, as
I was a UN official, protocol would have to be observed. According to
Ambassador Akhtari, any meeting with Sheikh Fadlallah in Damascus
would now be made public; the implication was that I would have to go
to Beirut if I wanted to see the sheikh. In addition, I would have to meet
a number of officials close to the Syrians as well as the Iranians while I
was there so that the formalities would be maintained and nobody would
feel ignored or considered unimportant. Of course, I would also have to
meet with Syrian officials in Damascus pour la forme.

As I was leaving Akhtari's office, I asked him to arrange some meetings with Syrian officials because I did not want to commit a faux pas
and ask for a meeting with the wrong person. At the same time, I counted
on him to make the proper arrangements with Fadlallah in Beirut. On
April 12, I had two meetings with Syrian officials and two meetings with
the Iranians. It was clear that I would not be getting out of Damascus by
Saturday.

I returned to UN headquarters, called on the administrative officer
and the chief of staff, and explained to them what I had to do. I needed
passes to be arranged so I could cross the Syrian border into Lebanon, as
well as a driver to get me there, and all this had to be executed with the
utmost discretion. At this delicate stage, I was especially keen to keep my
movements quiet and out of the rumor mills at UN headquarters in New
York. Thank God for a superb brigadier general from Canada, Butch Wal-

drum, the chief of staff of UNDOF. He took excellent care of all my logistical needs—transportation, communication, and security—at least
while I was on his turf.

On Saturday, April 13, 1991, I made my first visit to Beirut. The view
from the UN headquarters on the heights above Beirut was magnificent.
It was the base for Observer Group Beirut (OGB), a subsection of the UN
truce group established in Jerusalem after the first Arab-Israeli war more
than forty years earlier. At OGB, I was met by Major Jens Nielsen, a Dane
who served as the information officer. To say he was in charge of intelligence would be more accurate. He was to become a very important
source of information about Beirut while I was gone and a staunch pro-
tector while I was there.

Within thirty minutes of my arrival in Beirut, I received a phone call
from the chargé d'affaires of the Iranian Embassy informing me that a
meeting with Sheikh Fadlallah had been arranged for later that afternoon. I was to await further instructions. Naturally, the meeting was
postponed. At 9 P.M., an armored Mercedes with tinted glass arrived, the
guards armed with machine guns. Although the car had very sophisticated communications equipment, Major Nielsen insisted on following
us in his UN jeep. And so we descended into West Beirut, both cars traveling at high speed through checkpoints that would miraculously open at
the very last moment.

This was my first encounter with Beirut at night, and I could glimpse
various militias scattered throughout the city streets. As we approached a
compound that turned out to be the Iranian Embassy, we barely slowed
down, but the iron gates swung open for our minimotorcade just in
time. Nielsen remained in the courtyard while I went up to the second
floor by elevator, even though it was only up a short flight of stairs. The
inside of the embassy was dim; people would peek out through door-
ways, then disappear down hallways. I was escorted into a room decorated in typical Middle Eastern style and left alone. The chargé, Amir
Hossein Zamania, an old acquaintance from the Iranian Mission in New
York, came in and, without missing a beat, picked up the conversation I
had been having with Vaezi a few days earlier about Sheikh Fadlallah. I realized he was killing time until Fadlallah was ready to see me. He left a

few minutes later, and shortly afterward I was escorted out of the building. It was now almost 10 P.M. When I went downstairs, there was a new driver in the Mercedes, and we headed off down potholed roads through the rundown areas toward the south of the city, the heartland of fundamentalist and Shiite Beirut: Hizbollah country. Before long we arrived at a garage entrance, then walked upstairs to a patio with windows, a rather rustic but large place with wooden benches along the walls.

Sheikh Fadlallah was an imposing man dressed very properly, a mullah in a black turban indicating that he was a descendant of the Prophet. He had an impressive silvery beard and looked out of place living in the middle of a civil war in the slums of south Beirut, the home territory of the terrorists to which the more moderate mullahs had expelled him. Nevertheless, he seemed to radiate authority and inspire fear; this was not a man whose piercing eyes offered gentle reassurance.

All this enhanced his aura as spiritual leader of Hizbollah, a role he always denied in our conversations. The sheikh had received his theological education in Najaf in Iraq, the cradle of Shiism even before the rise of Qom, where he had met all the great ayatollahs during the 1960s, including, of course, Ruhollah Khomeini. Returning to his home in Lebanon, he had become a Shiite political leader and had eventually emerged during the shifting alliances of the Lebanese civil war as a member of a small council that supervised Hizbollah. The Party of God was, and still is, structured and organized in a fairly bureaucratic way with a council of advisers and subcommittees for various areas of activities. By the late 1980s, his prestige as a spiritual and political leader was unquestioned, and people called him the Khomeini of Lebanon.

I had traveled to visit Fadlallah alone, despite Major Nielsen's insistence that he accompany me, because I did not want both of us to run unnecessary risks. The United Nations' standard operating procedure in Beirut did not permit UN officials to travel to the Shia part of Beirut at night, although I doubt that would have stopped him. Frankly, I thought that if anything went wrong he would be more helpful to me on the outside.

It was now 10:30 P.M., and I was alone with Sheikh Fadlallah and his interpreter. The sheikh came toward me with a big smile. I immediately asked him how many Westerners he had met alone at night, and, still smiling, he replied, "You are the first." He warned me not to tell anyone in Beirut about my real mission. I was to communicate only with the Iranians, and they would help me contact the right people. I eased the conversation toward the deplorable condition of Beirut after the civil war, discussed the suffering of the people and especially the different communities, and moved gingerly toward the subject of how the United Nations might help.

He knew exactly what I was talking about and interrupted me even before I could play my Lebanon fund card. "This matter should be solved on its own merits, not with financial attachments," he said. "I think the time is right for resolving this issue, and the international atmosphere is becoming more realistic. Your presence is a good indication that the atmosphere is presently right."

He then shifted the conversation directly to the issue of strained U.S.-Iranian relations and expressed hope that the situation could be improved diplomatically. He seemed to be very familiar with the relationship between the United Nations and Iran and praised the role of the secretary-general in dealing with the hostage issue. He insisted that he was not a decision maker when it came to releasing the captives but was ready to give his assistance in whatever form he could. It was gratifying to hear him stress that the hostage issue could be solved on its own merits, without any other quids pro quos.

There were enough "prisoners of war" in the area, and they could all benefit from our negotiations, he said. It was important to have direct negotiations with the group holding the hostages, away from the glare of publicity. The secretary-general had been chosen as the channel, he said, because of the United Nations' role in negotiating the end to the Iran-Iraq war. He insisted that only the United Nations and the secretary-general could effect the exchange of prisoners so that all sides could save face; it was not to be seen as a quid pro quo. He was equally, and surprisingly, clear that in order to solve the problem I would have to continue my discussions with Iran and eventually with the groups holding the hostages, and nobody else.

"Remember," he warned ominously, "do not talk to anybody in Beirut."

He must have known that I could not have come to Beirut as the UN representative without meeting other officials. I realized, and presumably so did he, that I would still have to chat with them for appearances' sake. To end the meeting, he graciously accompanied me to the door, whereupon I was escorted to the street and to the car waiting for me in the pitch-black night, then driven directly back to OGB's villa overlooking the city. By then it was almost midnight. I felt that the principal goal of my mission had been accomplished. I had obtained Fadlallah's promise to do his best to help me, even though he had hastened to add, "Do not believe that I can solve this problem, because my connection with these people is not what you think."

I supposed that he was trying to distance himself from the kidnappers. He also insisted that taking hostages was objectionable to his religion. As I studied my notes, difficulties began to appear that had been less apparent when we spoke. I realized then that I had taken just the first step of a very long process in which there would be many difficult negotiations and many setbacks. We had a deadline to complete the release of the hostages by the end of the year, when Pérez de Cuéllar would leave office, and I constantly felt that I was running against time. I had pointed this out to the Iranians, though it was also clear to them since they could not know what the priorities and the political disposition of the next secretary-general might be.

At one point, the sheikh had said, "One of the reasons that your channel is better than any British or American channel is because they cannot meet directly with those people"—meaning the hostage takers—"whereas you can, with the help of Iran." The full import of this had not sunk in as he said it. I had thought that our meeting was a way of communicating with them in some way. I had not immediately realized that he was telling me I would have to meet with the kidnappers themselves—that without knowing it, I was moving step by step toward what the American hostage Terry Anderson would later call the lion's den.

The next day, playacting, I was treading water in order to keep everyone happy. On Sunday, April 14, I met with Sheikh Mohammed Shamsheddin, chairman of the High Shia Council in Beirut, a moderate and wise man, although not as influential in those days as he had been in the past. During our two-hour meeting I was also introduced to the son of Ayatollah Abu al Qasim al Mussawi al Khoei, an Iraqi cleric and holy man in the eyes of many Shia who was still living in Iraq and had been persecuted by the regime of Saddam Hussein. His reputation as a holy man who never engaged in politics was, according to some, even higher than that of Ayatollah Khomeini. His son pleaded with me to have the United Nations provide medical assistance to his father in Iraq. Despite our best efforts, the ayatollah died a few months later from a combination of old age and the duress suffered at the hands of the Iraqi government.

From there, I called on General Sami Khatib, the interior minister of Lebanon, a Sunni Muslim who was close to Syria. He received me in his apartment, a beautiful place protected by rings of security. We discussed the reconstruction of Lebanon, in which he displayed great interest. I raised the possibility of a visit by Bettino Craxi. General Khatib was someone to be reckoned with in Lebanon. He assured me that the Syrians would give me all the help I needed with the hostages and predicted that they would be free within two months

The following day, I met with two Hizbollah officials in what I suppose was a safe house—and was practically struck dumb when they handed me business cards identifying them as from the "Hizbollah Political Office." The Hizbollah officials listed all the misdeeds of Israel and the United States against the Shia of Lebanon, insisted that Hizbollah was detaining no hostages, and said that I would have to solicit the good offices of Iran if I wanted to get in touch with the hostage holders. Nevertheless, they reaffirmed the willingness of their organization to assist me in whatever way possible, and they expressed confidence in the United Nations and in the work I was doing, which they were certain would have positive results.

Finally, it was time to go. I was driven back to the OGB villa, packed my things, and was delivered back across the border into Syria. In Damascus, I asked to see the Iranian ambassador to thank him for his help, but he was away and I saw his deputy, who told me that his boss, Ambassador Akhtari, had arranged all my meetings in Beirut. In fact, the deputy was the operative who looked after me personally during my stays. I debriefed him and made it clear that I was still hoping that my visit with the hostages to verify their physical condition would take place soon because I was also trying to arrange visits to the prisoners in Israel—something both Fadlallah and the Hizbollah officials in Beirut had said would be a "logical" linkage.

My next stop was Geneva and a call on Cyrus Nasseri. He hoped that the Americans would now realize that I had established myself on the ground, and he encouraged me to secure a visit to Sheikh Obeid in Israel since this could move things forward. I had spent bits and pieces of two years on the hostage problem and had devised proposals on the fly to deal with something that seemed almost organic at times. Sometimes they worked, sometimes not. I was devastated, for example, when I discovered that my ace—the Lebanese relief fund—was a bust as a negotiating card. I had also worked with as few governments as possible, figuring that the more the actors, the more the headaches. But now Nasseri's comment about Obeid and my own reading told me it was time to begin working with another government. We clearly had to engage Israel.

It was also clear that the call to the Israelis would have to come from the Americans. The United Nations had delivered the Iranians, but our credibility in Tel Aviv in those days left much to be desired. We hoped that Washington would feel obligated, under the circumstances, to prevail upon the Israelis. This was something new. Major powers often exerted influence over their allies, but it was rare indeed for the United Nations to become part of such bargaining, and it was a measure of how far Pérez de Cuéllar had come in establishing us as peacemakers, not just peace-keepers.

The secretary-general raised the matter with President Bush when they met early in May. He told Bush that the Iranians had agreed to assist in finding a solution to the problem "quickly, completely, and not on the basis of money." We still hoped that we could avoid the complication of dealing directly with the Israelis by using Washington to do the job for us. Our first request was to arrange for Israel to accept a third-party visit to the Lebanese detained in south Lebanon or Israel itself. The Americans accepted the idea but suggested that if there were to be a visit at all, an official of the International Committee of the Red Cross would probably be more appreciated than a UN official. That was an understatement, given our credibility problems in Israel, but even so, the meeting with Bush did not lead to a visit.

By then the Israeli press had become very vocal about a possible deal that would involve freedom for the Western hostages, the resolution of the case of missing Israeli airman Ron Arad, and the release of Sheikh Obeid and other Lebanese detainees. A quasi negotiation through the media had begun in the Israeli and Lebanese press, which led to an understanding in the region that Israel and Lebanon would both have to be involved in the issue. During the month of May, diplomatic sources from various countries predicted an immediate solution to the hostage saga, which, of course, never came to pass. The British government, meantime, communicated to Pérez de Cuéllar that it would use only the UN channel for dealing with their three hostages.

British foreign secretary Sir Douglas Hurd in particular had made it clear to us that London feared that a partial solution of the hostage crisis in Beirut would not be the best outcome. On May 20, Hurd met with U.S. Secretary of State James Baker and pushed for a complete package to be executed through the good offices of the UN secretary-general. Baker apparently concurred. But no sooner had we received this briefing by the British than the message had to be corrected: Baker had not agreed to use the secretary-general as the only channel. Despite Washington's position, Foreign Office officials from London met with me wherever they could to brief and be briefed about our respective contacts with the Iranians, Israelis, and assorted Lebanese. By early summer, the German government had begun to do the same.

During this period, we were beginning to gain useful information from UNIFIL about the movements of an important Israeli official. Uri Lubrani, who had in his youth been both a student at Oxford and a fighter in the Jewish underground against the British, was something of a legend in Israel. Lubrani was career foreign service, but his office was in the Defense Ministry in Tel Aviv. He was also his government's leading expert on Hizbollah and the Ron Arad case, a former Israeli ambassador to Iran during the shah's reign, and, among other things, the man who had executed the airlift of Ethiopian Jews from Addis Ababa to Israel. Lubrani was to become Israel's chief political negotiator in the hostage exchange and a close collaborator for the next year. I came to respect him very highly as a professional, and, I have to say, we became very good friends. We established a rapport that allowed us to communicate openly and honestly, much more so than the formalities of state normally allow. But in May 1991, I had yet to meet the man.

At that point, information was being shared with and received from the Iranians and the British. Political intelligence from Washington was scarce for a number of reasons. The U.S. intelligence network in Lebanon had been totally destroyed when the CIA station chief in Beirut, William

Buckley, had been kidnapped and murdered in the mid-1980s. The return of his body was the last act I performed for the Americans kidnapped in Beirut. The other reason, I suppose, was that Jim Baker had still not decided if we were in a position to handle the hostage problem, and official Washington thus felt uncomfortable passing political intelligence to the secretary-general's office. I didn't know why Baker continued to distrust us, but it was awkward for me to work with the knowledge that the U.S. secretary of state did not want our involvement.

I would have liked to complete one grand exchange all at once. Israel would free Lebanese prisoners. The Lebanese terrorist groups and their Iranian sponsors would tell the Israelis what they knew about the missing Israelis and give up any prisoners they had or their bodies. The terrorists would release their hostages. That was the essence of the three-sided deal I would struggle to put together for the remainder of the year; it kept coming unstuck, and I kept trying to patch it up against a backdrop of distrust and enmity.

The hostage releases on the two sides, however, were grossly unequal in number. There were eleven acknowledged Western hostages left in Lebanon, compared with several hundred Lebanese prisoners held by the Israelis and only six or seven missing Israeli soldiers and airmen, of whom maybe only one was alive. The disparity in the figures meant that any deal would be lopsided. The kidnappers would hold out to get more, the Israelis to give less. Since no neutral party had ever been allowed to count them, the sides could not even agree on how many prisoners the Israelis held, and the estimates ranged from 300 to 600. Negotiations would be daunting. The other major hurdle was the question of who would go first. It would take a Herculean effort by both sides for even a modicum of trust to be established between Israel and Iran. By then they had been at each other's throats for thirteen years, and one would have to move first on the understanding that the other would follow. Somehow, the United Nations would have to provide the insurance.

The stalemate started to crack during two long private conversations that I had with Kamal Kharrazi, the UN ambassador from Iran, in New York during the first half of June. It had now been almost two months since I had seen Sheikh Fadlallah, and no one had yet come forward with a plan for my promised visit to the hostages. I summed up for Kharrazi what I thought was the basic understanding of the various parties involved, even though we had had no direct communication with the government of Israel. Everyone detained without due process should be released, be they Westerners, Israelis, Lebanese, or Iranians. The problem was how the releases could be carried out. That's where we could come in, I told Kharrazi, with a proposal by the secretary-general for consideration by all sides. We would make one to the Iranians for transmittal to the groups in Lebanon, and we would pass on the same to the United States for transmittal to Israel. In practical terms, this meant that we had to reach a common understanding on the numbers, or "inventory," as Lubrani would later call it. Furthermore, if the Iranians claimed that the groups had no knowledge of Israeli airman Ron Arad's whereabouts, a proper search could be agreed upon by all concerned to resolve the case. Finally, to make sure that none of the parties would be left holding the bag, proper "insurance" would be provided by the UN secretary-general.

Kharrazi helped clear the decks by assuring me that no hostage had died since the murder of Colonel Higgins in 1988. He also told me for the first time that the Iranians did not know Arad's whereabouts. Arad been shot down over Lebanon and captured in 1986, and his return had become a cause célèbre in Israel. His Lebanese captors were said to have sold him in 1989 to Iranian Revolutionary Guards, who denied that any such transaction had taken place. Kharrazi claimed they had known Arad's location for three years after his capture but had then lost contact with his captors and now had no idea what had become of him.

Our conversation centered on piecing together a package. Kharrazi kept asking how many people the Israelis were planning to release, whether his representatives would be permitted to see Sheikh Obeid in captivity in Israel, and whether in fact the Israelis would go along with the deal at all. I could not give him straight answers because I had yet to receive them myself. I could only stress that we wanted the offer from his side to be so appealing that he would get what he wanted.

Between our meetings I sent a brief and pointed personal letter to Javad Zarif, ambassador at large in Teheran. On June 18, the secretary-general handed Kharrazi a three-page memo I had prepared. It was not transcribed onto official UN stationery. The memo outlined, in some detail, the three points I had discussed with Kharrazi a week earlier but contained a sentence that could hardly be called a traditional diplomatic suggestion: "The UN Secretary General's envoy will continue his discussion in Lebanon [after the hostages have been released] at a site of convenience for the groups until the other side [Israel] reciprocates, i.e., until Sheik Obeid and the others are also freed. When this happens the UN envoy will leave Lebanon."

In short, I would be the "insurance." The proposal to Kharrazi essentially said that I was prepared to act as a guarantee inside Lebanon until the completion of the entire package. We did not know if the Israelis would reciprocate. I was, however, confident enough that if this were indeed to happen, my detention would be brief. Only the Iranians, myself, and the secretary-general were aware of the proposed exchange, since we wanted to avoid another Terry Waite situation. Waite, the archbishop of Canterbury's representative dispatched to Beirut amid great publicity to negotiate the release of hostages, had himself been kidnapped in 1987 and was still being held captive.

The next day, Kharrazi told me that Teheran had received the memo and that he would have to discuss its contents with the Iranian government in person. He was flying to Europe the following day to meet Deputy Foreign Minister Vaezi, and then on to Teheran. On June 22, I met with Vaezi in Switzerland. He made it very clear that he would never allow a UN official to be held hostage, but nevertheless my three-page memo had also been brought to the attention of the groups in Lebanon! The Islamic Republic of Iran, he said, would now increase the pressure on the groups in Lebanon to release their hostages. We also jotted down a program of hostage releases in bunches of two or three at a time, taking into account possible reciprocity by Israel.

We discussed the number of prisoners held by the Israelis at length. The International Committee of the Red Cross had put the figure at about 400; the Israelis had said the number was smaller, but the groups in Lebanon put it as high as 600. Most were being held at Khiam prison in south Lebanon, a buffer area under Israeli control. No neutral group had ever been allowed to visit them. The Hizbollah groups in Lebanon were holding six Americans and three British hostages. Two Germans were being held by the Hammadi clan as hostages for two brothers who had been tried and convicted in Germany, one in connection with the June 1985 hijacking of TWA Flight 847 in Beirut that had resulted in the murder of U.S. Navy diver Robert Stethem, the other for smuggling explosives into Germany. These numbers would be a matter of discussion for weeks, even months, and at times seemed to turn the negotiation into little more than a bazaar.

My next objective was to prepare a message for the White House. I wanted to know what its reaction would be to the idea of releasing the hostages two or three at a time, which seemed to be the most practical way to build confidence on both sides. When I met Scowcroft alone in his small office in the West Wing of the White House on June 28, he took copious notes as I briefed him on my work during the previous two months, starting with my first visit to Beirut. I particularly wanted to test his reaction to my discussions with and latest proposals to the Iranians. I also wanted him to know that the British had approached us and were providing us with information on many matters, including Hurd's meeting with Baker. I then gave him a detailed account of the concept of and procedure for a program of simultaneous releases.

Scowcroft said that anything that smacked of a deal with terrorists was against American policy. However, he added that if our proposal were implemented in the way the secretary-general suggested, he would look closely at it. "We are not in favor of a deal," he said, "but we are in favor of all parties who hold captives without due process releasing them. This could be communicated to Iran." In effect, he wanted a deal that wasn't a deal, or at least didn't look like a deal. Strictly speaking, he was right, since the act of restoring freedom to those who had lost it without having committed any crime was a matter of simple justice.

What I needed from him was help in dealing with the Israelis, who would be an essential part of the package. Scowcroft said he had contradictory information about the fate of Ron Arad and did not comment any further. He also stressed that the U.S. government could not guarantee that the Israelis would reciprocate in any way for the release of Western hostages. But when I suggested that Washington prompt Israel to contact us about an exchange, he did not demur. In other words, Washington would get in touch with Tel Aviv, but it would be up to the Israelis to decide whether to participate.

I suggested that to avoid conveying the pressure of a deal, both sides should communicate their commitments to the secretary-general. Scowcroft agreed that that would be a diplomatic way of handling things. He cautioned, however, that this was only his initial reaction, and he asked if he could call me in New York later on. But it was also clear that he was very interested in keeping the secretary-general out front so that the United States would not be exposed, a position I fully understood. In due course, we shifted from a triangle bounded by Iran, the United Nations, and the United States to one bounded by Iran, the United Nations, and

Israel. The secretary-general had accomplished that shift with diplomatic ingenuity and elegance. That left only one debt hanging over him if the hostages got home safely, the president's inaugural declaration that "goodwill begets goodwill."

With the Israelis slowly being drawn in, we turned back to the Iranians. In July, a solution to the entire issue was finally discussed, at first between Ambassador Javad Zarif and myself and subsequently by Ambassador Kharrazi and Pérez de Cuéllar.

Zarif called me in late July to arrange an urgent meeting for the next morning. On July 27, we met in my office. He stated that his government was now moving full speed ahead to assist the secretary-general in closing the hostage file before the end of his term in office. It appeared that all internal opposition had been overcome and that President Rafsanjani was now fully on board. Rafsanjani also wanted Pérez de Cuéllar to visit Teheran soon so that all agreements could be finalized for the conclusion of the hostage affair. Given that our bosses were holding us responsible, Zarif and I were aware as we discussed the various permutations that neither of us could count on what other governments would do. At the end of the day, it would come down to us. So we began to examine what was and wasn't there. There would be no money involved and no assurance that guarantees from other governments would stick. At the center of our work was the politics of the Gulf, which we both understood well. We had worked on the end of the Iran-Iraq war, we knew how the cease-fire had come about, and we knew why Iraq had finally accepted the border between the two countries and withdrawn its occupying troops from Iranian soil.

What else did Iran want after all that? It all seemed to fit into place. Zarif and I each had a big card to play, and we would argue for months about who would go first. But the core of our deal was clear, and if we both delivered, the operation could not be sidetracked by any other government. It was a deceptively simple swap: Iran would do its level best with the groups in Lebanon to free the hostages, and we would deliver Paragraph 6 of UN Resolution 598. If we could get more than that—freedom for Lebanese detainees in Israeli prisons, information about missing Iranians in Beirut and Israeli airmen and soldiers in Lebanon, American "goodwill" reciprocity—it would be frosting on the cake. But the game turned on Paragraph 6.

We knew that Teheran wanted a formal condemnation of Iraq for starting the war in 1980, but until then we had not realized how crucial it was for it politically. And, of course, the ability to deliver such a condemnation happened to rest in the hands of the secretary-general himself. Paragraph 6 of the Security Council's cease-fire resolution of 1988 specifically requested the secretary-general "to explore, in consultation with Iran and Iraq, the question of entrusting an impartial body with inquiring into responsibility for the conflict and to report to the Security Council as soon as possible." At the time Resolution 598 was drafted, no one could have imagined the role its sixth paragraph was to play in freeing the hostages. The mullahs—indeed, the Iranian people—saw it as a way to obtain justice, which mattered so much to them after all their suffering in the war.

I did not want to commit us too hastily because I wanted to play Paragraph 6 for all I could get—all the hostages, not just some of them. But I told Zarif that I thought we could go ahead with the idea, which in fact was a matter of conscience. The secretary-general's visit to Teheran could be even more successful if Paragraph 6 were implemented at the same time, Zarif responded. In private diplomatic conversations, no one ever expressed doubt that the Iraqis had initiated a massive military offensive on September 22, 1980, although only one person of international stature—German Foreign Minister Hans-Dietrich Genscher—had said so in public. Pérez de Cuéllar and I believed any impartial body couldn't help but reach the same conclusion, though we obviously could not guarantee the outcome.

When Pérez de Cuéllar met with Ambassador Kharrazi on August 1, 1991, he made it clear that he intended to be in touch with Iran and Iraq about Paragraph 6, but he made no formal commitment of how and when he intended to appoint a committee to assess the responsibility for the war. He also made it clear that he wanted a closure of the hostage file in the shortest possible time. Over the next couple of days, Zarif and I went through several iterations of our hostage-release plan, including my "detention" in Lebanon as insurance and the conclusion of the work on Paragraph 6 of Resolution 598. The Iranians also agreed that the search for Ron Arad would be part of the package. At that point, we had yet to make any contact with the government of Israel. Most important, Kharrazi and Zarif said that the groups in Lebanon were now prepared to proceed speedily with the first hostage releases to the secretary-general to make clear to the world that he was the channel to close the entire file.

On August 7, Pérez de Cuéllar briefed Scowcroft on our discussions
with the Iranians over the past two weeks. By that time I was already on
my way to Beirut. A day earlier, the Islamic Jihad in Beirut had indicated
that it would soon communicate with the secretary-general of the United
Nations and send a special messenger to him so that the release of all the
hostages could take place. The Iranians were trying to force our hand on
Paragraph 6 and the visit of the secretary-general to Teheran; we were trying to force them to get the hostages released. They blinked first.

CHAPTER 10

A Terrorist
Across the Table

Although we tried to keep the United Nations' role in the hostage negotiations confidential, it could hardly be called a secret mission. By
August 1991, the media—with the BBC and the British papers leading
the way—had become aware of my activities and had begun to refer to
me as the secretary-general's special envoy on the hostage crisis. So it was
no surprise that TV crews had staked out the UNDOF headquarters in
Damascus even before I arrived on August 7. Still, I was able to slip in un-
detected through a back entrance, as the media circus was being diverted
by the appearance of Alec Watson, the U.S. deputy permanent representative to the United Nations in New York, who could easily be mistaken for
me given our similar height and build. Watson, a good friend, later said
that he had thoroughly enjoyed his moment of mistaken identity.

At the time of my arrival, President Assad controlled Syria completely. His omnipotence was taken for granted. He had come to power at
the beginning of the strategic alliance between the United States and Israel, and he struck me, when I had met him years before, as a proud
player who'd been dealt a lousy hand but nonetheless would play
through with utter dignity. He and his nation were perceived as the same
entity. Within a few hours of my arrival in Damascus, I was conferring
with Iranian Ambassador Akhtari, who urged me to go to Beirut that very
night. He was rather spare in the details but did say that the Iranian Embassy in Beirut would make contact with me upon my arrival. When I left
his office around eleven that night, it was too late to arrange border-
crossing procedures with Syrian intelligence. But at the crack of dawn on
August 8, I was on my way. At the border, I was handed over to Major

Nielsen, who drove me straight to UN headquarters in Beirut. Amir Hossein Zamania, the Iranian chargé d'affaires, contacted me there and, like his colleagues in Damascus, conveyed a sense of urgency, although he too provided me with no operational details. Communications between us were frantic: the international press had gone hyper on the expectation that early releases were imminent. Before noon, British diplomats were visiting me at OGB to exchange notes. As we met, I received word that John McCarthy had just been set free.

McCarthy was a British television journalist who had come to Beirut in March 1986 to replace a colleague from station WTN who had taken a two-month leave. Within a few weeks of his arrival, McCarthy had been taken hostage and ended up spending five years in captivity as a close companion to Brian Keenan, a teacher and poet from Belfast. (Keenan's memorable book, *An Evil Cradling*, told how they had kept their sanity under intolerable conditions and explored the inner life of a hostage with passages that reminded me of James Joyce.)

McCarthy had carried a message from the Islamic Jihad to Pérez de Cuéllar declaring that the organization had chosen him as its messenger because the "oppressed and downtrodden of the world" were looking to the secretary-general for help. The message then aired a decade of grievances. McCarthy was dispatched home to London at once, and Pérez de Cuéllar flew to meet him there. The operation made front-page news throughout the world because there was a feeling that this was the beginning of the end of the hostage story. The secretary-general was publicly credited with securing the release, and Pérez de Cuéllar, who normally disdained publicity, made his first acquaintance with starlike celebrity.

McCarthy's release had not taken place without crossed wires, which would come to be the one constant in the hostage releases to follow. For example, the Iranians told me, as soon as I arrived in Damascus, that I should be prepared for a release that day. As it turned out, I never saw McCarthy. I took this as a signal that they essentially knew little of the details of the kidnappers' operations or their actual plans for the release of hostages. It also became apparent to me that the kidnappers regularly ignored their orders. As for the kidnappers themselves, they spoke with such bombast that they routinely sowed misunderstanding and confusion. They announced before McCarthy's release that they would be sending a message to Pérez de Cuéllar through a "special envoy," presumably a UN or Lebanese official. In fact, it was McCarthy himself who eventually carried their letter to London. More important, however, the movement had started. In the letter, the kidnappers had said that once all their freedom fighters were released, they would release their hostages, which was interpreted to mean within twenty-four hours—yet another signal that could be misinterpreted and indeed was.

The excitement of McCarthy's release and the hopes that it had raised were dashed the next day, when to the surprise of all, including the Iranians, a French national, Jérôme Leyraud, was pulled off the streets of Beirut in the first kidnapping since 1989.

It is not hard to imagine the mixture of tension and disappointment this news stirred in us. Beirut itself was tense, like a city under siege. As they often did when something unexpected happened in the city, Syrian intelligence and the army went on high alert. Checkpoints were stringently enforced, stopping or at least slowing movement across the city's zones. Soldiers suddenly became much more visible. If something like this could happen only hours after the first release, I thought, what shocks might we expect after the others? Leyraud's kidnapping seemed to imply that nobody was controlling anything, in which case all our complex diplomatic combinations to serve the interests of each side would have been in vain, jeopardizing the mission itself.

It did not take me long to realize that I had to come up with a more decisive plan, something far less diplomatic than what we had concocted thus far. So I got in touch with Zamania at the Iranian Embassy. He had no idea who had grabbed the Frenchman or why, he said; I believed him because he also insisted that the new kidnapping had only served to contradict everything we were trying to achieve. I then made a new proposal—that I meet directly with the kidnappers and hold one-on-one negotiations with them. I was prepared to accept whatever security conditions they might arrange. I did not consult with Pérez de Cuéllar first, in part because I was afraid he would be too concerned about my safety to agree. But if the kidnappers on the other end of the Iranian connection had indeed not taken the latest French hostage—and they quickly let it be known that they had not—it was obvious that we could no longer settle matters at a distance. The slow pace of the process was already a matter of concern; still, going backward was unacceptable.

When I met with Zamania at 11 A.M. on August 10, he confirmed that my request for a meeting had been passed on to the groups, who were now discussing it. I pointed out that we had previously agreed on two releases, but so far had received only McCarthy. Where was the second hostage? Not to mention the fact that the latest kidnapping seemed to breach our understanding. What I needed to find out from Zamania was who was in charge on the ground and not on some higher plane of politics. First I had been told by the Iranians to go to Damascus, so I had gone. Once in Damascus, I had been told by Akhtari to go to Beirut, and here I was. Now I found myself facing a seemingly hopeless situation.

I told him to tell the groups that if a splinter faction had taken the Frenchman hostage, I would still be prepared to proceed because not doing so would give any rogue element a veto over the operation. Then, once again, I asked Zamania who was in charge. I was deliberately challenging his authority by implying that whoever was in charge was weak. He could easily have replied that the Iranians were not in charge because they were not Lebanese. But I was trying to shame the Lebanese groups by making the point that they were not powerful enough if a splinter faction could so blatantly challenge their decisions.

I told Zamania that the problem had to be sorted out that very day, and I stressed that if the Islamic Jihad backed out of its promise to release a second hostage just because of some splinter group, its retreat would only prove its weakness, not its strength. He then surprised me: if the groups agreed to meet me, he said, I would have to go where they wanted, in the way they demanded. At that point, I had no idea of the real meaning of his words.

I waited at OGB the whole day. Then, in the evening, I got a message to meet with Zamania again. Major Nielsen knew I was on my way to the Iranian Embassy, and so did Lieutenant Colonel Timo Holopainen, the Finnish commanding officer of OGB. Both expressed their concern about my traveling through Beirut to the Iranian Embassy at night. As we walked outside to the garden with its magnificent view of the harbor, I told them that I might be on my way to another and perhaps even more dangerous meeting that would be much less diplomatic in nature. They volunteered to accompany me, but I insisted that they remain at OGB because I had said I would go alone; furthermore, the kidnappers would surely not countenance witnesses. I did not give them too many details, but, realizing that anything could happen, I told them that if I did not return before dawn, they should first call Zamania at the Iranian Embassy, then Kamal Kharrazi at his home in New York, and then Javad Zarif in

Teheran. Only after making those contacts should they inform Pérez de Cuéllar that I had disappeared. I gave them home phone numbers, including that of Pérez de Cuéllar's private residence on Sutton Place. Once again they insisted on accompanying me or at least giving me a portable transmitter so I could keep in touch. I knew, however, that this would be impossible. I did not want to carry anything with me aside from my UN identity card, a pen, and a leather folder with a notepad. No money and no credit cards; my pockets were empty.

The Iranian ambassador's Mercedes finally arrived to take me to the embassy, mercifully avoiding searches as it was stopped at the checkpoints going across Beirut. At the embassy, I noticed many people walking throughout the compound and cars coming and going. No one spoke as they went about their business. There was nevertheless a consistent flow of hospitality. I was taken to the formal divan, the sitting room for meetings, and offered tea, fruit, and cookies.

Zamania entered and informed me that the groups were prepared to meet with me. He warned me that there would be a few "formalities" involved in reaching them, which he hoped I would accept and for which he apologized. I did not quite comprehend what he meant by that. I thought of inconveniences as simply another facet of my job, although I was worried. However, I reasoned that I was talking to a diplomat in his embassy. I then asked Zamania if he was going to accompany me, half expecting that he would. "Oh, no, Mr. Picco," he replied. "I do not know these people. It is going to be between you and them!" Zamania said he had never before done this sort of thing, but he assured me that everything would run smoothly, then added with great diplomatic courtesy how much respect he had for me. He left the room, and I was alone.

At first I thought that he had just gone to the bathroom, but after a few minutes it became obvious that he was not coming back. Then a man I had assumed to be a junior diplomat came in and told me rather abruptly that I would have to leave because I could do nothing more here. I had no choice but to acquiesce, so I walked downstairs to where the Mercedes had been, only this time there was no car to be seen. The junior diplomat watched me from the doorway and told me to keep going. In broken English, he called after me, "Finished here. Go! Go!"

"Is Mr. Zamania still here?" I asked.

The man continued to wave me away, "Go! Finished here! Finish! Finish!" It was now about ten o'clock. In the distance I could see the gate.

The armed guard on duty opened it for me. I then walked out, leaving the embassy compound behind.

I was now alone, with no idea what to do or where to go.

I turned left from the gate in the general direction of south Beirut and the Shiite quarter, which seemed the logical thing to do. Nobody was in the streets. There were only a few streetlights, and in the distance I could vaguely see somebody at a street corner. I headed in his direction in search of human contact, but as I approached him, he started to walk away. He did not entirely distance himself from me, so I continued to follow. This went on for ten minutes, until we reached a street corner, where he suddenly disappeared. I stopped in my tracks. Within three or four minutes, I heard the sound of a car approaching at high speed. It screeched to a halt near me. I heard a car door open and instinctively turned away. Thinking back to Zamania's apologies, it had suddenly dawned on me that the most dangerous thing for me to do would be to see these people and be able to recognize them. The less I saw, the better. I think that they rather expected me to be a man of common sense, because when the car came to a stop, I was taken from the street and, before I knew it, shoved into the backseat. They shouted, "Don't look! Don't look!" and forced my head down as far down as it could go.

I am six feet, four inches tall and quite a package in the back of a car, but at that point physical discomfort was the least of my concerns. All I knew was that it was dark and that no one was talking. However, before my head had been shoved down, I had been able to glimpse a few things. I had seen two people sitting in the front seat, the driver and someone else, and a third person sitting next to me in the rear seat. During the split second when my head was being forced down, I also caught sight of major pieces of radio equipment on either side of the car. These were not the small radios or CB transmitters with which trucks are sometimes fitted, but two large electronic panels of command devices.

My handlers were naturally concerned about their security. As for myself, nothing had prepared me for this "diplomatic" experience. I now began to see the current predicament as a consequence of my heart ruling my head, anathema to a seasoned UN officer. My mind quickly raced from the practical to the worrisome and the fearful. Were these the "right people"? Would this be a one-way trip? What would happen next? Where was I going? For how long? And what about my son? I thought of my son and of the far too many times I had been away. Why was I here? That was one question for which I actually had an answer: I was here because I had chosen to be.

My idea of undertaking a rescue operation for the hostages, my request to meet with the kidnappers, my determination to do so whatever the cost, all had been personal decisions that nobody had forced me into or instructed me to make. I even remember smiling to myself for a moment as my face was being squeezed against the floor of the car. I had been told that a good diplomat never mixes his profession with his personal life. I literally said to myself: Picco, try to separate the two now! I had no regrets.

I thought then, just as I still do, that personal commitment meant credibility—and credibility, in turn, improved the chances of success in the Middle East much more than being a "good diplomat," which wasn't my strong suit in any event. At that moment, I had committed completely.

Yes, I was scared. Only a fool would not have been.

The car drove off at high speed, and I had a vague sense that I was going in circles. From time to time, a few inaudible words would be exchanged when we approached a checkpoint. At some point during this journey, I recall them telling me, "Down. Syrian. Down. Syrian." At each stop I could feel the tension mounting in the car, since the Syrian guards at the checkpoints were now searching for the French hostage. Nevertheless, we sailed through. The car then stopped in an alley, and I was told to keep my head down. We were alongside a waiting car. Both back doors were swung open, and I was pulled out of the first car and thrust into the backseat of the second, where I continued the journey with my head held down. The only thing I could observe about the second car was that it was not a Mercedes.

For about a half hour, I had the feeling that they were driving around and around to disorient me. Eventually we stopped, and before releasing the pressure, they slid a hood over my head. Then they told me to follow them. So, like a blind man, I put my hand on the shoulder of the person in front of me and started to walk. I think we went through a ditch, and then I heard my guide say, "Stairs," so I began to climb. We walked up three flights of stairs, at the top of which I heard a door open. From the sound of voices and movement, I could sense that there were a lot of people in the room. The men accompanying me led me to another room and sat me down. Then somebody removed my hood from behind.

I found myself in a room with walls completely draped in anonymous white sheets. There was absolutely no recognizable feature about it. I was told to remove my shoes. My "negotiators" rummaged through my folder with its pad and asked if I had brought a pen. I said I had. My jacket was now off. (During these trips I always wore a double-breasted blazer with a shirt and tie, and loafers—normal garb during my trips.) While my clothes and gear were being inspected, I was quickly frisked for weapons. About every five seconds I heard a beep from a machine of obvious sophistication, which I could not see. I sat on a sofa in the bend of what appeared to be an L-shaped room, facing a wall draped with a sheet. In front of me was a small table with a bowl of fruit, the ubiquitous sign of Middle Eastern hospitality.

Two people entered. One sat down opposite me, the other stood. Both wore ski masks over their heads with slits for their eyes. This was my first encounter with the kidnappers. One of them told me that the meeting was taking place because the Iranian government had assured them that the UN secretary-general could reach the Israelis and prompt them to reciprocate and also because the secretary-general was a man of honor who understood the plight of Third World people. Then he said, "You have to understand that for my brothers, Israel is armed by the U.S. and the West. It is financially supported by the U.S. and the West. So for us, Israel and the West are one and the same. We accepted you as emissary, as you have proven in the past to our people that you understand us and also for what you have done."

As he spoke, I took notes. Immediately after this quote, I put down a series of question marks because I had no idea what he was referring to. I assumed that the man sitting across the table was referring to the end of the Iran-Iraq war, but he also made it clear at once that he was a Lebanese Arab, not an Iranian. Then he asked me a question unexpected in this environment, one that revealed political sophistication: "Who sends you? Is it the secretary-general or the Security Council?"

Had we been sitting in a seminar at the Council on Foreign Relations, I thought this would have been a magnificent question revealing a genuine understanding of the structure of the United Nations. What was even more unusual was that the question had not been asked in jest. The question was, in fact, so serious that had I given the wrong answer, I could have paid for it dearly. If I replied that I had been sent by the Security Council, I would have been putting myself at risk, for that implied working for one of the major powers—the Perm Five members of the Council. I replied truthfully, stating that I had been sent by the secretary-general.

My interrogator was obviously pleased. "That is why you are here and why we will be dealing with you. If you had not come from the secretary-general, then we would have had a problem."

I could not help but think at that moment, as I did later upon reflection, how few ambassadors to the United Nations would have understood the implications of the question. It became clear from our meetings that I was dealing with a politically astute individual with a great awareness of the world, a man who spoke some French and English in addition to his native tongue.

The Iranians had learned, mainly through the Iran-Iraq war, that there were things that the secretary-general could do in the arenas of mediation and peacemaking that the Security Council could not. They had also learned with the rest of the world that there were things that only powerful nations could do in concert under the UN banner, such as turning back Iraqi aggression in Operation Desert Storm. The hostage crisis, I believed from the start, was tailor-made for the capabilities of the secretary-general.

I never did discover the identity of the two masked men in front of me. One may have been Imad Moughniya, the other his brother-in-law Mustafa Badruddin. According to Magnus Ranstorp from St. Andrew's University in Scotland, the core group of kidnappers of Western hostages involved only a dozen men from the Moughniya and Hammadi clans in south Lebanon. Imad Moughniya was by then a legend in the world of Islamic militancy in Lebanon—the head of the Special Security Apparatus of Hizbollah. He and Abdel Hadi Hammadi were able to manage the kidnapping operations because they worked mainly with family and clan members, ensuring a high degree of secrecy. Moughniya had also been a personal bodyguard of Sheikh Fadlallah in the early 1980s and had been involved in the hijacking of TWA Flight 847 in 1985, together with Mohammed Ali Hammadi, the brother of Abdel. The arrest and sentencing of

Mohammed Ali Hammadi by the German authorities had triggered the kidnapping of the German hostages in the late 1980s.

Mustafa Badruddin had been a major participant in the 1983 operations against the U.S. and French embassies in Kuwait and had been sentenced to death in the emirate. When invading Iraqi troops had opened Kuwaiti jails, Badruddin and the rest of the Dawa Seventeen had fled and made their way to Iran. He was known to have returned to Lebanon by the time I had my first meeting somewhere in Beirut.

During my stay at OGB, I began to receive bits and pieces of information from the most unthinkable sources. From what I had picked up in Beirut, I believed that Badruddin was indeed one of the masked men. Israeli intelligence would suggest that Moughniya was actually in the room during my visits. Certainly, if that were the case, I was the only foreigner to have survived an encounter with the legendary Imad Moughniya.

The kidnapping of the Frenchman, who had yet to be found despite the manhunt that Syrian intelligence had put into motion, cast a pall over our meeting. My interlocutor made it clear that he and his people were not responsible for the kidnapping and that, quite the contrary, they were ready to release the hostages. His own group was searching the town for the Frenchman, so far to no avail. The episode, he said, proved that there were still opponents of the political decision to free the Westerners. The operation was not going to be cost-free for anybody! Therefore, the release of a second hostage had to be delayed because there was a danger it could lead to the death of the kidnapped Frenchman. He explained that the Syrians and Iranians had put pressure on his group to release the hostages. The pressure, however, had been exaggerated and had produced the opposite effect. He specifically referred to excessive Iranian religious pressure.

Then it was my turn. A delay in the release of the second hostage because of the Frenchman's kidnapping, which according to my interlocutor had been perpetrated by just two or three people, meant that the entire Islamic Jihad was being blackmailed by a few renegades. If that was the case, I asked in a replay of my conversation with Zamania, who was really in charge? Further, I suggested that if two or three people could blackmail the group, didn't that say a great deal about the weakness of the group itself? I then softened my tone and told him that "your credibility is our credibility." The second hostage had to be released now if the group and, by extension, the UN secretary-general were to remain credible.

They took the point but insisted that the Frenchman be rescued before the matter got out of hand. A second release would require some type of reciprocation, which only the Israelis could provide. The principal questioner warned that if they went ahead with a second release and it were not reciprocated, the consequences for the remaining hostages would be "devastating." He assured me he was speaking with full authority for the groups holding the American, British, and German hostages. He then added that I would have to prove to him that the secretary-general was prepared to ensure that the countries involved—in particular the United States, Britain, Germany, and Israel—would reciprocate. He handed me a message from the groups for each of these governments.

From the Germans, the groups wanted to know about the condition of the imprisoned Hammadi brothers, both of whom they believed were being mistreated by their jailers. They warned that the German hostages, who were being held by the Hammadi family, would suffer if the mistreatment of the brothers continued. By the United States, they wanted pressure brought to bear on Israel to release its Lebanese prisoners and to stop putting pressure on Germany to keep the Hammadi brothers in jail. As for the British, they also would have to exert pressure on the Israelis if they wanted the remaining three British hostages freed.

In the middle of the conversation, one of the two masked men, who would remain the principal interlocutor throughout our talks, introduced himself as Abdullah, which I assumed was a nom de guerre. Abdullah insisted on knowing the response to each of the messages they sent to the governments before another release could take place. Moreover, he wanted to hear the replies directly from me and not the Iranians. In effect, there were two surprises: first, we would need another meeting, and, second, the release of another hostage would have to be further delayed. I vehemently objected to the latter, while I confirmed to him my readiness to meet again—as if I really had a choice. I then raised the question of the Israeli soldiers missing in action. I wanted to learn how far we could go.

To say that things were tense is putting it mildly. There were people behind me and the unseen machine beeping in the background—probably some sort of a radio-wave detector. The men behind me were obviously armed: I could hear the metal of their weapons swinging and clicking. They whispered, and occasionally my interlocutor's eyes would shift and I would catch him looking past my shoulders to them. From time to time, he would rise and vanish behind me to consult quickly with one of them before returning to continue our discussion.

He asked when he could expect another meeting. I was concerned that this question would signal an end to our conversation without my having achieved any practical results. I was not prepared to leave as yet, and I told Abdullah that we had much to accomplish here and now. I raised the principal concern of Israel, which was to learn the fate and whereabouts of the airman Ron Arad. He said a separate group was responsible for the Israelis but that he would bring me its reaction, which would include whether Abdullah and I would negotiate about the Israeli prisoners or whether I would negotiate with the other group directly.

Then, apparently as a show of his goodwill, Abdullah announced that they would now bring out a hostage for me to see. I quickly replied that I had no interest in seeing any hostage unless he could leave with me. This was a reversal of my original position of seeking to visit the hostages to determine their physical condition—but by now we were past that. Too many expectations had been raised for me to accept a mere inspection, and the whole thing had assumed its own powerful dynamic. Nothing ever worked out according to my intricate plans, and I always had to be prepared to change them on the spot.

Abdullah replied that I could not take a hostage with me because that would require special security arrangements. I insisted that if I saw one of the hostages, I would have to be able to tell him that he would be freed, if not that night then the following day. Abdullah said that a release would raise "complications" (already the familiar catchall excuse) not only because of security but because the problem of the French hostage was still unresolved. I told Abdullah that in that case, I did not want to see any of the hostages lest I raise false hopes.

He then got up and walked behind me. A few minutes later, he returned and told me that they had agreed then and there to release one of the hostages into the hands of the United Nations. I was asked when I would like to receive him. I replied that if it was possible I was ready to receive him that very moment, but I wanted the release to be carried out so that Syria would not be upstaged and possibly offended. In Lebanon, where Syria was the dominant and sometimes implacable power, doing anything to antagonize it was unwise. When I told him that, I could hear people laughing behind me. He then went into a description of the groups' relationships with Syria and Iran. Syria and Lebanon were two entirely separate entities, he said, even though the groups had to acknowledge Syria's strength. As for Iran, just because the groups shared spiritual and political beliefs, it did not imply that Iran could tell them what to do and when to do it.

Then he said, "We are prepared to accept your decision as to when we should release this hostage."

"As soon as you can," I said.

In a very emphatic manner, he conveyed to me in words and gestures their demand for reciprocity by Israel—and the negative consequences for the West if it were not done promptly. He got up to fetch me a Coke, and a few minutes later the hostage was brought in.

Edward Tracy was a man who had led a very difficult life even before his capture. Estranged from his family, he had come to Beirut during the civil war to sell Bibles and ended up selling pornography. His family had never inquired of his whereabouts and had refused to have anything to do with him after he was kidnapped. He entered the room wearing a light blue tracksuit with a white stripe across it, a very popular color combination in the Middle East at that time.

It was a very emotional moment for me. I rose and embraced him, saying, "Mr. Tracy, I'm so glad to see you. You will soon be free."

He hesitated and replied in a voice loud enough for all to hear, "I am not Mr. Tracy."

Someone exclaimed, "This is a trick! Mr. Picco tricked us!"—as if the whole thing were some grand American plot.

"Picco tricked us! Picco tricked us!" another voice called out. At this point, I did not know what to do. In fact, no one knew what to do.

Then I said, "Wait a minute. This man is Tracy. I have his picture to prove it."

Tracy once again responded, "I am not Mr. Tracy."

Confounded, Abdullah looked around and asked something along the line of: Who is this man? What is his name? Not in English, of course, but I understood what he was getting at.

For a moment there was panic on both sides. I thought I was literally lost as Abdullah tried once again to establish his captive's identity. The hostage looked up with almost a hint of a smile and said, "I'm not Mr. Tracy. My name is . . ." and he babbled something incomprehensible. At this point I said, "Look, I have seen his picture. This is Mr. Tracy."

I could still feel their eyes on me, as if I had betrayed them. Once again I turned to the hostage and said, "Mr. Tracy, you are going to be freed."

He answered, "You mean I have to leave this place?"

"Aren't you happy?" I inquired.

"Do you know what cordon bleu is?" he asked me. I replied that I certainly did. "Well, I have three cordon bleu meals a day here, and I don't pay for them."

"But Mr. Tracy, don't you understand what we are talking about here?" I asked him.

About then, everyone in the room began to realize that this unfortunate man's mind had gone. Suddenly, the emotional tension dissipated as what had been surprise, fear, and a sense of betrayal gave way to relieved laughter and, finally, disbelief. Tracy and his comments were so utterly inappropriate as to be truly funny.

Finally, he admitted the obvious: "Yes. I am Mr. Tracy." I will never know how he regained his senses, but it did not come a moment too soon.

As a calm of sorts returned, I once again tried to convey to Tracy that he would be released the following day and that I would probably see him again. They took him out of the room, and Abdullah agreed that Tracy would be released despite the uncertainty about the fate of the Frenchman.

Expressing his trust in me once again, Abdullah approached me and apologized for the procedure that I had had to endure to reach them; there simply was no other way. It was 1 A.M. when I finally got up to leave. I was again blindfolded and led down the stairs and into a car, and I followed the same procedure of keeping my head down in the backseat and swapping cars, only in reverse. I was driven back at high speed and left very close to where I had been picked up, near the Iranian Embassy. I walked over to the embassy, where they appeared never to sleep, to find out how I could get home.

I identified myself and asked for Zamania. Upon hearing my name, one of the guards opened the gate from the inside. When Zamania saw me, he exclaimed, "I'm very glad to see you back!" When he told me he had been concerned about the whole encounter, I believed him. After what I had just been through, finding myself in the Iranian Embassy at almost two in the morning gave me a sense of safety and security. I cannot think of another diplomat who would have felt that way in that place at that time. I was glad to brief Zamania and explain the circumstances of Tracy's imminent release, making it clear to him that it would happen regardless of the search for the French hostage. In fact, the Frenchman, Jérôme Leyraud, an aid official, was released the following morning and three people involved with his abduction were said to have been executed by the groups.

Tracy was released on August 10. The Organization for Islamic Justice issued a press release referring to our conversation the night before and the agreement we had reached: "Consultations were undertaken with [Pérez] de Cuéllar and carried out by special envoy Gianni Picco to open an important field for negotiations on influential international levels. . . . The release of an American hostage will take place in 72 hours and we asked Picco to go to Damascus to assist in his handing over and to assure the presence of the United Nations which we want to play a role in solving this crisis." The press release also referred to the need to release Sheikh Obeid from Israel and all other detainees in prison in Israel and other countries.

They had done me no favors by setting off the Syrians' role against ours. But there had always been bad blood between the Lebanese groups and Lebanon's Syrian overlords, and they found it hard to resist a chance to put a thumb in the eye of the Syrians. One place we did not want to meddle was in Syrian politics, so I stayed out of sight when Syrian intelligence officials handed Tracy over to the American ambassador in Damascus, who rendered them homage, which in fact they deserved for ensuring that everything flowed smoothly at the end.

Ahead lay a more difficult job, for which I would need the help of Pérez de Cuéllar and the Americans. That was to bring the Israelis around so I could make good on my promise to the groups. I returned to OGB that night around 2:30 A.M. and found Nielsen and Holopainen standing on the porch of the villa looking at the road climbing up from Beirut. With their military self-control, they proved to be the best company I could have asked for at that moment. They were clearly relieved to see me back; they asked no questions but were prepared to listen should I decide to speak. We had a soft drink sitting at the bar of OGB as I sought shelter from the emotional storm. Perhaps a Scotch would have been more appropriate under the circumstances, but I had not touched alcohol in eight years. Finally, at 4:30 A.M., I managed to get to sleep.

The next four weeks proved to be as complex a period of diplomatic bargaining as any I ever spent as I tried to assemble a package with something in it for everyone. For the Israelis, we needed news of their MIAs. For the groups in Lebanon, it was the return of a sizable number of Lebanese prisoners by the Israelis. For the Germans, it was reassurance from the Hammadi clan that the two German hostages would be part of the releases. For us and for the stability of Lebanon itself, it was the return of the Western hostages, who had become a symbol of anarchy in that troubled country. For the Iranians, it was a chance to provide a contribution to the solution of the problem that had marked Iran as a rogue state. Pérez de Cuéllar would be visiting Teheran on September 11. This became a deadline for me to tie everything together.

My first visit to Jihadland was over, and two hostages had been released. We had yet to meet with the Israelis, who would soon take on a much more significant role in the hostage operation. General Scowcroft had arranged for Uri Lubrani to meet with Pérez de Cuéllar in Geneva on August 11. I was not present at that meeting because I was flying back from Damascus. But I would join them the next day. The meeting was my first with Lubrani and would begin my professional relationship with a tough and wily negotiator who was disliked by some, liked by others, and, during the many months we faced each other, respected and befriended by me.

It became very clear that the entire matter was of the highest political importance to Israel and was in the hands of the security establishment and not the Foreign Ministry, although diplomats were occasionally called in as window dressing. Lubrani set the stage for his country's position during that first long meeting with Pérez de Cuéllar. Israel would be prepared to free the Lebanese detained in south Lebanon and would even consider a visit by the ICRC to Sheikh Obeid in Israel, he said, provided that similar visits with the Israeli MIAs could be arranged. There were six Israelis on Lubrani's agenda: two who had been lost in a battle in June 1982; three who had been captured during the same year in a different military operation in Lebanon; and airman Ron Arad, whose plane had been shot down over Lebanon in 1986 and whose whereabouts Israeli intelligence had been aware of until late 1989.

Lubrani was the point man for dealing with these issues because he had become Israel's top expert on Hizbollah, Iran, and their close relationship. And Israel believed that the Shiite militants, and Hizbollah in particular, probably had controlling authority when it came to the issues on the table. At their second meeting, the Israeli negotiator asked, and Pérez de Cuéllar agreed, that I go to Israel to be briefed on the Israeli MIAs in greater detail. My task was to obtain evidence and information about the missing Israelis and seek their return. It was in this meeting that Lubrani used an expression that became his trademark throughout our association. It was important, he said, not to be "led down the garden path" by the Iranians, whom he considered extremely astute and tricky to handle. I felt that the two greatest chess players, Israel and Iran, had now begun a match. The only difference was that the pawns on the board were human lives.

Lubrani also delivered a letter to the secretary-general from Israeli Prime Minister Yitzhak Shamir, in his youth a guerrilla fighter against the British, who was thus no stranger to the use of terrorism for political ends. The letter broadly reaffirmed the points Lubrani had made the previous day regarding ICRC access to Lebanese captives, including Sheikh Obeid, as part of a package that would lead to their release in exchange for the freedom of all Western hostages and the return of Israeli prisoners and MIAs. But there was less in the offer than met the eye. The Israelis had completely ignored the significance of the two Western hostages already released by the groups. Instead, they wanted to turn the bargain on its head, demanding "reliable and irrefutable information" about all Israeli captives before releasing any of the Lebanese whom the groups expected in exchange for the hostages they had just set free. Shamir was saying that before he made any move, they would have to make another.

Now that the United Nations seemed to be empowered to conduct the deal, Lubrani then asked, what should the Israelis tell the Swiss? He had been working the Swiss channel for some time and did not want to damage what had become a good relationship. Pérez de Cuéllar said flatly that efforts should not be duplicated, that the United Nations and Israel should keep in close touch with each other, and that both of us should remain in contact with the Swiss. If we needed their help, he said, we could simply ask for it. Lubrani ended by pledging Israel's full support to the secretary-general's efforts, but he and Shamir had front-loaded the deal and put me into a tight spot.

On the one hand, I had the groups demanding a payoff for their gestures to date; on the other, I had the Israeli prime minister demanding to be paid up front before he would agree to the release of Lebanese prisoners, which I had already promised to work on when I faced Abdullah across the table in Beirut. From the Israeli point of view, the release of the Western hostages was of little relevance if it was not accompanied by movement on their own MIAs.

When I briefed the Iranians, they put in their own demands, which I fully expected. They wanted information about the four Iranian citizens who had been missing in Beirut since 1982. Kharrazi joined us in Geneva on August 12 and was briefed on the discussions with the Israelis. When he was told of the strength of Israel's position with regard to its MIAs, he repeated that to the best of his knowledge the groups in Lebanon could be helpful with information on two Israelis who had lost their lives in the area; but as far as others were concerned, and specifically Ron Arad, his government had no knowledge of them. He agreed, however, that a search would be mounted provided it would also be extended to the four missing Iranians.

When I arrived in Tel Aviv on August 21, I was escorted off the plane first and whisked into a windowless van waiting on the tarmac. I found it to be as comfortable as a den. During the ride, we received a phone call. I was told that it was the prime minister, checking to see if I had arrived. I was also told that my identity would be protected and that I had already been registered under a false name at a hotel, where I was not to answer the phone with my own name. When we arrived at my suite at a grand hotel by the sea in Tel Aviv, I discovered that the problem of answering the phone would never really arise. I had a guard, and Israeli intelligence had arranged everything. I did not even have to pick up my key at the desk.

I met the full Israeli team who would become my counterparts in so many meetings in the months ahead: Lubrani; Ori Slonim, a lawyer involved in the MIA issue; and the deputy chief of military intelligence. For two days, I was briefed by military intelligence about the Iranians, Hizbollah and its bases in the Bekaa Valley of Lebanon, and anyone else who might lead the way to the six missing Israelis. In addition to Ron Arad, there were two soldiers, Joseph Fink and Rahamim Levi Alsheik, who were thought to have been taken prisoner in south Lebanon by Hizbollah in 1982 and were now believed dead, and three more soldiers, Zacharia Baumel, Zvi Feldman, and Yehuda Katz, who had been involved on June 11, 1982, in a battle just outside Beirut known as Sultan Yacoub, where they were believed to have been captured and taken to Syria. Over the years, several Israeli prime ministers had asked various heads of state to approach Syrian President Hafez al-Assad, seeking help in solving the mystery of the Sultan Yacoub battle.

I also asked for and obtained from the Israelis information they had about the missing Iranians. They marked on maps what they believed to be the burial sites of the four (Mouhsen al-Mousawi, Ahmad Motevaselian, Kasem Alkhavan Alaf, and Tajhirastejar Mogedam), who had been killed by Lebanese Christians in Beirut in 1982.

Lubrani made it clear that, before handing over a single Lebanese prisoner, the Israeli government first wanted to know everything known by the other side about its missing men. "If the Iranians think the ball is in our court," he said, "then we have a problem." I knew that if I were to report back to Abdullah and his people with that response, it might short-circuit our work right there. I let the Israelis know that their position was untenable by presenting them with a counterproposal, which was that I would search for the Israeli MIAs with the help they had given me.

I hoped that if I could come up with more information from inside Lebanon to satisfy the Israelis, they would release some prisoners. In other words, I was suggesting a release in exchange for information to keep the ball rolling. More specifically, what I needed to get from Lubrani was Israeli reciprocity for information on any of the MIAs, not just on Arad, since I knew his would be the hardest case to crack. I also knew by then that the groups were holding the bodies of two Israelis. I needed Lubrani's confirmation that if I brought back information about these two bodies, Israel would reciprocate by releasing prisoners. At one moment in our conversation when we were alone, Lubrani agreed and also said that a letter from Sheikh Obeid could be given to me for his family if that would be useful.

On August 28, I was in Teheran to plan for Pérez de Cuéllar's visit, now only two weeks away. I needed to get as much information as I could

about the two Israeli bodies held by Hizbollah so that the Israeli reciprocity could take place before or during the visit of the secretary-
general. Reciprocity, of course, could be used by Pérez de Cuéllar to
obtain a further commitment by President Rafsanjani on more releases of
Western hostages. With that outcome, we would advance the cause of the
hostages with a diplomatic coup of our own. (I also asked that the Iranians release a number of Iraqi prisoners of war as part of the humanitarian activities of the secretary-general in the region.)

On the day of my arrival, Velayati and I met at his home. It was 10
P.M., and since early morning I had been on the go with meeting after
meeting. The foreign minister's main concern was the outlook for the
UN-sponsored study on the responsibility for the Iran-Iraq war, or what
we now referred to simply as "Paragraph 6." Three European professors
had been entrusted by the secretary-general to study the matter, I told
him. Velayati and the foreign minister of Iraq had already received a formal letter requesting the presentation of their respective versions of the
facts as a basis for the professors' study. I could not predict the results of
the study, I said, and in any event the results would need to be announced
in New York, not Teheran. I then asked if the secretary-general's visit
would be a success, to which he answered that he was pleased that the
study was definitely under way. We understood each other perfectly.

That day, other Iranian officials had been pressuring me to reveal
what the secretary-general's conclusion on Paragraph 6 would be, even
though the three professors had yet to complete their work. For my part,
I had insisted on the need to get some information on Ron Arad. By then,
two names seemed relevant in the search. Mustafa Durani, a Lebanese
Shiite militant whose allegiance over the years had varied between pro-
Syrian and pro-Iranian groups, had held Arad in captivity at some point
in 1989. The second person was Mohammed Hassan Azkari, commander
of the Pasdaran, the contingent of Iranian Revolutionary Guards in
Lebanon's Bekaa Valley. If I could gain access to these two, I told my Iranian interlocutors, I might learn something about Arad. They were non-
committal but said they would think about my request.

By the time I left Teheran for Switzerland in the early hours of August
30, I knew that if the Israelis were to reciprocate for receiving precise information about the bodies of Fink and Alsheik with the release of some
fifty prisoners, we would be able to move ahead. Later that day, I met
with Lubrani at the Savoy Hotel in Zurich. Preparations for the deal dis-

cussed in Teheran proceeded well. I had begun to know Lubrani, and although he did not confirm a precise count for release, I knew he would not let me down. However, he had to discuss the matter with the prime minister's inner cabinet. He flew back to Israel, and I went back to New York. Twenty-four hours later, the inner cabinet had approved the minideal and Lubrani wanted to meet again to discuss the specific information I would need to provide on the two Israelis' bodies before the Lebanese prisoners could be released. Back in Zurich on September 2, Lubrani gave me a list of detailed identification marks required by a rabbi to certify that the bodies were, in fact, those of the missing Israeli soldiers—teeth, fingerprints if possible, photos, hair and eye colors, blood type, skull X ray if possible. He stressed that the cabinet also wanted the secretary-general to obtain information about Arad.

Lubrani said that Israel would release 55 men, 5 women, and 15 bodies, all Hizbollah, out of their "inventory" of an estimated 250 to 280 Lebanese prisoners, but he warned that without any information about Arad, the deal would be off. I tried to raise the number from 60 live Lebanese to 100, but for that he wanted even more information about Arad. The Israelis had included information about Arad then and there as part of this first exchange, and I did not know whether I could deliver. Upon leaving the hotel room in Zurich, I asked the Israeli deputy chief of military intelligence, a general, whether I could indicate to the groups in Lebanon that they would receive 80 prisoners, in whatever combination—dead or alive. He made no comment. We took a car to the airport, the general and Lubrani speaking between themselves in Hebrew during the entire trip. As we arrived, the general confirmed that I could use that number.

When the secretary-general and I met with Iranian Ambassador Kharrazi in New York upon my return from Switzerland, Pérez de Cuéllar said the Israelis were promising 70 to 80 Lebanese, without mentioning that some of them were dead. In exchange, the information about the dead Israeli soldiers would have to be impeccable, and the Iranians would have to be able to give us solid information about Arad's status—not necessarily where he was but whether he was dead or alive.

In Zurich, Lubrani, the general, and I had also discussed the Swiss channel, which seemed quite active just about then. Swiss Ambassador Edouard Brunner in Washington had become his country's point man on the hostages, and I was told he would probably contact me shortly. I found the persistence of two channels not constructive, to say the least, and events soon confirmed my skepticism. On September 3, only a week before the secretary-general's trip to Teheran and a day after my meeting in Zurich, Lubrani called to report that the Swiss had proposed a deal. The groups would hand over one of the two bodies held by Hizbollah as well as the remains of 6 soldiers in the pro-Israeli South Lebanese Army (SLA) in exchange for 50 detainees from Israel. The swap would take place before Pérez de Cuéllar arrived in Teheran on September 10. I feared that this was a blatant attempt to sabotage our efforts, and perhaps Lubrani felt some of the same suspicion. He had declined to answer the Swiss until consulting me on how it would affect our efforts. The Swiss also claimed to have learned, through a contact in Beirut, that Ron Arad was alive and that his captors were prepared to give a "sign of life" in exchange for the release of Sheikh Obeid. This was clearly a better deal for the Israelis than the one I could offer, and I encouraged Lubrani to take it. On my side, I had already arranged to go to Beirut in forty-eight hours to secure the information the Israelis sought about the two bodies. I also made it clear that I could not guarantee information about Ron Arad before or during the secretary-general's visit to Teheran.

I asked Lubrani if he wanted to go through the Swiss channel, which seemed so promising. "You must be joking," he replied.

During the next five days, Lubrani and I exchanged messages and phone calls on what kind of commitment the secretary-general could make on the Arad case as part of the package that would lead to the release of the Lebanese detainees. This, in turn, meant elaborate discussions with the Iranians. We finally reached an agreement on the following formulation: The secretary-general is ready to start the search so that he can say at the end of it whether Ron Arad is dead or alive. For this search, the secretary-general has been assured by Iran that it will provide all available tools to make him successful.

On Sunday, September 8, Pérez de Cuéllar and I met in Paris with the entire Israeli team. There were two points in our discussions. One was a clarification of the Lebanese releases by Israel, imprecisely referred to as "some 70 to 80." The other was the duration of the search for Ron Arad, a key point for the Israelis. Ambassador Kharrazi had mentioned ten to fifteen days, which Pérez de Cuéllar passed along to Lubrani. During that meeting, Lubrani's team also told Pérez de Cuéllar that Israeli intelligence was sure Iran knew exactly where Arad was—in the control of the Iranian

Revolutionary Guards and Azkari himself, who at that moment was in Teheran.

The deal, in my view, was still too soft on both sides to guarantee that I would get the information I needed in Damascus and Beirut, or that it would be enough to satisfy Israel. But time was growing short, and I set out for the Middle East that evening to find out what I could.

CHAPTER 11

From a Mullah
to a Rabbi

◢

T HE PLAN WAS TO FLY FROM PARIS TO DAMASCUS on the evening of September 8 so I could spend the next day in Beirut working the forensic material on the missing Israelis, head for Cyprus to pass along the information to Lubrani, then return to Paris to hook up with Pérez de Cuéllar in advance of his September 11 visit to Teheran. Nothing went according to plan.

Throughout my first day in Damascus, Iranian Ambassador Akhtari, who was to arrange for me to obtain the information, made himself unavailable. His underlings told me that he was in his office but very busy. Another setback surfaced when Javad Zarif called to alert me to a logistical problem involving Teheran, Damascus, and Beirut but refused to elaborate. When I met Akhtari at 5:30 P.M. on September 9, he confirmed in vague terms that difficulties had arisen and said he would do his best to make sure I received the information later that day. Clearly I would not be able to meet the Israelis in Cyprus and be in Teheran on the eleventh. As a result, I switched my meeting with Lubrani to Israel on the tenth and hoped I could catch an Iran Air flight from Damascus to Teheran that evening.

Near the end of the day, Akhtari told me that the information on the two missing Israeli soldiers had been prepared with some difficulty and that the file was not yet complete. I warned him that I could not present incomplete documentation to the Israelis and still expect the release of the prisoners. He promised to do his best.

Well behind schedule, I called Zarif in Teheran for help in pressing the ambassador to move faster. Realizing that I now did not have enough time to go to Beirut and then make it to Teheran, Zarif said he would arrange for the forensic material to be brought to me in Damascus at 5 P.M. on

September 10. I did not like the idea because it would give me very little time to take the material across the border to the Israelis, have them examine it, then return to Damascus and take a plane in time to meet up with the secretary-general in Teheran the next day. But Zarif promised an Iranian plane to ferry me directly from Damascus to Teheran to join the meeting with Pérez de Cuéllar and President Rafsanjani. The schedule was tight, but I could still make it. Not by air, however; now I would have to make special arrangements to drive across the Golan Heights by car after dusk, deliver the goods to the Israelis, who would examine them on the spot, then beat it back to Damascus to catch the plane the Iranians were sending. Communicating by coded messages, I asked Lubrani and his team to meet me as close as possible to the dividing line on the Heights.

In the late afternoon of the tenth, I once again went over the forensic requirements with Akhtari, who said the bodies had been well preserved even though the men had been killed several years earlier. Turning to the other side of the bargain, he asked me what Israel would be giving in return. I told him we were trying to get seventy Lebanese. He asked, "And what about the fifth missing Iranian in Beirut?" Until that moment, I had been aware of only four! At the last moment, they always tried to throw something else into the pot. I told the ambassador I knew nothing about a fifth Iranian.

I also called on Deputy Foreign Minister Shakour Nasser Kaddour of Syria to deliver a letter from Pérez de Cuéllar to President Hafez al-Assad on the Arad case. The Iranians and Syrians each claimed that the other had information about the Israeli airman. Two weeks earlier, Assad had assured U.S. Secretary of State Jim Baker that Iran was the place to find out about Arad. On this one, the Israelis agreed with Syria.

Kaddour, it seemed, wanted a piece of the action. He responded by presenting me with a list of twenty-six Syrian civilians being held by Israel for opposing the occupation of the Golan Heights. I promised to do what I could. Even my own embassy, the Italian Embassy, called to remind me that Italy had a hostage, Alberto Molinari, in Lebanon. I had already been inquiring about him in Beirut, but to no avail. Molinari was a longtime resident with dual nationality who had been caught up in one of Lebanon's many clan feuds.

At 7:30 P.M., the new appointed hour for me to receive the information, Akhtari called and invited me to have dinner with him.

"Ambassador," I said, trying hard not to lose it, "I have something to do right now!"

"Yes, but we must have a nice dinner before your important achievement."

I said that I thought that it had already been achieved.

"There's been a slight delay," he admitted without apology or apparent concern that this would affect the meeting between his president and my boss the following day.

So I went to his embassy, where we sat down to a lonely dinner, just the two of us. At 9 P.M., I looked at my watch and said that I had no wish to appear impolite, but I did have pressing business.

"Stay and be patient; that material will arrive shortly."

"Where is this material coming from?"

"It will be delivered at the airport."

"Then we should go there to receive it."

He conceded that that might be a good idea but added that "if you want to go back to your office and relax, I'll let you know when it arrives." I told him I was certainly in no state to relax! I suggested we go to the airport and get the material and that I jump into a car to cross the Golan—immediately. He agreed and said he would let me know when the material arrived so we could proceed to the airport together.

I went back to UN headquarters, just down the street from the Iranian Embassy, and told my UNDOF military contacts to again rearrange my trip across the Golan Heights and my return to Damascus for much later. Lubrani was informed by coded fax. He would meet me at what was for him the farthest Israeli outpost on the Golan Heights, accompanied by a rabbi, who would scrutinize the documents from Beirut.

It was now midnight in Damascus, and I was still waiting for Akhtari's call. Finally the ambassador signaled that he was ready to meet me at the airport. It was nearly 1 A.M. when I arrived in a UN jeep equipped with a radio and telephone and carrying a small security detail that would be no match for the forces deployed at the airport. The scene at the airport was surreal. The Iranian ambassador was sitting in his Mercedes in the airport parking lot with his security people. An Iranian security car was parked in front of him. Thirty yards behind them was our white UN jeep, followed by a second as a backup. All around us, Syrian security forces formed an outer perimeter.

I approached the ambassador's parked car. The Iranian guards surrounding him opened the door, and I stepped inside.

"Mr. Ambassador, it is a pleasure to see you. May I have my material?"

"It is not here yet."

"How long do you think it will take?"

"It should be here at any time," he replied calmly.

I asked if there was nothing he could do to speed things up. What had happened, according to Akhtari, was that the material had been sent from Beirut to Teheran and now was being sent back from Teheran to Damascus so that I could pass it along to the Israelis. It had arrived on the very plane that would fly me back to Teheran during the night, he said. Since the Iranian plane had landed, I asked what the delay was.

Akhtari explained that the Iranian messenger was being detained by Syrian intelligence inside the airport. I then suggested that he could send one of his diplomats to retrieve the briefcase containing the material so I could have it immediately while the Iranian messenger was being questioned by Syrian intelligence.

Alas, the briefcase was chained to the courier's wrist.

It almost seemed as if there were a conspiracy to delay so that the meeting between Rafsanjani and Pérez de Cuéllar could not produce any results. But I had no intention of waiting and doing nothing.

I returned to my car and called the UNDOF chief of staff on the radio, asking him to approach Syrian intelligence at the highest possible level to speed up the release of the Iranian messenger at the airport. I then called Zarif in New York from the car phone; he was unaware of the confusion but was very sensitive to the fact that I needed success with the Israelis to convey to Rafsanjani during his meeting with Pérez de Cuéllar the following morning. We had several conversations, and finally, at 2:15 A.M., the courier approached the ambassador's car with the briefcase chained to his arm. The ambassador produced a key, unlocked the briefcase, and extracted some papers.

I looked at my checklist of forensic materials. "Ambassador, this is not enough. What do we do now?"

He replied, "I suggest we go get a good night's sleep."

I told him I appreciated his sense of humor, but we still had a problem. It seemed to me that I had complete information on one body but limited details on the other. I made it clear to Akhtari that if I were the Israeli in charge, I would not fulfill my side of the bargain, certainly not at the numbers originally promised.

He conceded that this might mean fewer prisoners would be released.

Our conversation ended at 2:45 A.M., and I told my UN driver to floor it to the Israeli border. I certainly hoped the Syrian Army had been informed of our plans to travel across the border, because I had no more time left for formalities at the Golan Heights checkpoint. The driver had cautioned that no one had crossed that border at night since the 1967 war, especially without stopping. "Whatever you have to do, you do," I replied, and we were off.

It was dark as we approached the Golan Heights, but the news had preceded us, and we were waved through after a cursory check. On the Israeli side, a guard stopped us. I hadn't even thought about the Israelis, since I assumed Lubrani had handled the formalities on his side. Then the guard asked, "Is this the car that was supposed to be here at 11:15 P.M. last night?" I said yes. He made a few phone calls and let us through. At 3:45 A.M., I arrived at the forward outpost, where the Israeli team was waiting.

I handed Lubrani the papers, explaining that I knew they were not all he had asked for but that I still hoped I could expect something in exchange. Lubrani replied, "Look, the rabbi is in the next room waiting for you. He has to certify that the information is sufficient."

The information on the first Israeli soldier turned out to be good. The rabbi said that the information on the second was a bit sketchy but that the evidence nevertheless confirmed the identity of the missing man. Lubrani said that the following day Israel would release fifty-one live prisoners and twenty-five bodies due to the incompleteness of the forensic reports. I thought it was a fair decision. It was now 4:30 A.M. on the Golan Heights but 6:30 A.M. in Teheran. Pérez de Cuéllar and Rafsanjani were scheduled to meet at 11 A.M.

After this incredible twenty-four hours, the engine for the release of the hostages had refired. We returned to Damascus at full throttle. The Iranian plane was at the airport, and one of the pilots could not resist remarking, "You're a bit late."

Look who's talking, I thought, but granted him the point. "Yes, but let's take off as soon as possible."

"Sure, as soon as the Syrians give us permission."

After what seemed an interminable delay, we took off, landing in Teheran at 10 A.M. I joined the secretary-general as he was meeting with Velayati and whispered to him that he could tell the Iranian foreign minister that, thanks to his efforts, many Lebanese prisoners would be released in a few hours.

The release of the Lebanese detainees went ahead as scheduled a few hours later, while Pérez de Cuéllar and I were meeting with Rafsanjani. The story was broadcast around the world and sparked new speculation that another Western hostage would soon be released.

The logistical chaos of the past seventy-two hours hadn't prevented the one meeting that counted, the one between Pérez de Cuéllar and Rafsanjani. The Iranians had Paragraph 6—what they hoped would be an official judgment naming Iraq the aggressor in their eight-year war—front and center in their minds. My Iranian interlocutors over the past half-dozen years—Nasseri and Zarif, Kharrazi and Vaezi—were all in Teheran, and they peppered me with questions about Paragraph 6, to the point where I felt psychologically tortured by their repeated inquiries.

First and foremost, they wanted to know about the secretary-general's "expectation" for the report being prepared for him and how he might respond. A satisfactory answer, they seemed to suggest, was their quid pro quo for further assistance in the release of Western hostages.

Not surprisingly, the private meeting between Rafsanjani and Pérez de Cuéllar started with Paragraph 6. The Iranian president tried to pin down the secretary-general as to the date when the report would be complete. I wanted to say it would be finished only when the entire hostage slate had been wiped clean. Pérez de Cuéllar said it was his wish that the report be finished by the end of October. By that he really meant he expected all the hostages to be released by then.

For Rafsanjani, the report on Paragraph 6 was so important that he openly stated that any previous linkage between the Iranian frozen assets in the United States and the hostage crisis "had been cut by his government." "We have no intention of linking the two things," he said.

When the conversation finally turned to the details of the hostages, Pérez de Cuéllar was pleased to point out that we had been able to obtain the release of fifty-one live and nine dead Lebanese. All the prisoners could be released, he told Rafsanjani, if only the mystery of Arad's whereabouts could be unraveled.

"The Iranian government received a lead from Mr. Picco, and we followed it," said the president. He was skeptical that Mustafa Durani, the

Lebanese Shiite militant who had allegedly had Arad in custody in 1989, had "lost" him during an Israeli raid. A rather disingenuous story was circulating that Arad had been left unguarded during a battle and had then escaped. He also said that he had no evidence that Ron Arad was dead.

Rafsanjani promised to try to squeeze more information out of the Lebanese, but he emphasized that there were only two methods that could be used. The first method, literally physical pressure, was ruled out because he found it distasteful. Indeed, torture had been the method used to free Jérôme Leyraud, the French aid worker who had been kidnapped. Rafsanjani felt it was an option only of last resort. "We had to put a lot of pressure on those responsible for this, and this has not been good for Iran in Lebanon because it was a bad method." Though the kidnappers were rumored to have been killed, no one officially admitted it.

The other method would be for Syria to interrogate those suspected of having information. "If everything is hanging on this, maybe in Syria, though I have no evidence of that, we will follow one of these two solutions. This is all we can do," Rafsanjani said. But that still meant we were moving on the Arad case, and Rafsanjani confirmed it by promising to send an emissary to Assad to discuss this matter.

Although we did not get all we wanted—we had asked the Iranians to release one thousand Iraqi prisoners—we did agree that the hostages had to be freed before the secretary-general completed his term of office at the end of the year, now less than four months away.

During the rest of our stay in Teheran, we worked through a list of objectives that needed to be accomplished in order to move forward. We received the support of the government of Iran to get the body of Colonel Higgins; to obtain the list of people I needed to interview on Arad; to receive further information about Alec Collett; to secure the release of perhaps two Western hostages; and to receive the complete forensic information on the second Israeli soldier. Pérez de Cuéllar stopped in Paris to brief the Israelis about the results of our meetings in Teheran before we returned to New York to prepare for my next visit to Beirut. I had to make sure that the government of Iran would inform its ambassador in Damascus and the groups in Lebanon that I would be returning for the release of the hostages. Ambassador Akhtari also had to summon two or three people to Damascus to discuss Arad's fate; he specifically mentioned Durani and Azkari in the Bekaa Valley.

I spent three days in New York urging the Iranians to follow up on our discussions and specifically to impress upon both Akhtari in Damascus and the groups in Lebanon the understanding that Rafsanjani had achieved with the secretary-general. Meanwhile, Pérez de Cuéllar received from Iran its complete version of how the war against Iraq had started. The Iraqis never replied to a similar request, so the European professors did not have Baghdad's input for their study on Paragraph 6.

I was hoping that during my next visit to Lebanon I could bring about the release of two more Western hostages, but on September 17 I realized that there were some problems, or, as Akhtari would say, some complications. The Iranians informed me that the groups would discuss the release of another British hostage but not another American. The Islamic groups in Lebanon, however, issued several press releases about the same time saying that Jackie Mann and Joseph Cicippio—the first British, the second American—would be released soon. Matters were getting more muddled, not clearer. I would have to return to Beirut to talk with Abdullah.

Aside from Pérez de Cuéllar, my one constant source of support and comfort were the British. They shared their information about the Middle East and thanked us unstintingly for our efforts. The day we returned from Teheran, the secretary-general received a letter from Prime Minister John Major praising him for our work and supporting our activities.

Most of my seventy-two hours back in New York were spent shuttling in and out of meetings and being buffeted by conflicting and sometimes escalating demands. As I was preparing to return to the Middle East on September 19, everyone seemed to want a piece of the action and a piece of me. The Germans reminded me not to forget their hostages and dutifully reported to me on the prison conditions of the Hammadi brothers so I could pass this on to the groups in Beirut. They refused only one request, that the brothers be allowed conjugal visits, although they said they might relent upon receipt of solid assurance of the safety of the two German hostages. The Germans were still concerned about the lack of information on their people. The lack of news would continue for three more months as Abdullah focused on the American and British hostages and treated the German hostages as a special case under the control of the Hammadi family.

Again I had to go back and forth between the sides to settle new difficulties. Lubrani insisted on more information about the second body, as originally agreed. He again offered to help obtain it by passing on a let-

ter from Sheikh Obeid to his family. But he was offering to release only
about four or five more prisoners, a small number that was certain to
anger the very groups in Beirut that it was supposed to impress.

Both the Israelis and Hizbollah sent signals that other channels were
offering them a better deal. Only God knows whether this was really
true. Sheikh Mussawi, the leader of Hizbollah, announced that a British
hostage would soon be released, after which Hizbollah would expect
Sheikh Obeid to be released by Israel. Lubrani phoned in astonishment,
and I assured him I had never heard of any proposal for such an exchange. I knew I would have to return via Tel Aviv to let him know what
the Israelis could expect from my search for Arad.

The Iranians met with me to try to extract the nature and timing of
the report on Paragraph 6. They were certain that any honest professor
could reach only one conclusion, so for them the only remaining question was when and how the professors' conclusions could be presented
to Iran's best advantage. Through an off-loading of responsibility by the
great powers in drafting the cease-fire resolution, the secretary-general
alone was responsible for the report. It was the only leverage on the Iranians that he and I had as individuals, irrespective of what governments
might do. I would never recommend that the secretary-general give this
up for anything less than a full resolution of the hostage problem. The report was really all that mattered now to the Iranians, and the hostages became only a means to an end in obtaining it.

Then, out of the blue, the Iranians told me it would be advisable to
have a chat with the Libyans. The Libyans! I had been on this case for almost three years, and this was the first reference anyone had made to
Libya. I began to realize that I was unlikely to be able to tie everything together in a coherent fashion; it just wasn't going to work that way. Zarif
was starting to balk at having the groups deliver two more hostages in
Beirut despite Rafsanjani's hints; now it would need a couple of days and
my own persuasive powers, in addition to those of his own president. I
reluctantly agreed to talk to the Libyans, but there would be a price: the
Americans, who ranked Colonel Muammar Khaddafi of Libya high on
their enemies list, would surely taunt Pérez de Cuéllar for this gesture.
But I told them, and the Iranians, that I was prepared to speak to the Devil
if it would help free the hostages.

When I called on Ambassador Ali Abdul Salaam Treiki, the Libyan ambassador to the United Nations, I asked if he could put me in touch with

any Libyans who knew the situation in Lebanon. He replied that he was just the right person to talk to. My purpose, however, was not to seek information from him but simply to make a point. If I could talk to Treiki in New York and thus satisfy my Libya commitment, it would be relatively harmless and only a little time-consuming. Now, if some other Libyan were to seek me out, I could tell him that Ambassador Treiki in New York was my official channel. Little did I know at the time that things would not be that easy.

CHAPTER 12

Jackie Mann

The First Marathon in Beirut

FLYING THE CONCORDE WAS QUITE AN EXCEPTION for a UN official. But Pérez de Cuéllar had authorized me to get to Damascus and Beirut as fast as possible, and catching a connection to Larnaca, Cyprus, via London was the fastest way on September 19. We needed a Western hostage release after the visit to Teheran by the secretary-general; it was now a week later, and nothing had happened. I had arranged to be picked up in Larnaca by a UN plane for the flight to Damascus. But it was not to be: in London, I discovered that the Cyprus Airways flight had been canceled. The British Airways lounge at Heathrow became my temporary working base as my assistant in New York, Judith Karam, and I tried to rearrange the logistics. I found a flight to Tel Aviv and let Lubrani know I was coming. He and his colleagues told me when I got to Israel that they were not thrilled with the delays in starting the search for Ron Arad. Things took a bit longer than I had anticipated, but on September 20, I was back in Damascus.

Akhtari told me the groups were angry at me because the number of Lebanese detainees set free by Israel a week earlier had been smaller than promised. They had expected between seventy and eighty rather than the sixty Israel had actually released. But he knew full well the reason for the difference: the groups had not delivered all the required information, a fact he himself had acknowledged in the car at the airport earlier in September. Moreover, he now seemed less sure that all the agreements in Teheran between his president and the secretary-general could be implemented. To top it all off, he introduced the need for Israel to release some Palestinian prisoners, since some bodies of Israeli soldiers might be held by Palestinians.

It was as if he had set off a bomb. If we were to bring the Israeli-Palestinian equation into the mix, I would need three more years, not three months. The issues, intricate and deeply rooted, defied prompt solution and would only cause further delays if we had to deal with them in all their interconnections. We couldn't do it, I told Akhtari; the players were to remain the Lebanese groups and Israel, with Iran assisting on one side and the secretary-general on the other. If the Palestinian dimension were included, I added, we could only conclude that someone wanted to sabotage the entire operation.

Discouraged by my meetings in Israel and Damascus, I went on to Beirut. OGB had begun to pick up some hostile noises about me in the street. We took extra precautions: I booked myself into a small hotel in town, checked in with an empty suitcase, and left. I never slept there. Instead, I alternated nights between Nielsen's and Holopainen's houses. A few days later, I went back to the hotel to pick up my suitcase and pay the bill.

A diplomat named Alizade was the new chargé d'affaires of the Iranian Embassy in Beirut. I didn't like the idea of changing team members so far along in the game, but then I didn't have a vote. Alizade turned out to be hardworking and reliable and was fully briefed about the subject. At our first meeting, he also warned me of the discontent I would face when meeting the groups and added that Iran's influence should not be overvalued.

I insisted to Alizade that I needed the rest of the forensic information about the second Israeli soldier, Joseph Fink, as well as some help in arranging a meeting with Durani and Azkari, who were supposed to know much about the fate of Ron Arad. Alizade was more interested in the number of new releases I would be able to secure in exchange for the extra forensic information and hinted at possible releases of women detainees from the Khiam prison. Like every other Iranian official, he also raised the issue of the Iranians missing or held hostage. I, in turn, stressed the need to release the South Lebanese Army prisoners held by Hizbollah. It was another request that Lubrani had put on the table.

Alizade needed to do some more homework for me. While the Teheran agreements had been reached at the highest political level between our principals, very little had been implemented so far. The following day I met Alizade again. The groups wanted to see me that evening, September 21. Were they going to proceed with the release of another Western hostage? When we met at the embassy, Alizade told me I would have to do what I could to obtain one—and at that point, he left the room. I went downstairs, but everyone was gone from the normally bustling embassy. I was totally alone. Then a man appeared at the door. He did not respond to my greeting but simply waved me to the gate and let me out. I walked down the same deserted street in the same direction as before, trying to convince myself that the situation would be the same but knowing it would not be. I was concerned because I knew the groups were angry at me and I assumed they were tracking me in some way. Sure enough, after a few minutes a fast car pulled up and stopped. I turned toward the wall of a nearby house. They pulled me into the backseat.

This time, their physical behavior was extremely rude. The car was smaller and a tighter squeeze. We were driven at high speed until the car suddenly stopped in a small alley. I could see that in front of us a van was blocking the street, a change from past procedure. The men in the car opened the door, pulled me out, ordered me to look down, then shoved me into another car waiting nearby. My anxiety increased. The car sped away, then came to a stop about twenty minutes later. My escorts placed a hood over my head, conducted me into a building, and led me up four flights of stairs. When we arrived at our destination, I looked down at my feet and saw a small welcome mat. It was in Italian—SALVE—of all things! Such mats had been very popular in Italy at one time, and the surplus must have been sold for export by the thousands.

Once inside, I was stopped in a narrow corridor not quite the size of a small walk-in closet with two small chairs facing each other. My interlocutor from the previous meeting—the man who called himself Abdullah—approached me wearing a ski mask, but I recognized his eyes and voice. He had the voice of a young man heavy with responsibility who had grown up too fast after seeing too many horrors in a civil war all around him. He spoke in spurts and seemed very worried. The situation was obviously not comfortable for either of us, but he also seemed to be concerned about his personal security.

Abdullah sat with me for a few moments, whereupon we moved into a larger room and the real meeting began. We were surrounded by the ubiquitous white sheets, and his invisible comrades were behind me. A coffee table held four platters, one holding grapes, one apples, one pears, one bananas. There was also a bottle of Coca-Cola.

At the beginning of our discussions, a technical problem arose: I had to go to the bathroom. This was entirely unexpected, and they became agitated, discussing the problem among themselves because they had to do some preparation along the route to the bathroom. Apparently I caused a small logistical crisis. When I got to the bathroom, they asked me not to close the door.

"Let's compromise on that. I'll leave the door ajar." I said.

On the way back to the interview room, they warned me to bow my head for my own safety. I knew that if they thought I saw even one of their faces clearly enough to identify it, I would likely have to stay on as a hostage. I could feel that their trust in me had ebbed since our last meeting. They asked me to take off my watch, belt, and shoes.

Abdullah reminded me that they had been told that eighty people would be released instead of sixty and said they felt they had been had.

Then he said, "Please explain." I did not, at least not immediately. First, I outlined my discussion with the Israelis and explained that they, too, had felt shortchanged thus far. I told him of the treatment of the Hammadi brothers in German prisons and of the British approach to the Israeli prime minister in support of the UN negotiations as well as of the support of President Bush. Then I went into the numbers for the releases. In reply, Abdullah said that the Iranians had not informed him that the forensic information had been insufficient. Then he made an extraordinary statement: Perhaps we should negotiate directly and leave out the Iranians!

He reminded me that I was the one who had asked for our first meeting. They had been reluctant to agree because they had had problems with outsiders in the past. Two or three hostages had been killed, he said, because the groups had found "the road in front of us blocked." I supposed he was referring to William Buckley, the CIA station chief in Beirut, who had been murdered in 1985; Michel Seurat, the French doctor who had been killed in 1986; and Colonel Higgins, who had been murdered in 1988. If they could find someone they could trust, he said, they would continue negotiations, and they had put their confidence in the UN secretary-general and in myself. Now, he continued, I had to maintain their confidence as an interlocutor.

"Everything that you tell me, I discuss with my comrades," Abdullah said. "We can make an agreement, and we can break an agreement. You and I can decide things here, and this will have nothing to do with the Iranians or the Syrians. What we agree here with you, we will do."

He explained that families were holding all the hostages because the small, separate, and ordinary locations meant less chance of discovery. By "families," he meant groups of blood relations who were also part of the militant Islamic organization. Each family held two or three hostages at a time. During this meeting, as at all others, I was taking notes, and I wrote down these words precisely: "For the negotiations to succeed, we want to speak directly with you." Abdullah's method took away my strongest card with the Iranians; what mattered most to them was Paragraph 6, which could not matter less to the men who actually held the keys to the hostage cells.

I had come to discuss the release of two Western hostages, which surprised and angered Abdullah when I told him. His people had been told, by the Iranians I assumed, that I was there to discuss the release of one. For him, this was a strong argument in favor of direct talks and cutting out Teheran.

Still, he said that if I could promise them twenty more people from Israel, they would give me Jackie Mann, a retired Royal Air Force pilot who had lived in Beirut. I knew the Israelis would not free another twenty without further forensic information on Joseph Fink, so I asked Abdullah to produce the rest of what he had, as Rafsanjani had promised the secretary-general. In truth, Abdullah did not seem interested in that grand bargain at all, just as the Israelis were rightly concerned more about their own than about Jackie Mann. The information Tel Aviv wanted would produce the prisoners Abdullah wanted. But twenty was a big number.

He then said that if the Israelis freed the twenty prisoners, the groups might agree to release everybody, but he cautioned that he and his comrades needed to think about it. I said that I also wanted to know about the fate of the Germans and about Ron Arad. He said that we could not discuss that now but would meet again the following night. He came over to me, put his hand on my shoulder, and said, "Tomorrow we will have a personal surprise for you." I had no idea how to take this, but at least I knew the process would not die.

I was driven back in the usual way, but this time they dropped me off in the Christian part of the city so I would not be kidnapped by some splinter group.

The Iranians were anxious to hear what had happened and called me at 1:30 A.M. to say they were sending an embassy car to pick me up. I was emotionally drained by my meeting with the kidnappers but could not refuse. When I arrived at the embassy, I found them as cheerful as ever. The Iranians said the most important thing was that the kidnappers wanted to meet me again and continue negotiations. They felt that I had a better chance of success than they did, although they said the kidnappers were, if anything, being too cooperative.

Our discussions of the various offers and counteroffers continued the next day at the embassy. The possible permutations were getting just too detailed to keep Pérez de Cuéllar, or anybody else, for that matter, constantly briefed.

The situation required me to speak with Lubrani to see how we could fine-tune a new release of Lebanese prisoners in exchange for the complete information on Fink. Thus began my version of shuttle diplomacy—round-trip journeys between Beirut and Rosh Haniqra, the northernmost coastal outpost of Israel, close to the Lebanese border. These trips would require one-hour helicopter flights from Beirut to Naqoura, where the UNIFIL headquarters were located, followed by a drive across what Israel calls the Security Zone in south Lebanon, then into Israel proper. The logistics of the trips were all carried out by UNIFIL and UNTSO. The armored helicopter that would shuttle me to Naqoura was Italian, since Italy provided (and still does) the helicopter contingent of the UN Interim Force in Lebanon, deployed in the south of the country since 1978.

I met with Lubrani and his team at a military barracks in Rosh Haniqra. As I had expected, he wasn't prepared to release more than ten prisoners for the remainder of the information on Fink. He agreed, however, to my request that of the people set free, "there would be no more than ten percent dead." I also needed more than ten prisoners and said so to Lubrani on my way out. I looked at him and knew he would do it for me, though he didn't say a word.

After I flew back to Beirut, my first port of call that day was the Iranian Embassy. Alizade seemed optimistic about my forthcoming meeting with the groups, but he also indicated that he didn't believe it was possible for the groups to do anything about the SLA prisoners in their hands.

I traveled to meet Abdullah that night, thinking all the while about the surprise that he had mentioned to me during our previous session. These nighttime excursions were becoming more and more worrisome. On this evening, I walked to the same place I had before, but nothing happened, so I walked a bit further. After a while, a car drove up, I was hustled in, and we followed the same routine as the night before.

This time, however, one of the handlers failed to warn me about a step while I was blindfolded and I took a bad fall. I suddenly thought these escorts might not be from Abdullah's groups and that my fall was a sign to prepare myself for a blow.

Abdullah had told me about the forthcoming release of Jackie Mann, but he needed to convey to his comrades that between ten and twenty prisoners would be returned to Lebanon. Of course, I could not commit to that because I had a promise of only ten from Lubrani and still had no further information on Fink.

"Ten is not so bad," I told Abdullah. "The median point between zero and twenty is not ten, because ten is much further from zero than from twenty. So if I were to give you ten, it would mean more than fifty percent of the twenty you ask." I said that only partly in jest. I would use anything I could. I asked them for the forensic information, but they said they did not have it. We fenced for hours. The proposal to release women prisoners went over well. Sometimes the kidnappers would ask me which hostage I wanted released first. I would always reply that I wanted all of them released together. Who could dare play God and choose in such a situation? I also offered them a letter from Sheikh Obeid and a videotape taken in his Israeli jail—providing they would furnish me with a tape of Ron Arad. Another possibility was a visit to Obeid by the Red Cross or by me.

They agreed to show me the hostage, since he would soon be released, although I did not wish them to hand him over to me. In the division of labor, that was up to the Syrians.

I had good physical stamina at the time because my hobby was long-distance running and I trained almost every day no matter where I was in the world—except Beirut. I would eat nothing during my sessions with the kidnappers—I was at once too agitated and too focused to take food—and I drank only sparingly. It was the dead of night, I did not know where I was, and neither did anyone else except my temporary captors, who seemed to fear an Israeli commando raid at almost any time.

As I was taken to the car, one of my handlers whispered into my ear in French, "If you bring us news of the Iranians missing in Beirut, we will give you news about Ron Arad."

He asked me to confirm that I had understood him. Then we were in the car and gone. I quickly reflected on his statement. Such things were quite typical in the Beirut of those days. Did someone really want to open a separate channel behind Abdullah's back? I wasn't buying. It could easily have been a trick to test me, which would then spoil the negotiations I was conducting with Abdullah. If anybody really wanted to communicate something on Arad, Abdullah was the right person, and he could use the information as a negotiating tool with me. I decided it was a hoax. I had too much on the plate with Abdullah to fall for a message conveyed to me by somebody whom I could not even look in the eyes.

When I spoke to Alizade thirty minutes later, he gave me some information about Alec Collett. He had been kidnapped by a group close to the Libyans, and perhaps the Libyans could assist in retrieving his body. It was another twist I could have done without.

Each morning after the meetings I would go to sleep for a few hours, then head back to Beirut airport for another helicopter flight to Naqoura and Rosh Haniqra. September 23 was no exception.

Lubrani held fast to his offer of ten more prisoners and said we were being cheated. His colleagues threatened to go public and accuse the secretary-general of failing to deliver on his promises. Lubrani softened the hard-liners' threat by promising to override it if I could persuade Hizbollah to yield a body, living or dead. He was pleading for something because the Israeli public, and especially the families of the missing men, had become aware of my negotiations and would criticize the government if Israel were left out of the bargaining.

Invoking the secretary-general to help me obtain more releases had little effect on the Israeli team. Then I informed Lubrani that the kidnappers were about to release another hostage, Jackie Mann, in twenty-four hours or so, and if Israel refused to cooperate it might jeopardize the release. Lubrani told me I could assure the groups that if they released Mann, Israel would release six men, three women, and one body. However, he needed the complete forensic evidence on Joseph Fink.

I returned to Beirut by car and helicopter, my body running on pure adrenaline in lieu of sleep. The meeting with Abdullah on the night of September 23 seemed to have no end. He insisted on securing the release of twenty prisoners before confirming when Jackie Mann would be freed, and he was not ready to let me have the remaining forensic information. It had now become a battle of wills among Abdullah, Lubrani, and me. Even if they were not prepared to release the complete forensic package, I was still expecting a hostage release as a result of the Teheran meeting between Pérez de Cuéllar and Rafsanjani. By early morning, around 4 A.M. or so, we had been at it for several hours. Abdullah, clearly under pressure by his comrade standing behind me, finally blinked. He said to me, "It's time for you to go home."

I interrupted him: "I'm not going anywhere without a hostage release."

There was a moment of silence. I sensed that he was smiling under his mask. "Do you know what you just said to me? I offered you to go home, and you want to stay? Should not this be the other way around?"

We laughed. But I stayed.

He was near collapse from fatigue and plainly concerned about his safety as daylight approached. It was time to go at last. I would not get Jackie Mann that day after all.

Before Jackie Mann was turned over to the Syrians the next day, I was driven to see him just before dark in somewhat relaxed security conditions. Still avoiding even a quick look at the driver, I got into a Mercedes, which eventually pulled up next to some kind of jeep. On the backseat sat Jackie Mann, bent over with his head between his knees. I got out, reached in, took his hand, and said, "Mr. Mann, I'm Gianni Picco from the United Nations, and I'm here to tell you that you are now going to be freed."

Mann did not move, but he took my hand and squeezed it. He repeated my name several times, possibly because he had not heard it before. Some of the other hostages had been permitted radios during the last year or so of their captivity and had heard my name on the BBC, but he had been kept under a harsh regime and might not have had one.

The Lebanese driver of the car said that Mann would be taken to Damascus and turned over by the Syrians to the British ambassador so he could go home.

"Is this true?" he asked me, his head still between his legs.

"Yes. You're going."

"I have to inform my wife," he said. I told him that his wife would be informed in plenty of time.

Then, holding my hand tightly with both of his, he said, "Oh, my God! I don't have the key to my apartment!"

I told him not to worry; we had his keys.

He could not believe that his freedom was imminent. He asked me if he could move, and I said, "Yes. You can actually move, you can raise your head a bit if you like."

He said, "But they have not given the order."

He had apparently been programmed by beatings and other punishments to move only when ordered to do so by his captors.

"Just keep your eyes closed," I said. "Don't look at the driver. But you can rest assured that your ordeal is over."

He said he did not know how to thank me. Once again he wanted to be reassured that what I was saying was true. Could it be that I was "one of them"? I told him, "I am one of you, Jackie, not one of them, and you are free."

The brief encounter was over, and I was pulled out of the jeep and shoved back into the Mercedes. Jackie Mann was then driven away, but as he records in his own book, the emotion of that moment stuck in his memory. He was seventy-seven years old, had tried to escape three times, had been caught, and had been beaten severely. But he was still an indomitable fighter pilot of the RAF. It had taken three nights of meetings and three days of traveling, had been physically and emotionally taxing, and had required changing scenarios on the ground. It was worth all that and more: Jackie Mann was going home.

When I returned to the UN office, I telephoned the British Embassy and informed them that Jackie Mann was on his way to Damascus. I also called Pérez de Cuéllar in New York. I returned to Damascus on September 25 and had a few hours to decompress before boarding a plane for New York at 4 A.M. the following day. In the interim, the Revolutionary Justice Organization, as it decided to call itself on this occasion, released a statement "in the name of God, holy, dear, and powerful," thanking the secretary-general and praising "the UN and its representative [who] proved to be highly diplomatic, which ended in a new improvement in solving the impossible complications and reaching conceivable and acceptable results." This was more than enough to enhance my credibility in the ongoing negotiations. It hailed Mann's release as "the first step in the next phase aimed at closing the affair of the hostages and the prisoners. We would like to thank those who helped and cooperated with such a positive result, namely Syria and Iran, hoping that there will be more progress toward keeping the good interest of everyone in mind."

I felt we were genuinely on course, and I wrote in my diary, "My long struggle for the hostages continues. This time in Beirut I was detained a little bit longer than expected. In some way Abdullah seemed to me to be like the Phantom of the Opera with his face covered all of the time. He had the same air of tragedy and hopelessness." That night he seemed of a piece with his entire nation and with the poet Kahlil Gibran's admonition: "Pity the nation that wears a cloth it does not weave, eats a bread it does not harvest, and drinks a wine that flows not from its own wine-press. . . . Pity a nation divided into fragments, each fragment deeming itself a nation."

Over the months of this operation I got several glimpses of the personal identities of Abdullah and of the other militants I encountered. They made it very clear to me that they were Lebanese first. But I could see little hope for them or their country if they stayed the course they were on.

"The glimpse of Beirut that I see at night when I am face down in the back seat of a car traveling into the forbidden quarters is almost an 'unreal' Beirut, a 'sad' Beirut," my diary continued. "I can only see floors, ground, stairs, and road and occasionally a piece of a door. When I do see something in its entirety it is always a masked face and white sheets. They are indeed the scenery of a tragedy." I began feeling for Beirut and for Lebanon much more deeply than I had thought possible, given the limited time I would spend in the country.

Jackie Mann was handed over to the British ambassador in Damascus on September 25—the first release to occur without Israeli reciprocation but not the last. The Israeli team would not have made further concessions without first receiving something; domestic public opinion would not have understood. But a Western hostage release with no "contribution" from Israel was certainly a new twist. "We need to regroup and rethink the strategy," Lubrani had said. "We need some time out."

I was back in New York on September 26. The General Assembly had brought together a number of foreign ministers, including Britain's Douglas Hurd and America's Jim Baker. In a private meeting on September 27, Baker caught us by surprise: he asked Pérez de Cuéllar to let Foreign Minister Velayati know that Washington was ready to reestablish diplomatic relations with Iran. Baker said he was prepared to meet in secret with Velayati at the private residence of the secretary-general.

On the plane home I realized that operating by remote control from the relative safety of Damascus was merely a dream. In the end, every deal had to be recast on the spot. I also realized that future meetings with the kidnappers might not turn out to be as smooth as they had thus far. The Iranians had begun to warn that as the "hostage inventory" became smaller, the threat to my personal security would grow larger, with the last release the greatest gamble of all. I had known that intuitively, but hearing it from the Iranians made it seem more emphatic and ominous. I did not confide my difficulties and fears to Pérez de Cuéllar when I returned to New York, because I didn't want him to think I was parading my courage. He was already concerned about my safety and had told me repeatedly to avoid unnecessary risks. Nor did I want to confide in my family because it would only have created more anxiety, which they could do nothing to assuage. I was left alone to contemplate my secret double life. I had asked for this dangerous assignment and had even invented a good part of it myself. Now there was no turning back.

So it was with a sense of letdown, not only from the high of Jackie Mann's release but with the realization of what kind of bargaining lay ahead, that I returned to New York. It wasn't a quiet time. Lubrani phoned upon my arrival to say that his people needed time to think up a new strategy. The Germans were asking me to fly over to Frankfurt to give them any news I might have on their two hostages, about whom they had heard nothing thus far. Kharrazi told me that Iran had paid a very high political price to the groups in order to free Jackie Mann. Meanwhile, the forensic information on Joseph Fink that the Iranian ambassador was supposed to send me never arrived.

When Lubrani arrived in New York on October 2, he brought information on the four missing Iranians in Beirut. According to Israeli intelligence, Christian militias had entombed them under concrete in a mass grave. The Iranians were skeptical. Lubrani told me that the fate of the Israeli bodies was not nearly as important as learning about any live ones, especially Arad. I told him that I was trying to pursue that as part of another hostage package, but he was skeptical, too, and believed that the groups were reneging on their promise to the secretary-general. It was Lubrani's normal tactic to start with strong criticism, then try to work with us, but this time our conversation went nowhere.

I could understand Lubrani's bind. The Israeli team was under attack at home, since Western hostages were being released and the Israelis were freeing Lebanese prisoners without receiving any news about their own MIAs. Now, Lubrani said, it was time for me to become theatrical and tell Iran that "Israel has gone mad" because this would change the pattern of promising information and not delivering. Given the unfilled promises, he wanted Arad "front-loaded" in any deal—that is, he wanted solid information on the missing Israeli airman before yielding another prisoner. I was as committed to finding a solution to the Arad case as I was to the entire process, and I intended to feature the search for him prominently in the new package I was putting together.

The idea behind the new package would be to create a number of steps that would allow the search and the hostage releases to proceed in parallel. I hoped that this would gradually create reciprocal trust as the process continued. But Lubrani wanted a firm deadline for the search for Arad and, if possible, penalties imposed if either side did not live up to the deal I negotiated. "You can tell them that Israel has become paranoid about Arad," he said. "Tell them whatever you like, but make sure you tell them that Israel has gone mad and Lubrani has blown his top."

Then he told me something that made me wonder if the world at large might be going slightly mad, too. He had received a call from someone at CNN who wanted to know if Israel would object to a split-screen interview with Ron Arad on one side and Sheikh Obeid on the other. Be my guest, he said. CNN's renowned correspondents couldn't find Arad either.

Judith Karam and I spent the first week of October putting together a comprehensive package. We met Lubrani at the offices of the Israeli Defense Ministry in New York and Javad Zarif either in my office or at the Iranian Mission to the United Nations. The Germans' apprehension that their hostages would be left out of the deal kept growing, and they reiterated their wish for me to go to Bonn for discussions with Foreign Ministry and Interior Ministry officials.

Lubrani remained in New York for a full week. He kept in contact with his masters in Israel as we devised a nine-point plan that would lead to the freedom of all Lebanese detainees, Western hostages, and Israeli

MIAs in thirty days. Each step, number, and permutation involved fierce debate. Our version was still different from Lubrani's when he presented me with two papers on October 7. The first was the "Principles for a Comprehensive Agreement," the second "A Nine Point Plan," and both had already been approved by somebody in Israel. Our plan differed in terms of the number of prisoner releases by Israel. But it did not totally front-load the search for Ron Arad, which made it more realistic in my view. The search would end, however, before the thirty days of the comprehensive agreement ran out. It was basically what we had been discussing but with smaller numbers.

When I presented the plan to Zarif, he complained about the numbers but not about the details on Arad or the concept of a comprehensive deal. More important, the gap between Zarif and Lubrani on the detainees held by Israel was getting smaller—325 according to Zarif, 270 according to Lubrani. The numbers were within striking range for a good negotiator.

I discussed with Lubrani the fact that Washington might still be trying another channel. He said that he might decide to leak the news to the press in order to kill the channel. I asked him to refrain from doing so.

I had made known my suspicions about another channel to Larry Heinzerling, the AP man assigned to monitor Terry Anderson's case. Unbidden, he did me a good turn by taking it up in Washington, and on October 9, I got a call from Peter Burleigh of the National Security Council staff. Burleigh, an old acquaintance from my Afghan days, said he had heard from Heinzerling about rumors that another channel was active. Speaking on behalf of the NSC, he confirmed that there had indeed been two U.S. channels—the Swiss channel and the UN channel. But the Swiss channel was currently dormant, and the NSC was operating on the assumption that the United Nations was the only game in play. Furthermore, as far as the president was concerned, there were not two channels because the NSC and Baker's State Department were combining their efforts. If I had any further doubts, he added, I should not hesitate to get in touch with him.

We also received support from an unlikely but extremely welcome source, the hostages themselves. Occasionally, the kidnappers would release a videotape of a hostage sending an obviously scripted message to the world. They always had an effect. The latest, from Terry Anderson, cited the efforts of the secretary-general as the only thing that could solve the hostage problem and thanked him for what we were doing.

On October 10, there was good news: John Pattis was released from Evin prison in Teheran. Pattis had been employed by an American engineering firm working at Iran's main satellite ground station when he was arrested in 1986 and sentenced to ten years in prison on a charge of giving bomb-target information to Iraq. On one of my early-1991 trips to Teheran, I had arranged for our office there to provide his wife, Ellen—then in town trying to obtain her husband's freedom—with any assistance it could. His release was a great relief for the Pattis family and a sign of movement on the Iranian side. Mrs. Pattis called to say that while her husband was very reluctant to talk about his experience, it might be helpful for me to know that about a year earlier, prisoners in Evin had heard guards bragging about an Israeli pilot who was being held in the same place.

As my discussions with Zarif continued, he warned me that if Israel raised the stakes too high, the groups in Beirut might decide to do a deal with me alone. I told him I had no intention of doing a solo deal because I was seeking the release of all illegally detained prisoners regardless of nationality; their continued detention was an affront to civil society. Nevertheless, Zarif's warning was confirmation to me that if I had to do a deal directly with the groups, I had enough cards in my pocket and credibility to do so.

Then he reiterated what the Iranians had suggested before. His government, he said, was fully aware of the danger that I could be seized myself. As the groups got closer to releasing all their hostages, he cautioned, I might become the last one, thus guaranteeing their safety from retaliatory raids as they scattered throughout Lebanon. I told him that I was aware of the possibility but that it was only a slim one in my mind. In any event, the reward—the release of all the hostages—was certainly worth the risk.

CHAPTER 13

Jesse Turner

Lost in Beirut

B Y OCTOBER 7, LUBRANI HAD LEFT NEW YORK, although we remained in constant touch. The meetings with Zarif and Kharrazi had become almost hourly events, and the phone calls were so frequent that it was hard to keep anyone fully briefed. We were leaning on the Iranians for the hostage releases, and they were leaning on us about Paragraph 6 of Resolution 598. My assistant, Judith Karam, and I seemed to be the only ones on the UN side aware of all the details—a commando team essentially reduced to two people.

I flew to the Middle East on Sunday evening, October 13, hoping I wouldn't have to go to Beirut but knowing somehow that I would. I was worried that the kidnappers would think they were being shortchanged and would vent their anger on me. We were trying to keep things moving and satisfy the groups through the three-step plan we called the "old page": receiving more complete information on the second Israeli body, releasing one Western hostage, nine Lebanese prisoners, and one body. We were not yet ready to move on to the "new page": the comprehensive plan and its carefully drafted nine points.

No such subtleties were in the minds of the press awaiting me as I changed planes in Cyprus. As I approached passport control, I could see a crowd of journalists waiting. A flight attendant from Cyprus Airways approached, claimed she recognized me from my time there fourteen years earlier, and said she could get me to a small office, where I could wait in privacy for my connecting flight to Damascus. However, once I had collected my luggage, she led me straight through a nest of TV cameras. She smiled at them, pleased to know she would be on the evening news. I tried to hurry past as she continued to lead me to the Cyprus Airways office and the much welcomed privacy.

In Damascus it was easier to keep out of the public eye since I stayed at the Bjornssons' residence instead of a hotel. Originally, the arrangement had been designed to avoid journalists, but during that intense period, the Bjornsson home served as a retreat of home-cooked meals, rest, and relative safety. Bjornsson also provided me with transportation and a means of communication.

The Iranian embassy was, as usual, my first stop. I wanted to brief Ambassador Akhtari on the new package, in the hope of obtaining his support. When I explained to him that we regarded this as a truly comprehensive package, he said it would mean much more to him if it included the Palestinians, the Lebanese detained in Europe, the Iranian prisoners, the Syrian prisoners in Israel, and on and on. "This would be comprehensive," he said gravely. So much for the understanding I thought I had had in New York.

The ambassador was around sixty, a mullah with a portly and imposing figure, about six feet tall and wearing a white turban. He came from a culture that taught the greater a man's power and authority, the more softly he should speak. Listeners therefore had to be silent to hear what he had to say. A huge gray beard framed his face, and when he spoke, his expression would change from an occasional smile to expressions that were serially serious, authoritarian, and fierce. Hanging on the wall behind the desk was a picture of Imam Khomeini. Adjacent to his armchair was a white telephone on which he would take phone calls. The office was not especially grand, nothing at all like that of the oil minister in Teheran, where the door and desk seemed to be in different time zones. But Akhtari was a key person in the Iranian setup in Syria and Lebanon and regarded himself as such.

In our conversations, he left no doubt that he was the inheritor of a very important position, not only as ambassador to Damascus but also as Iranian proconsul in Lebanon. Thus, a supposedly comprehensive package developed in New York by a forty-three-year-old Italian and two Western-educated Iranian ambassadors (Zarif and Kharrazi) did not exactly leave the eminent Akhtari awestruck. Eventually, he told me that he would do what his president instructed him to do, although he quickly added that there were limits on what they could do to pressure the groups in Lebanon to cooperate. He wanted to know how long the plan would take and how I would execute it. It was necessary, he said, to conduct a review of the "inventory" on both sides, after which things might be resolved in two or three months.

That worried me. It was too vague and could not be taken literally; we didn't have that kind of time. As he detailed his objections, it was clear that my briefing was his first. He claimed to have received—via another channel he did not reveal—a much better offer than the release of nine-plus-one by Israel. As always, when confronted with such counteroffers, real or imagined, I would always recommend accepting the better one. But his instructions from Rafsanjani, Akhtari said, were to entrust me with the operation. He then accused the Israelis of trying to slow down the negotiations and asked me to put more pressure on them, saying that he could offer me no further help and that I would have to go to Beirut. I knew that such a trip would be successful only if he helped pave the way.

He invited me over for dinner on the evening of the same day. When I showed up at 8.30 P.M., Akhtari had changed his robe. His attire was brighter, a white undertunic with a light beige tunic. We were joined by Amir Hossein Zamania, an Iranian diplomat whom I had first met in New York when he had been a press officer at the UN mission. We started a conversation on Islam and the treatment of women by various religions. We then talked about the ambassador's great wish to meet the pope, before he started to complain about Iran's being mistreated by the world and wrongly considered a terrorist state. Most of the upheavals in the Islamic world, he claimed, had simply been autochthonous events during which the oppressed of a region or state had followed Khomeini's lesson that even they could rise up and win.

When we turned to more immediate issues, he reminded me of his definition of "comprehensive." Nevertheless, he said that continued cooperation between Iran and the United Nations would be the key to solving the problem. He then went on to say that I was encountering the same problems that they had encountered with the groups. He used the German hostages as an example, mentioning them for the first time. They were being held by the Hammadis, a Lebanese family who worked with the Hizbollah security apparatus but who often preferred to do things on their own. Akhtari said the Hammadis had initially complained that Iran was doing nothing for their two sons imprisoned in Germany and that they would therefore have to kill their German hostages. To this I replied that the families would be receiving German visas to visit the two brothers; I also reminded him that I had told the Western press that Iran was committed to working toward the release of the hostages.

The ambassador said he realized this and added that he would work with me but that I would still have to go to Beirut on Tuesday for a meeting with his colleagues at the Iranian Embassy. Zamania would be traveling there, too. I asked if that meant I should be hopeful, and he said yes. But he warned that I would now be meeting with difficult groups. I asked why, and, as was his habit, he quickly changed the subject and said that he hoped I would not encounter bigger problems. This was not at all reassuring.

I was back in Beirut on October 15 to find a Reuters dispatch reporting that I had already met with members of Islamic Jihad and that they had expressed concern for their safety if they let all the hostages go, since U.S. intelligence would immediately start tracking them down. The dispatch went on to say that the kidnappers might have asked Picco to give them international guarantees for their safety. All this was news to me. The rest of the dispatch said that while Iranian officials had suggested that they seek safety in Iran, the kidnappers preferred to stay in Lebanon because they would be more effective in their own country and be able to move around more freely. The story ended by reporting that the kidnappers had reorganized to better protect themselves from infiltrators and had indeed discovered one suspect guard who was accused of working for Israeli intelligence. He had allegedly been taken to Teheran for interrogation.

This business of guarantees was crazy: the issue had never been raised. No government would ever give me such a commitment—and if it had, it would hardly have been credible.

But the Reuters report didn't make my life any easier. It was therefore no surprise that when I presented myself at the Iranian Embassy just before 9 P.M., Zamania, who had come to Beirut as promised, told me that the situation had become more difficult. Later that night, as I waited to meet the Islamic Jihad group, I asked him if he thought one meeting would be enough. He would not give me a clear answer. Every "meeting" in the unknown world of the kidnappers was a risk.

As it turned out, on this trip to Beirut I would have four nighttime meetings with Abdullah in four different locations in Lebanon, with trips by helicopter from Beirut to the UNIFIL headquarters in the south, then by car across the border into Israel to negotiate with the Israelis, and for good measure a side trip to Libya.

I left the embassy at around 10 P.M., only to be summoned back to a midnight meeting and informed that there were further complications. Zamania told me that times were hard for both of us—whatever that meant! However, he hoped that because of the trust the groups had in me, matters could be handled. A man from the embassy then accompanied me out the front gate.

At that time of night, no one was in sight. I walked to the first pickup place and waited. No one came. As I walked further down the street, I heard a car coming. It screeched to a halt. As was my practice by now, I averted my eyes. The door opened quickly, and I heard steps approaching from behind. A hand pushed my head down and then turned me around toward the car. Once I was in the backseat, a third person made sure that my head was against the seat. Then we took off at the usual Grand Prix speed. The ride lasted twenty minutes, but when we stopped, it was only to switch cars. The two cars were positioned to prevent my seeing anyone's face. I simply had to exit one door, take two steps, and enter the next car. No fewer than five people were involved in this journey. There was no conversation, only the sounds of steps, doors opening and shutting, car engines, and the sounds of the night. Everybody knew exactly what he had to do.

In the second car, a hood was placed over my head and face. It was a longer ride, taking about forty-five minutes to reach our destination. Then there were stairs to climb, and occasionally I could hear a door opening a few flights up. When I arrived at the apartment, the security procedure was tightened yet another notch. The hood covering my head was lifted from behind. I was then asked to remove my shoes, watch, belt, and even wedding band to be inspected for any radio devices that could broadcast our location.

It was now 2 A.M. on Wednesday, and Abdullah was waiting for me. I knew my speech by heart. I repeated the comprehensive plan and the "old page" and told him that we should try to limit our discussion to what we could achieve at this point. My worry was that they would raise some new issues and that I would be unable to satisfy them.

Abdullah thanked me for coming and said he hoped that I had a solution for the entire issue, even though new developments—he did not elaborate—suggested that, for the time being, we could make only limited progress by finishing the "old page." I had been given the false impression that everything had been explained and sorted out and that we could thus proceed with another Western hostage release. I now realized that this was wrong. He said that they had been much more hopeful the first time they had met me and that now we would have to think of practical solutions. The next round of bargaining had begun.

Abdullah said he was sure that the Israelis had told me they were prepared to release fifty prisoners in exchange for the rest of the forensic information.

I said no, I did not think that was correct.

He claimed that they had received the information from another channel. He assured me that it was a "very real one" and that I could check this out with the Israelis. Nevertheless, he said, the groups wanted to use the United Nations as their channel to the Israelis.

I asked myself why I should expect anybody to tell me the truth. Perhaps both sides were lying to me and trying to sabotage my mission.

Abdullah then changed the subject to the problem of freeing the Lebanese prisoners in Europe—which Akhtari had included in his version of a comprehensive plan. He suggested that perhaps the Israelis could facilitate their release. Then, suddenly, he scaled his numbers down to a more realistic figure, proposing that the Israelis release between ten and twenty prisoners.

This meant that I now had the makings of a deal. I told him that I could offer the Hammadi family a visit to their imprisoned menfolk in Germany as well as a public statement from the secretary-general confirming that we were talking to the groups, that they were cooperating, and that we had confidence in their fulfilling their role. I knew that I could offer these gestures on my own and that they were well within the rules of national and international law.

However, I still needed to get Israel to agree on the number of releases if I wanted the process to continue. If I could not persuade the Israelis to raise the number above ten—and I knew that would be difficult—I wished to know which prisoners they considered the most valuable. Abdullah handed me a list of some fifty names. They had to understand that this was not a separate request but a compromise on their part if I could not obtain a higher number of releases. In the meantime, I had to take his word that I would receive the complete forensic information that I needed about the missing Israeli.

It almost seemed as if Abdullah had forgotten that I was there to secure the release of the Western hostages. Later, however, he indicated that he could not help me yet: I needed to get a bigger concession from Israel. The meeting with Abdullah ended at 3:40 A.M. I had no choice but to go to Israel and come back the following night for the next encounter.

The return trip was much faster, but the security procedures remained the same. This time I traveled in a more comfortable car and was let out about ten minutes' walking distance from the Iranian Embassy. All of the Iranian embassies I had visited around the world had given me the impression that they were open for business twenty-four hours a day. In Beirut, that was a real plus. I rang the bell. No words were exchanged. An efficient guard ran inside the building and led me into a simple waiting room. A few minutes later, Sayed Tokhteh, a young diplomat I had met earlier, asked if everything was fine and called for a car to take me back to OGB. I was tired and worried because of the lack of progress. I knew that the next release would be a protracted affair.

OGB had arranged for me to sleep at its headquarters on a small cot adjacent to the communications room. The routine proved to be exhausting. I got very little sleep and food. Before going to bed, I had to list my requirements for the following day: a helicopter to fly me from Beirut to Naqoura, the UNIFIL headquarters; a car to clear my passage into Israel; and a message to be sent to Uri Lubrani for the meeting on the border at Rosh Haniqra. The OGB officers had become an efficient family, seeing to my logistical needs whatever the hour.

To arrive at Rosh Haniqra in Israel by 1 P.M., the UN military officials wanted me to take off from Beirut airport at 11 A.M. That meant leaving OGB at 10.30 A.M. I had to review the discussions of the previous night, organize my thoughts, check to see if there were any relevant news in the Beirut press—which was often used to negotiate in the open—and prepare a brief note for Pérez de Cuéllar estimating how near to or far from the next release we were. After an hour of listening to the BBC and RFI (Radio France International) on the radio, I was ready to go.

At 1 P.M., I was at Rosh Haniqra. Lubrani was there.

I now had several cards in front of me. I reported on my discussions in Syria on the case of the three Israeli soldiers missing at Sultan Yacoub in 1982. We focused on the "new page" and the beginning of the search for Ron Arad, which had now been on the table for two months. Was he still alive? We often asked each other our respective impressions—and concluded that until there was proof of Arad's death, there was still hope. Uri then passed me a list of questions to ask during the search, questions that would prove whether or not Arad was alive because only he could answer them. What was his wife's nickname? His daughter's? What was his cat's name? What did he call his car? (We never got any answers.) It was then that we agreed on the device of an interim report on Arad if this could speed up matters. It did not.

Then there was the "old page"—for immediate implementation, we hoped. I handed Uri the prisoners' names and urged the Israelis to release more from the list as a goodwill gesture. Indeed, I told him that I was counting on him for this, because if he were unable to deliver to the groups at least some of what they expected, I would probably be the one who would pay. He could give no commitment, not even a reply. But he and I had begun to know each other, and I knew that when I left the simple military barrack at Rosh Haniqra, he would not let me down. He would give me more than ten but less than twenty, I thought—maybe fifteen. And Abdullah would accept that, just as he had told me. I knew I had a deal.

A car took me through the border checkpoint to the UNIFIL helicopter pad, where the Italian contingent was in charge. It was a pleasure to see my compatriots. The Italians took quite a series of risks with their helicopters in those days and were recognized as thorough professionals. They lost a few pilots along with some of their aircraft but saved many Lebanese lives with their daring flights between the hills and the bombs. In a rare moment of national feeling, I was proud of them. The commanding officer's only complaint was that I would not stay for dinner, but, as always, he found a way to offer me something to eat and drink. By 5 P.M., I was back at the Iranian Embassy in Beirut.

I wanted another meeting with Abdullah, and soon. I needed to receive the forensic evidence on Fink, the second Israeli soldier whose body had been found during my early visit to the region. Unsatisfied with my meetings with Zamania, I returned to OGB and called Javad Zarif in New York. The role Zarif played for me in this story is unparalleled. He had a difficult brief. He had to translate our agreements, understandings, requests, and pressure in ways that connected to the Iranian domestic scene, and he had to get positive and timely replies. I needed to know if the Iranians were prepared to support my request for a comprehensive plan—the "new page"—and whether the search for Arad could start within the next fortnight, before the end of October. He said it could start by the middle of the following week if I returned to New York within twenty-four hours. I told him I would return only when I could obtain another hostage, but I felt that his readiness to go ahead was a positive sign.

I spoke with Zarif at 11:30 P.M., Damascus time; within an hour, Zamania invited me to visit him at the Iranian Embassy.

This was a meeting I could not refuse. The timing would imply a possible new encounter with Abdullah. Zamania had heard that I would once again be meeting with the groups that night, which meant I was doing well. I expressed some concern about traveling alone to an unknown location. Zamania could not do much about that. He did reassure me, however, by adding that I now had better relations with the groups than the Iranians themselves did. President Rafsanjani had instructed the embassy to help me.

"And, Mr. Picco, Allah be with you," he said.

I left the embassy. It was 1 A.M. in Beirut, not the best time to be strolling alone in Western clothes through the Shiite area of town. I had to think about being picked up by the "wrong" people. Some of my handlers had occasionally expressed regret for the treatment I had to endure. There was rarely any communication with the handlers aside from such grunted orders as "Get out" or "Down." Until I would actually arrive at the rendezvous and find myself facing Abdullah, I always had the secret fear that the cars, handlers, and drivers represented not Abdullah and his groups but some splinter group that had come to kidnap me for its own reasons. They could have been the Hammadis, who, I learned a few months later, wanted to kill me because I could not free their relatives in Germany. I never had a problem with Abdullah himself, who was always the model of courtesy. Whenever we met, he apologized for my treatment. But I could never be totally certain whether the journey would end with an apology from my masked interlocutor or a lonely cell of my own.

This time we got right down to work, and I told Abdullah that he could probably obtain more than ten prisoners, including some of the names he had given me. For the comprehensive plan to click, I needed the groups' promise to work in a four-week time frame. I told them that

Sheikh Obeid would be freed if Ron Arad were freed, and Khiam prison would be emptied.

Abdullah accepted the names and numbers. He needed time to discuss the schedule and said all those released must be members of Hizbollah or Palestinians, which they were in any case. He explained that one of the Western hostages was being held by Palestinians calling themselves the Jihad for the Liberation of Palestine, so we would have to do something special for them.

I replied that I had already told him what I could offer and that there was no time or place for new requests. He knew that I was negotiating with Uri Lubrani, but I said that if I had to include a Palestinian name the deal would collapse.

Abdullah reminded me that among the original prisoners who had been released, there had been some Palestinians. That was not my information, but it did not matter. What was relevant was that if I allowed the introduction of the Palestinian dimension into the negotiations for the Western hostages, there would be no deal.

Abdullah then said that he had never realized that the term "Lebanese" specifically excluded Palestinians. How could I expect him to bring out more hostages if some were being held by Palestinians and they got nothing in return? The Palestinian jailers, he said, were demanding the release of four hundred Palestinian prisoners. He said that the problem could be sidestepped if I agreed to exclude some of the hostages from the negotiations. I refused that outright.

It was now 2:30 A.M. He disappeared behind me for a discussion with his comrades. When he returned, it was clear he wanted to pursue the Palestinian issue a while longer to see what he could get out of it. I reminded him that we were trying, at that moment, to complete the "old page," and nothing about Palestinians was written there.

"Do you know who can help you?" he said brightly. "Colonel Khaddafi. He can influence these Palestinians."

I promised to keep the Libyans in mind but insisted on sticking with our agenda, which meant obtaining more information on the second Israeli soldier. He said that Ambassador Akhtari would give me photos and a video in Damascus the next day—which actually meant that day—with the remaining forensic evidence on Fink. In return, he wanted some of the people on his list to be freed, and he wanted me to go to Libya to persuade Khaddafi in person to intercede with the Palestinians. Now I knew why the Libyans had been popping up for a couple of weeks. I also knew that if I paid court to Khaddafi, the Americans might react badly. There seemed no way out because Abdullah said a Libyan envoy was already on his way to Damascus tomorrow to meet me and arrange for my journey to Tripoli.

"Can I have my hostage?" I blurted out, adding that we could deal later with whichever hostages were held by the Palestinians. The Libyan connection was most upsetting. At the least, it would cost me something politically; at worst, it might be sugar in the gas tank, gumming up the works. I had a history with Teheran, but I had met Khaddafi only once—with Pérez de Cuéllar in 1984. On top of that, I was Italian, and Italy had been the former colonial power in Libya. At that point, all the signals were flashing red.

We ended the night with a rapid-fire exchange. Abdullah insisted that no group could intervene in another's business because each had its own arrangements. I reminded him that I had come for the second successive night and had nothing to show for it. He said I had to work harder. I said *he* had to work harder, too. This was as far as he could go tonight because he was very tired, he responded, and I had to go to Damascus anyway because the Libyans would be waiting for me. I said testily that I had been in Damascus only the day before and that if he had sent word to me, I would have stayed there.

The meeting ended at 4 A.M. I was dropped off in front of the Iranian Embassy, again wondering what kind of madness was entangling me. I rang at the front gate, and Sayed Tokhteh came down. I complained to him that nothing was happening, none of the timetables were being met, and, on top of that, I now had to go to Libya.

He replied inscrutably that once I solved this problem all the others would be solved.

"What problem? I don't even know what the problem is!"

Working with the groups, he cautioned me, was not like working a light switch, and he echoed Abdullah in saying that I had to go to Libya because of Colonel Khaddafi's influence with the Palestinians. I said that if a meeting with Khaddafi could free another hostage, I would do it. But could he help me arrange the trip? What were my objectives? Did the Libyans know something about Ron Arad? Was I to discuss only one hostage or more? I said I was returning to my UN quarters for some sleep and that if he did not come up with a plan for my trip to Libya, I would not go. Then I left to make my way nervously through the checkpoints across Beirut in the Iranian Embassy's armored car. I lay down on my cot at 5:30 A.M. I had to be at the Iranian Embassy in Damascus at noon.

When I met Akhtari in Damascus on Thursday, he was adamant about the trip to Libya. It did no good for me to remind him that a month had passed since the secretary-general and I had met with his president in Teheran and discussed the release of two Western hostages and the body of Colonel Higgins, and we had seen little progress. He said that he had received only an incomplete report of the current situation, but he knew that the groups wanted me to go to Libya and that I had agreed. Iran, he admitted, did not have good relations with Libya or the Palestinians, so I had to help.

I had heard earlier from the groups that Alec Collett had been kidnapped in Beirut by some Palestinian group associated with the Libyans. But I had little hope that any of them would help locate him, dead or alive, just because I was making a dash to Tripoli.

The ambassador had already met the Libyan envoy to prepare the way for me. He hoped that when I got to Libya, Colonel Khaddafi would be helpful and not too tough, and that I could work things out in two or three days. "Two or three days in Tripoli? I don't have two or three days to go to Tripoli! It's not possible."

Changing the subject to one that was more pleasant to him, Akhtari said it would be fine if I could get what the groups wanted from the Israelis.

"I have already told them that!"

He started talking about Israel freeing more than twenty prisoners, but I interrupted him: "Mr. Ambassador, I have already discussed this with the groups, and it is not twenty or more, it is ten or more."

Then he switched back to Libya and said it might be better if I were to go on Saturday instead. Procrastination was a way of life with him; he had a mullah's sense of time, more closely connected to the hereafter than the here and now. In the most matter-of-fact way, he warned that if there were any further changes, things might take seven or eight days. I had ceased to understand what he was saying.

Since he was throwing out suggestions that had little or nothing to do with what I thought I had just agreed to with Abdullah, I thought I might get around him by simply sending a message to Khaddafi and not making a trip. He replied that a message would never be accepted. Everyone had confidence in me, he said, and as soon as we received confirmation from Khaddafi, we would proceed as fast as I would like.

Since there seemed to be no other way, I began to outline my objectives for Tripoli. I told him that if I could meet Khaddafi, I would ask him on behalf of the secretary-general to use his influence on the groups in Lebanon to assist in our humanitarian efforts when I returned to Beirut. I said that I would also ask for his cooperation in the search for the missing Israeli airman, Ron Arad, and the UN hostage, Alec Collett. The UN staff member had been taken in 1985, and since then, only an unclear photograph, purporting to portray his body being hanged, had been released. That was not conclusive proof, and the secretary-general had urged me to do my utmost.

Akhtari said that sounded fine. We would meet with the Libyan special envoy that evening, and the next day I would go to Tripoli. At that point, he reminded me that he knew I was looking for the body of Colonel Higgins and that when I returned he would help me.

At 10 P.M. on Thursday, I returned to the Iranian Embassy to meet the Libyan envoy, who focused on how to arrange for an audience with Khaddafi.

"Gentlemen," I said, "you are the ones who say that I must meet with Colonel Khaddafi. I don't want to disturb him, so I'm not going to tell you what to do. You tell me what to do. You want me to meet with him, you solve the problems."

They said that I had to see him in person, and that since the weekend was approaching—Friday is the Muslim holy day—perhaps I should wait until next week. The logistics would be easier then. This was totally unacceptable. I said that I had been given permission by the secretary-general to meet with Khaddafi but that time was critical. I had to be back in Beirut by late Friday to pursue my operations there, and any delay always had consequences.

"At every moment, things in the world change," I said, hoping it was a quote from the right holy book or at least a Bedouin proverb. I finally scored a point they appreciated. The Libyan was not certain he could bring a Libyan plane to Damascus in time, and suggested I rent a plane, with the cost to be paid by his government. I quickly agreed to his idea.

I went to my UNDOF office, just a hundred feet from the embassy, placed a call to Aero-Leasing in Geneva, and asked it to send its smallest, cheapest jet to Damascus first thing Friday morning. It had to fly me to Tripoli and back in one day. I had repeatedly reminded the Libyan ambassador that I had no intention of being forced to stay in his capital for any longer than one day. My plan was to resume my negotiations with the groups in Beirut Saturday night.

Renting a plane may seem as banal as renting a car, but in a bureaucracy it is not. Papers have to be signed by several offices, and authorizations have to be satisfied. The cost, $50,000 in this case, is large enough for most companies to demand a fistful of signatures. I had no time for that, so I spoke to the manager, pleading our long-standing business relationship, which went back to our flights into Kabul with Diego Cordovez, as an excuse to cut the red tape. He agreed to do it, so the trip to Libya was on.

I took no luggage with me to emphasize that I was not staying. I was very worried about this mission, and I did not know much about Libya and its leader.

After a three-hour flight from Damascus, we landed at Tripoli airport, which turned out to be completely empty. There were no planes taking off and landing aside from ours, and no sign of life. My rented plane stopped on the tarmac about five hundred yards from the nearest building, and I got off carrying only my briefcase. It was hardly a red-carpet welcome. In the distance, I saw the silhouette of one man coming toward me. We both walked across the paved expanse until we met. He introduced himself as the chief of protocol. He asked about my luggage, and I told him I had none because I would be staying for only a few hours. He said nothing. This was not a good sign.

We drove to a big hotel in Tripoli, the name of which I cannot now remember. He collected the key and conducted me to the top floor. I saw no one else in the hotel or, for that matter, on the road from the airport. My official escort showed me into a huge apartment. I reminded him that I had come for an official meeting, but all he said was that someone would talk to me. I asked him for the key to the room, but he said nothing, let himself out, and locked the door with me on the wrong side of it. I dived for the telephone, but it was dead.

I waited for three hours. I had no communication with anybody and no idea what was happening to my plane and its crew. Finally the phone rang, and a voice informed me that it was time for the meeting, which would be with the foreign minister.

The minister informed me in impeccable French that he was ready to listen to my request. I had no real request, of course; this was just a necessary step in a ballet I could have done without. So I spoke in general terms about the situation in Lebanon and my work. He seemed oblivious to my mission and the ongoing negotiations. He stated that his country had no relationship with the groups in Lebanon but had helped to solve hostage problems in the past. (Terry Waite had gone to Libya in the mid-1980s on hostage matters.) He said that he would need two or three days. I replied that I was not staying for two or three days and that it was up to him if he wanted to help me, but I had to return to Beirut that very night to resume my discussions with the groups actually holding the hostages. I added that the secretary-general of the United Nations would, of course, welcome any help that his leader wished to offer and emphasized that I had made my special trip on the express understanding that I would meet Khaddafi.

The foreign minister said that he understood my position but a meeting with his leader was impossible at the moment. He pointed out that the Libyan government had been helpful in securing the freedom of French, Swiss, and Belgian citizens kidnapped in Lebanon over the years. He asked me to give him a few days to study the matter; then we could meet again. Colonel Khaddafi would have met me personally if he had been in Tripoli, he added, but he was out of town.

At that point I decided definitely to leave, but I made a plea for his help anyway. "Some in Lebanon would find your encouragement for the humanitarian work of the UN secretary-general very important," I told him. "For my part, I will not fail to inform the secretary-general of the United Nations of the result of my mission and of all those who have contributed to it." And those who have not, I implied but left unsaid. I then told him that the secretary-general had instructed me to seek Libya's help in obtaining news of Alec Collett's fate and its advice on how best to proceed on his case. He did not seem to be familiar with the case at all.

He promised to work with us if I could spare him a few days and meet again tomorrow.

"Mr. Minister," I said, "I will not be here tomorrow."

"Why?"

"Because I am leaving now."

"I need a few days to do this."

"I don't have a few days, because the people that I'm trying to help are in bad shape, and for them a few days is a long time. So I cannot stay here. I must go and do my best."

I never quite understood what the trip was supposed to accomplish, but Islamic Jihad chalked it up as a show of goodwill on our part. I never got to see Khaddafi, and, incidentally, the Libyans never paid for the plane rental. The bill had to be picked up by the United Nations. It turned out to be the largest single cash expense we incurred in freeing the hostages, a small enough price for the lives that were saved.

The jet brought me back to Damascus just before 1 A.M. on Saturday, much behind schedule. I went directly to the Iranian Embassy to obtain the forensic information on the second body. On the way the car had a flat tire, which had to be changed in the dark. I should have probably taken that as an omen of what would happen over the next twenty-four hours. Here I was scurrying through four countries to obtain the release of another hostage in a drama that would have been close to farce if the political disappointments and the physical dangers had not been so palpable.

Zamania expressed great disappointment that I had not met Khaddafi, but I said that it had been Libya's responsibility to arrange an audience with him, not mine. What I wanted from him there and then was the material I needed to take to Israel to facilitate the release of at least ten more prisoners expected by the groups. He did not have it. I paused. I could not believe it.

It was time for theatrics: I blew my top, which was easy because by then I was exhausted—physically, mentally, and emotionally. I told him that if the information were not ready by 6 A.M., the time I was planning to leave for Israel, I would call New York and tell them to spread the news that the United Nations had been asking for something that had been promised more than a month ago and still had not received it.

At 1:30 A.M., I called Zarif in New York and was equally stern with him.

At 3 A.M., I received a call from Zamania. The material was ready for me. I went to the embassy a half hour later, got the missing forensic material, and was told that the groups wanted to see me again in Beirut on Saturday night—in other words, later that very day.

As dawn began to break on October 19, I had barely slept a night since I left New York on the thirteenth. And I wasn't about to get any rest for a while. Lubrani wanted me to go to Israel for something urgent, a full day of discussions in Israel. It did not sound good. It was not.

I had left Zamania at almost four in the morning. I was at Damascus International Airport to board a UN plane to go to Tel Aviv at 6:15. The UNDOF official who was supposed to clear my way through customs was not there. The Syrians at the airport actually knew me, so they ushered me to the UN plane on the tarmac. But when I boarded, the pilot told me that the flight plan had not yet been cleared. Perhaps all these small hitches were there to test my stamina. In the meantime, the BBC—always carefully listening in on the Middle East—was saying that in a communiqué issued from Tripoli in northern Lebanon, Islamic Jihad had indicated that Alann Steen and Jesse Turner might be the next releases and called on Turner's wife to come and meet him. I knew this was not in the cards, and in any event it was too late to change my plans to fly to Israel.

I met Uri Lubrani and handed over the additional forensic evidence. He passed it on to the chief rabbi, and we began a long day. Lubrani offered fifteen live (thirteen men and two women) and two dead prisoners for the forensic information I had brought—but not until more Western hostages were freed. I also promised that the search for Arad would begin by the end of October. He said that he would try his best for an earlier release, but in any case, he thought they were being "led down the garden path."

Uri looked worried. His political support had been eroded by the lack of movement on the Arad case, he said. Both the defense minister, Moshe Arens, and the chief of staff, General Ehud Barak, wanted to see me personally. Accompanied by a group of Israeli defense officials, I was taken first to Arens's private residence later that Saturday morning—11 A.M. Israeli time, 10 A.M. Damascus time. The plan I had discussed with Uri in early October, with the back-loading of Ron Arad, would not do. Arens wanted Arad up front. I began to understand that Uri had been overruled and wanted me to hear it from the man in charge, to make me understand the strength of the argument and why Lubrani could not continue on the same road.

I then asked Arens why he thought Teheran would accept this complete reversal of priorities, with Israel being satisfied up front about Arad and everyone else getting what they wanted only afterward. He replied that he had impeccable intelligence to that effect.

"May I venture to say that intelligence is not a science but an art," I said. "What if your intelligence is not correct? We know the Mossad is a superb organization, but it is not God. What if I present this to the Iranians and they say, 'Mr. Picco, go to Hell'?"

He answered with confidence, "We know that they will accept this."

It was a tense and disappointing moment for me. I knew that we had been overruled and feared that my comprehensive plan was about to go down the drain. During the entire meeting, Lubrani said nothing. I realized that this was a question of high politics, so I told Arens that if he insisted on maintaining his position, I would present it to the Iranians and see what they said. Then I left.

General Barak is a legend in Israel because he is the most decorated officer in the country. I was flown to Tiberias to meet him, another helicopter ride I could have done without. The general was very hospitable, and so were the other military staff around him. He, too, wanted frontloading on Arad. Then he asked for even more: Barak wanted a commitment from the secretary-general not to release the Paragraph 6 report until the Arad case had been cleared up.

I offered no comment on this shocker. Rafsanjani wanted the Paragraph 6 report from the secretary-general, and he wanted it yesterday. The issue posed by Barak's request went to the moral core of what we had been doing. I knew then and there that I would have to make a recommendation to Pérez de Cuéllar—and that in doing so, it would be tantamount to making the decision myself. Should I renounce the possibility of having the other Western hostages released until we had cracked the Arad case, or should we proceed with the release of the Western hostages and therefore weaken the effort to resolve the Arad case? And what if, by delaying, we missed the opportunity to free anyone at all? Worse yet, did I have the right to decide that the hostages should remain in captivity even a day longer? At that point, the dilemma remained my own, unshared by the Israelis, who still believed that the entire operation could not proceed without the release of more Lebanese prisoners on their part in exchange for Picco's hostages. They did not fully understand the power of Paragraph 6.

In any case, Uri told me that the package—meaning the release of the fifteen prisoners from Khiam prison—could be unwrapped the following day, if need be. It was a consolation prize but a further step nonetheless. In the incredible list of items on the table, there were also some Syrians who had been jailed by Israel on the Golan Heights. The Syrians had asked me to intercede. That day I was informed that three of twenty-six prisoners on the Syrian list had already been released. What mattered was to keep the entire machine moving. It seemed to me that we were proceeding at a snail's pace.

Getting to Beirut from Tiberias was a torturous journey of several hours. I had to take an Israeli car to the border, then another to the UNIFIL camp at Naqoura, where a UN helicopter waited to take me to Beirut. I did not arrive at the Iranian Embassy in Beirut until 8 P.M. Saturday. I met Tokhteh, the young Iranian diplomat, who sounded optimistic about what lay ahead. I couldn't remember the last time I'd slept—and my day wasn't over.

The groups were awaiting our nighttime rendezvous. When I expressed my hope to Tokhteh that the meeting would be short, he simply replied that it would depend on me. To this, I replied that, especially after the involvement of Libya, the secretary-general would be very disappointed if a hostage were not released in the near future because we had lived up to our side of the bargain, the same bargain that we had made in Teheran a month before. I then left to meet the groups in the way that by now had almost become routine. Of course, the trips were never routine; each was different enough to raise new doubts and fears. Why was this trip so short? Why the use of three cars this time instead of two? Why was nobody sitting on the backseat with me tonight?

I arrived at Abdullah's by 10:30 P.M., early by past standards. Of course, it was quite late for me—several days late, in fact.

This was my third encounter with the hostage holders on this visit to Beirut, all to free one more hostage. At this pace, I thought I would never make the December 31 deadline.

The groups' security arrangements seemed to have become more and more stringent. That night, as I was chaperoned into a room and relieved of my hood, I was once again asked to allow them to check the few items I had on me that could conceivably hide electronic equipment. My pad and pen were always with me. This time, after checking my pen, they did not return it to me. I felt uneasy. There was nothing wrong with the pen. However, I was afraid that, by retaining the pen over time, they would tamper with it, then present it to me with some alleged or planted bug inside, thus accusing me of spying. I could hardly bear to imagine the consequences. I did not like this one bit, but when I asked for my pen back, I was given another in its place.

During our meetings, I was a commando force of one playing all the roles at once: note taker, speaker, listener. It is not easy to speak and write while you must also listen attentively to the other side—taking notes on what is being said while, at the same time, planning how to phrase your answer.

At this particular meeting, Abdullah, his face well masked as usual, had at his side another person, also masked. He seemed almost angry at the fact that Khaddafi had not met with me. He appeared to think that this might create a problem.

Trying to keep up my resolve, I said that there would be no problems, our problems were finished, and that tomorrow he would give me an American hostage.

He confirmed that this would indeed happen, and in return I affirmed that he would receive fifteen prisoners from Israel. Abdullah wanted this to be announced in advance by the United Nations, which, in my view, seemed to present no problem.

There was, however, one small twist. The hostage to be released was Jesse Turner, and Abdullah wanted Turner's wife to meet him before he was freed. When I asked why, he would only say it was important. I then pointed out that Mrs. Turner, who had previously traveled throughout the region, was currently back in America, but he claimed that they had asked her to return to Beirut in a press statement released the previous morning.

Abdullah left for a moment to talk to his comrades—literally behind my back. When he returned, he said that they all wanted to be sure that there would be no delay in the release of the prisoners by Israel. Then he added yet another twist: they wanted to release Turner directly to me.

Until now, all of the hostages had been turned over to Syrian security, which had transported them to Damascus. They had then been handed over to their respective ambassadors in public. The relationship between Hizbollah and the Syrians who controlled Lebanon was peculiar and at times unstable. The kidnappers, who prided themselves on being Lebanese, were always looking for ways to show their independence of action. But releasing a hostage directly to me might make the Syrian authorities resent me. I certainly did not want to make any television appearances with a hostage. My intent was to obtain their freedom. It had been my belief that as long as the role of the secretary-general's office was that of actual participant, it should be played away from the limelight. Irritating a government by stealing the publicity would be silly and would only create more problems. But no matter what I said, this issue could not be resolved. Abdullah said that we would reconvene to discuss the matter the following night. Another meeting? Why? I then asked for my pen and was once again told no.

The pen had suddenly become a bigger thing; their insistence on keeping it and asking for yet another meeting made me wonder what use or abuse they had in mind for my writing instrument. I demanded it back then and there. "No, no. We can't give it to you now." I asked them what the problem was, but they would not tell me. They then disappeared, so there was nothing I could do. I simply had to leave.

This time I was driven directly back to the UN base, where I had a driver take me to the Iranian Embassy. It was now 1 A.M. Sunday. I expected the release of Turner and the release of Lebanese detainees by the Israelis.

Tokhteh was surprised to see me so upset. He thought I had received good news. Instead, all I could think of was my pen. "I want my pen!" I said. "I do not play tricks with others, and I do not wish others to play tricks on me."

Given the hour, the Iranian official regarded me rather quizzically. I explained that the longer the groups kept the pen, the more time they would have to plant something in it. I then told the official to warn the groups at once that I would refuse to continue negotiations with them if my pen were not quickly returned.

"Please let them know that I am most upset. It is a matter of principle, and I find it very offensive. I want this settled right now," I said.

It was not hard to imagine someone among the groups wishing to discredit me by taking the time to plant a radio device or some sort of directional beacon in the pen. Later on, they could produce it and accuse me of bringing in a pen that was bugged.

Tokhteh was clearly taken by my unusual mood. He must have gone to work immediately, because we met at the embassy again at 4 A.M. For me, there was now no more day or night. It was all of a piece.

The official said gravely, "We have followed the matter of the pen. The groups have told us through intermediaries that your pen will be given back to you on the next day. Abdullah has expressed apologies for the misunderstanding. He might have been a little overconcerned because of your trip to Israel."

So I was right. They suspected me because I had spent the entire day in Israel and they thought that, known or unknown to me, someone could have "played around" with my silver pen.

"Please understand that the Israelis have never asked me to take off my shoes or my jacket or anything," I told the Iranian. "They have never touched me and never touched my pen. Case closed."

As agreed, I had also prepared a text that I would make public in a few hours, indicating the secretary-general's satisfaction concerning the forthcoming release of Jesse Turner. Such statements always included a word of appreciation for all those who had helped in the process, including, of course, Abdullah. But this statement was the first, and only one, where I personally gave advance notice that a hostage would be released. I needed to push matters by going on record that we had an agreement. It was very risky politically. Would they let me down? Was my political judgment wrong? The procedure of the release had not yet been defined. I was supposed to meet Abdullah again in the evening.

Finally, I slept for a few hours on my cot at OGB. At 11 A.M., Uri let me know—we had established a communication line between the Israeli military and the United Nations in Beirut—that he would proceed with the release of fifteen, of whom three were on the list I had given him. The list I had received from Abdullah.

On Sunday, October 20, everything was ready for Turner's release—or so I thought. I issued my press release at 6 P.M., naming Abdullah for the first time as my interlocutor in the negotiations for the imminent release of an American hostage. The United Nations never recognized it as a formal press statement, which was the least of my worries. If Turner was not released after this UN announcement, my credibility would vanish.

I went through my routine of leaving the Iranian Embassy at around 9:30 P.M. and waiting for a car to approach at high speed, but this time I had to wait half an hour, and I wondered if the operation had somehow been blown. After several cars came and went, the right one picked me up, and I was taken to meet Abdullah. There were signs of nervousness among the handlers as they exchanged words. And they were in radio contact with somebody else.

When I met Abdullah, masked as usual, he was nervous, too. He said he doubted that the Israelis would keep their word. I said that instead of inventing problems that did not exist, we should proceed on what we had agreed. He asked about Mrs. Turner, and I told him to forget about her because she was not in Beirut. But he insisted on releasing Turner to me and not the Syrians. This was why there was so much concern. To defy Syrian intelligence in Beirut was a political and practical gesture not to be taken lightly even by Islamic Jihad. I was not pleased. Why defy the Syrians?

Abdullah informed me that during the night they would issue a declaration that Turner would be freed within twenty-four hours. Just then, the pen that had previously been taken from me was returned with apologies.

"Unfortunately, he cannot be released tonight," Abdullah went on to say. "We must have another meeting."

I thought he was joking, but he was not, and I began to suspect I was being used in some ploy. I insisted that he reconsider and release Turner to me now. He said they would think about it and either release him to the Syrians tomorrow in the middle of the day or to me on Monday night. At least I knew a hostage was coming out, but I didn't know how. The meeting ended before midnight, and I went back to my UN base at OGB, where, exhausted, I slept—but not before sending Uri a message asking that the "entire package" be delivered on Monday. I needed the fifteen Lebanese detainees to be released.

At 2 P.M. on Monday, an Iranian Embassy car came to the UN compound and left a message at the gate asking me to meet with Tokhteh at 7 P.M. that evening. I surmised that the Syrian option had been discarded. At 6:40 P.M., as I was in the UN car being driven to the embassy, I got a call telling me to wait. I returned to OGB and waited. The Iranian Embassy car did not arrive to pick me up until 10 P.M. By that time CNN and the Iranian news agency were already reporting that a hostage had been released. I asked the Iranians what had happened. They said they didn't know.

The Iranians wondered why I was so worried, and I snapped, "I'm not waiting for a package of pistachios!"

I asked how the operation was going to work, and Tokhteh replied, "Don't ask me! I don't know the details of these things!"

I said, "If I can't ask you, then I'd better go out on the street and ask somebody who knows!" Then I asked to have the embassy car drive me to the meeting place, but he said that would endanger his driver.

I walked away from the embassy on foot until an Islamic Jihad car arrived. I was prepared to follow the usual procedure. Instead, to my surprise, a voice inside beckoned me to enter the car. I did and found Abdullah hastily putting on his mask and obviously agitated.

"Abdullah, what's happening?"

"They are looking for you, and now they are looking for me, too, because they know that I am going to release Turner to you. The whole Syrian intelligence force is out. We have to move very fast."

He took my hand. His palm was very sweaty. The car was going at top speed, and as he held my hand, I felt for the first time that this young man, surrounded by his security apparatus, dealing with me from behind the anonymity of his mask, and feeling in a position of great power, was afraid. I felt as though I were holding and consoling a young man with a family and children. He spoke quickly: "We will give you the hostage very shortly. . . . I wonder if this is going to be our last meeting."

I replied as calmly as I could, "Why should this be our last meeting? We have before us a lot of work still to do."

But he was a different man, a man on the run who did not know if he had a tomorrow. I had the distinct impression that he actually needed me to hold his hand until he steadied himself. I asked him what I ought to do after receiving Turner, and he advised me to go to a hotel, where Syrian intelligence would be waiting for me. This arrangement was obviously part of a political message being sent by Hizbollah to the Syrians, and I was not pleased to be the messenger.

As the car slowed down, Abdullah said he was not pleased with the names of those released by the Israelis. Then the car pulled up next to another car. As the door opened, I still had Abdullah's hand in mine.

"Go now, you have to go." But he did not let go of my hand.

I looked at him. Before me was someone who, whatever power he might have exercised over others, was a human being in terror behind his mask. I had to be careful not to look at the others because they were not wearing masks. They told me to look down as the door of the other car opened. Someone pulled me out and pushed me into the other car.

Abdullah's car sped away, and through the rear window I could see the back of his head, no longer covered by his mask.

In the second car I turned my head sideways. Crouched down next to me was Jesse Turner. I took his hand and said, "Professor Turner, you are going to be freed now. I am Gianni Picco from the UN."

He said, "I am so grateful." I was also asked to bend my head between my knees as the car was moving. We finally stopped in a very dark place. The driver ordered us out, and I told Turner to slide over and get out on my side, lest the car speed off with him. I lifted my head to see where we were and noticed that he was still bent down, head on his knees.

"Mr. Turner, what are you doing?"

"Well, I haven't been given the instruction to lift my head."

"No, no. You're free now. You're a free man. And I am very happy to be the one to tell you this."

He was holding my hand, and he was trembling. He said, "Oh, I'm glad that you know where we are, because I don't."

In fact, I had only the vaguest notion. It was one in the morning in downtown Shiite Beirut, and it was dark. The streets were deserted. Syrian intelligence was looking for me. Where could we hook up with the Syrians before their frustration with us turned to anger—or worse?

But I did not share my thoughts with Turner. On the contrary, I bluffed and said, "We just need to walk a little while." I was also concerned that another group could actually seize both of us. But Abdullah had clearly given instructions to let us out where he thought we could make our way to more familiar places. On the one hand, he was wrong because I did not know Beirut that well; on the other, he was right because we finally made it. I eventually spotted the UN symbol on a doorpost with the name of a Norwegian officer I vaguely knew. It was his home. The sky blue UN symbol had always given me hope, but never more than at that moment. I rang the bell, hoping to gain entry and put my charge in safe hands before we were kidnapped again or even killed. I rang again, then again. Nobody would easily open the door in Beirut at 1 A.M. in those days. Eventually, the officer came down two flights of stairs and opened the door, surprised to see me. I asked if I could come in.

"Sure, if you have to," he replied, still puzzled.

I addressed Turner: "Mr. Turner, this is a Norwegian officer. He is a wonderful man. Stay here with him. He will make you some coffee or tea. You are free now and among good people."

Then I told the officer that if anyone else but me came looking for Turner, he was to hide him in the bedroom! Turner was thoroughly perplexed, but the officer quickly grasped what was happening.

"Major, do you understand who this is?"

"Well, I can guess, if he is with you."

I then telephoned OGB looking for Timo Holopainen, the commanding officer who was always waiting for me at all hours with his deputy, Major Nielsen. I needed transportation to go looking for Syrian intelligence officers, who by now must have been furious.

Several days before, while waiting for the groups to contact me, I had been interviewed by a famous and beautiful Italian journalist, Carmen La Sorella. She had asked when the next hostage would be freed, and while I could say nothing then, I had promised her she would be the first to know. I had no problem giving her a scoop, provided I was sure that Turner was safe. When I called OGB, I explained that I hoped someone would call from Syrian intelligence looking for me. Somebody did call, but it was Carmen. She had managed to get the address of the Norwegian officer's residence and to get to the house before Holopainen. When she appeared at the door, I could only improvise, telling her that things were not yet done and that I would call her later. She must have understood that something was fishy, but she also realized that I was very serious and had no intention of letting her in. "Carmen, I can't speak to you now! Tomorrow, tomorrow." So she left. Colonel Holopainen arrived shortly thereafter.

A well-known hangout for Syrian intelligence was the Summerland Hotel on the Corniche, or what was left of the Corniche. I put on my UN cap and left in a UN-marked jeep bearing a UN flag that I had asked Holopainen to put up for easier recognition. We wanted to be conspicuous, something I normally tried to avoid. It must have been quite a sight—a Finn and an Italian decked out in UN regalia and looking for Syrian intelligence in the dark of an October Beirut night. In the lobby of the Summerland at that hour, there were four people, tops. Nothing. We got back into the car and drove slowly into a rundown quarter, where I hoped we would be spotted immediately by anyone actually looking for me.

Holopainen had been posted in Beirut twice during the civil war. He knew more than he ever said aloud about the city. He knew that it was not healthy to make Syrian intelligence unhappy. It was not a joke. "You know, Mr. Picco," he said, "it's not a good idea to meet Syrian intelligence at night here."

Then I left the car and walked for a while—a Westerner in a double-breasted blazer and a UN cap. I was fearful that the Syrians would feel that I was stealing the glory from them by taking Turner to Damascus and turning him over to the U.S. Embassy myself. Syrian intelligence was under strict orders to bring in Turner, and any officer who let him slip through the net could expect serious trouble for the rest of what would probably be a very short career.

My options were narrowing fast. We drove to the Iranian Embassy, and I asked to see Tokhteh. He was even more frantic than I was: someone had already reprimanded him because Picco had disappeared with the released hostage. Disappeared? Were they looking for me? I was looking for them, too.

"I thought that they were in control of all Beirut. Where are they?"

He replied, "You don't understand what is happening. They are furious with you, Mr. Picco, you have to make contact immediately!"

I told him to phone the Syrian military command and inform them that they could find us in a square, or rather an open space, not far from where Turner was now safe. Meanwhile, Major Nielsen, the OGB information officer, had also done his homework to find the Syrians. When we returned to the Norwegian's house, I asked Holopainen to go upstairs with Turner. I would wait alone for the Syrians; if there was any problem, it was mine, not his.

I walked into the middle of the square and positioned myself to be visible from any approach. Within a few minutes, about twenty cars converged on the square and focused their lights on me. An officer approached and asked if I were Mr. Picco, and I said yes. He coldly informed me that they had been looking for me. He was not pleased. I told him calmly that I had also been looking for them and thought they would surely find me first. Then they demanded the hostage.

"I'm not giving anybody to anybody unless I see an ID card."

"Mr. Picco, you cannot ask for ID cards from us," said a Syrian officer.

I asked to speak to the officer in charge, and a Syrian major emerged from one of the cars and walked toward me.

"Can I see your ID, Major?" Except for his superiors, I must have been the first person who had ever asked him that. He was irritated. I insisted, adding, "You can do whatever you like to me. I've been looking for you, and I don't mean to deprive you of the possibility of taking the hostage to Damascus. I just want to make sure that we understand what we are doing here. Maybe there is a misunderstanding, maybe someone has not informed you properly. These things happen. But I want to know."

"Where's the hostage?" he snapped.

"No. I want to write down your name. I want to know to whom I am giving this hostage."

"Mr. Picco, I think the major is very upset," said an adjutant.

"I'm very upset, too. Here is my UN card. Will you show me your card?"

So the major showed me his card. I took down his name and told him to follow me to the house where Turner was waiting. A detachment of Syrian intelligence officers started following. I held them off.

"No, no, no! Two people, two people! No need for all this."

As we entered the building, I could see they were on alert and ready to pounce, as if they were conducting a police search.

"No, wait. This is a normal house. Major, you are about to meet Professor Turner. If I hand him over to you, do I have your word that you will take him to the American Embassy tomorrow?"

"I will take him to Damascus to my superiors."

I reminded him that Turner was supposed to be delivered to his embassy. The Syrian major said he had no instructions to answer such questions.

"Do you want me to wait here while you get those instructions?"

Then he conceded that Turner was to be taken to the U.S. Embassy, and I asked him again if I had his solemn word as an officer that Professor Turner would be taken to the embassy unharmed.

"Nothing will happen to Professor Turner, because we are here to help him."

"Good." And I presented him to Jesse Turner. I told Turner not to worry, that he would sleep well in Damascus and that the next morning they would deliver him to the U.S. Embassy. He departed with a very unhappy Syrian major.

Abdullah had also provided some reassurances because a press release he had arranged to issue at midnight that evening said that after the successful negotiations I had had with the groups, Israel had released the Lebanese detainees and Turner had been set free. It was signed by the Islamic Jihad for the Liberation of Palestine. Was the Palestinian-Libyan connection a factor? I still doubt it. It was a domestic matter inside Islamic Jihad.

I went back to the UN compound for some sleep. At 4 A.M., I got a message from the secretary-general asking why the hostage had not been freed as promised. I assured him that he had been freed. At 7 A.M., I awakened and turned on my radio for what I hoped would be a BBC report confirming Turner's imminent release in Damascus. No news. I listened again at 8 A.M., then 9 A.M. Still nothing, and I began to worry. The news came at twelve noon. The BBC reported that Turner had been released to the U.S. Embassy. The delay was the Syrians' way of making a point.

CHAPTER 14

Waite and Sutherland

Raising the Ante

I RETURNED TO NEW YORK VIA ISRAEL, where I met with Lubrani and his team for a few hours to assess where we stood. From their point of view, we were in trouble. We had yet to take even one step forward in the search for Ron Arad. While the release of the hostages continued, there was no movement on the Israeli front, and it had become clear in the meetings with Arens and Barak that Israel intended to take a stronger position with Iran, the groups, and me as well.

On October 23 in Tel Aviv, we devised what we thought was a clever way to marry the front-loading of Arad demanded by Arens and Barak and the back-loading sought by the Iranians. The plan called for the secretary-general to receive some information from either the groups or Iran about Arad. He would keep it to himself, however, while Israel would proceed with the release of other Lebanese detainees based on Pérez de Cuéllar's word that he had the information. At the end of the process, the news on Arad would be given to Lubrani.

The idea went nowhere. When the Israeli team arrived in New York two days later, Lubrani handed me a written proposal. It was a straightforward front-loading of Arad: "The search for Ron Arad will be completed and Israel will receive an irrefutable sign of life, information about Ron Arad's state of health, the name of the country in which he is being held, and the 'address' for conducting negotiations for his release. Everything else would follow."

The Iranians' first reaction to this "missile," as I described it, was fin de non-recevoir—diplomatic jargon that means the other side has not even agreed to receive the proposal. It's worse than a nonstarter; for the Iranians, the message didn't exist. Nevertheless, we made sure they sent it to Teheran, and Lubrani wanted me to go to Iran to discuss it personally. The Israelis also were convinced that the Iranians were so desperate to close the hostage file that they would eventually accept the proposal. They based this assessment on their own intelligence. I felt uneasy about their analysis and went so far as to ask the Americans their opinion of Israel's intelligence network in Iran; the Americans, it turned out, had their doubts, too. They believed, among other things, that poor Israeli information during the 1980 U.S. Embassy hostage crisis in Teheran had led Tel Aviv to misread the real position of the Iranian government and its ability to deal with the matter.

I also realized that Lubrani had been overruled. His plan of October 8 had, in my view, more chance of being implemented than the latest one. I believe he knew that as well, but he had been criticized back home for being too soft when it came to dealing with his UN interlocutor.

If he had problems in Israel, I had them in Syria. Damascus, as I feared, had not been happy that Turner had been released to me first, and now there was something new. On October 29, Lubrani told me that the Associated Press was going to run a story that Ron Arad was alive in Syria—and that Damascus planned eventually to exchange him for a Syrian pilot held in Israel for years. Syria, the AP story would also say, was upset with Picco because he had made it clear all around that the Syrian pilot did not want to go back to his homeland and therefore could not be considered barter. The story also mentioned Syria's upset over the Turner release. The original source for the story appeared to have been Syrian, although it was also confirmed by a Hizbollah official. Iran and Hizbollah did not wish this matter to interfere with the hostage saga, and some tension had arisen between Damascus and Teheran. In fact, the Syrian pilot had already defected to another country and there was never any confirmation that Syria was holding Ron Arad.

The official Iranian reaction to the new Israeli plan was given to Pérez de Cuéllar by Ambassador Kharrazi on October 30: if Israel were front-loading Arad, the groups would front-load the release of Sheikh Obeid and the others. Kharrazi said he also hoped that the United States could review its legislation labeling Iran a state supporter of terrorism. The hostage operation, however, was more important to Iran, he added: "We are losing time and credibility. We have to delink the issue of the Western hostages from any other." Kharrazi's point was clear: in Iran's view, there was no need to have Israel as part of the hostage-release plan anymore. By front-loading a comprehensive package with Ron Arad, Israel had cut off any possible deal with Teheran. Israeli intelligence, after all, had not been accurate. The Israeli missile had met an Iranian counterstrike.

By the end of October, seven Western hostages remained in captivity and we had two months to bring them home. There were four American hostages: Alann Steen, a teacher at the American University of Beirut (AUB), kidnapped in January 1987; Joseph Cicippio, a financial director at AUB, kidnapped in September 1986; Thomas Sutherland, the dean of agriculture at AUB, kidnapped in June 1985; and Terry Anderson, an AP journalist, kidnapped in March 1985, who had become an international rallying point through the tireless efforts of his sister, Peggy Say. In addition, there were Englishman Terry Waite, the negotiator-envoy of the Anglican Church, kidnapped in January 1987, and two Germans, Heinrich Struebig and Thomas Kemptner, aid workers who had been kidnapped in September 1989.

Although each case was complex, Waite's and Anderson's were particularly so because of their symbolic value. The case of the two Germans was also complicated by the fact that their kidnappers seemed unwilling to accept the German government's steadfast refusal to release the Hammadi brothers, who had been legally tried, convicted, and imprisoned as terrorists.

For more than two weeks, I shuttled back and forth among the Iranians, the Israelis, and the secretary-general. Through the shared experience of our tough negotiations, I became friends with Lubrani on one side and Zarif and Kharrazi on the other. There were still many items on my agenda requiring follow-up. The Germans continued to press me not to forget their own, and the Canadian and Italian governments reminded me of their nationals who had disappeared in Lebanon during the civil war. The Syrians were also keen to get my reply about the Golan Druze imprisoned in Israel, the Iranians were pushing me on the fate of their missing in Beirut, and the groups were agitating about the Lebanese detained in Western Europe on terrorism charges. As for the three Israeli MIAs of Sultan Yacoub, Syria claimed that they had already been returned to Israel. Three bodies had indeed been delivered and buried, but Israel contended that they weren't their missing men. With Israel's agreement, I had asked the Red Cross to disinter and examine the three bodies. When the job was done, Israel's doubts were vindicated: the bodies Syria had sent were not those of the Israeli MIAs.

Meanwhile, I kept in touch with some family and friends of the hostages as requested. Larry Heinzerling of the AP, along with James Foley, who had been in Beirut with Terry Anderson when he was kidnapped, kept me informed of their work. They wanted to be in Damascus when Terry was released. I agreed to alert them in enough time for them to make their way to Syria, but I did not want them or Terry's family to be misled by a premature announcement. When the time was right, I told them, Judith Karam would call and say, "Mr. Picco invites you for coffee."

I suggested that Pérez de Cuéllar sound out Washington on the annual certification by the administration naming terrorist states, which was due in November and would normally list Iran. If Iran were delisted, it would be able to increase its trade with the United States. But the Americans said it was too late to change the report, and in any case their intelligence indicated that Iran had been involved in the assassination of thirteen opponents abroad in the last eighteen months, which to them indicated only that Teheran was switching from kidnapping to killing.

The Iranians, even as they were delinking Israel from the hostage issue, were asking Pérez de Cuéllar to involve the United States in the negotiations. Despite intelligence cooperation with the coalition united against Saddam Hussein, Teheran felt there had been no positive signals from Washington. The secretary-general spoke to Jim Baker about it in early November, but to no avail. My mantra was still "Goodwill begets goodwill," and I was sure these words of an American president would not prove empty: the White House would keep its promise. Nevertheless, even Pérez de Cuéllar began to feel that we were carrying the burden of the negotiations in almost every respect—politically, financially, emotionally.

The whole operation for the release of the hostages over four years cost less than $100,000, one quarter of which was to be covered by the United States through its regular dues, the rest by other governments. The unreimbursed side trip to Tripoli cost $50,000. The other major transport expenses—twelve two-hour helicopter trips between Beirut and Naqoura—never went onto our books. I was flown with great panache by the pilots of an Italian Air Force unit attached to UNIFIL, with all costs paid by the Italian government. The bottom line for the U.S. government would have been $25,000, but all the expenses were charged to a little fund for peace that an elderly American lady had donated to the secretary-general some fifteen years earlier. In effect, the entire hostage operation didn't cost U.S. taxpayers a cent.

Zarif left me with little doubt that Teheran believed the secretary-general was wasting his time pushing the Israeli line because the comprehensive plan of October 8 had already been presented to the groups and it was impossible to change it now.

If the Israelis had painted themselves into a corner, I said, I would have to help them get out of it, just as I would if Iran found itself in a similar fix. I asked the Iranians to proceed with the search for Arad because it was the right thing to do. Zarif was in no mood to yield anything to the Israelis and replied, "I believe that this is impossible and even wrong at this point."

With further confirmation from Kharrazi that Iran had counted Israel out, the good news was that Iran wanted the release of the Western hostages to continue and that we would have to find different ways of dealing with the groups. It was politically unfortunate that Israel was left on the sidelines—only temporarily, I hoped. But since we could get nothing from Washington, I would have to look for other negotiating cards.

So at the beginning of November, Zarif and I sat down to examine our hands. I told him I could look into a new approach to foreign aid for Lebanon. But I also knew that Amnesty International was completing its report on the conditions of Lebanese prisoners at Khiam, in south Lebanon. The publication of that report, which I knew would be critical of Khiam's Israeli wardens, could be timed to our operation. In fact, some of the nongovernmental organizations (NGOs) had been in touch with offers of help over the years. Once the report was out and the two remaining Israeli bodies were released, a search for Arad could be completed.

Zarif wanted the secretary-general to let Teheran know what the report on Paragraph 6 said before all the hostages were released, but I was not going to waste my only trump card. I argued that if he pressed for an early release of the report, it would appear that Iran doubted the secretary-general's word. On the contrary, I said, the greater the gap between the release of the hostages and the release of the report, the greater the weight would be accorded a document we both assumed would identify Iraq as the instigator of the Iran-Iraq war.

Iran wanted to conclude the hostage saga by November 25. But true to form, the dates and procedures suggested by Iranian officials would not come to pass. Zarif now asked specifically if the report on Paragraph 6 could be issued during the week of the twenty-fifth. I reminded him that I had received nothing about the body of Colonel Higgins, nor about the fate of Alec Collett and several others.

Three days after my talk with Zarif, the British briefed me on a meeting between one of their senior officials and the Iranian deputy foreign minister. He had offered to strike a separate deal with the British to obtain the release of their last hostage, Terry Waite. What he had demanded from London in exchange for Waite was a public statement accusing Israel of sabotaging the negotiations. The Brits had refused.

Actually, the message I was receiving from Iran was that its negotiators had now focused mainly on the U.S. hostages, with Waite and the two Germans playing second fiddle. It was time to return to Beirut to ensure the comprehensive nature of our efforts.

We received the report on Paragraph 6 from the European professors in early November but told no one. I took all three copies home and hid them among my other books. The report was academically solid and nonpolitical, and avoided the more inflammatory accusations the Iranians wanted. But it did accuse Iraq of entering Iran with ten armored divisions on September 22, 1980. Although there had been other border skirmishes, the academics judged that the Iraqi tank attack had been a disproportionate reaction and a violation of international law. The freedom of the remaining hostages now depended on this report.

En route to Damascus on November 12, I changed planes in Frankfurt so I could meet with German officials. They told me that the Hammadi family was in Germany to visit their sons under the auspices of the Red Cross. They could do no more: German law, coupled with U.S. diplomatic pressure, prevented the Germans from giving an early release to Mohammed Ali Hammadi. After all, he had been convicted of a hijacking in 1985 in which an American had been killed, his body dumped out of the plane onto the tarmac. The return of the German hostages therefore lay in the hands of the secretary-general alone.

The British team also met with me in Frankfurt and promised $24 million for the Lebanese reconstruction fund. At British insistence, we met in a different location from the room my German hosts had prepared. "Do you really suspect that there are microphones in this room?" I asked. The answer was obvious, and one of their negotiators punctuated it: "We would have done the same." They then served a timely warning for someone about to face a group of Middle East terrorists alone: Scottish prosecutors were about to issue an arrest warrant for two Libyan intelligence officers in connection with the bombing of Pan Am Flight 103 over Lockerbie almost three years earlier.

In Damascus I tried to mend fences by explaining the nighttime fiasco with Syrian intelligence in Beirut. But the colonel to whom I told my story refused to believe it. He always believed my briefcase carried bundles of money to ransom the hostages.

Upon my request, Zarif had followed me to Damascus to serve as liaison and avoid the misunderstandings and delays that had resulted the last time. Javad Zarif was a friend to whom I could say things as they were and know they would be understood. The time and the circumstances required such a forthright relationship if we were to make the deal happen.

Iranian Ambassador Akhtari was not in Damascus and was not expected back for at least a couple of days. The press, which in the past had always heralded my arrival with rumors, was ominously silent on the subject of the hostages. I wrote in my diary, "In theory, I am 24 hours away from the next release if my homework has been done properly, and yet there is no indication of anything." When I met Zarif, I understood why.

The first thing he said was "We have complications." Even after the detailed conversations in New York, our schedule and other proposals for an exchange had been rejected in Teheran. Amnesty International's report and possible foreign aid to Lebanon were not good enough.

Akhtari was in Lebanon working on my behalf. It was a good sign that a big man was willing to dig into frontline dirt, but the Hizbollah leader, Sheikh Abbas Mussawi, had not accepted my request for a meeting because I did not have enough to offer.

I drew myself up and said that it was a matter not of whether the leader of Hizbollah wanted to meet me but of whether I wanted to meet him, and he should thank me if I did because I would give him political credibility rather than the reverse. I knew I had to summon some bravado or I would be pushed around.

"I don't meet him, he meets me," I said, "and if he doesn't meet me, it's his loss, not mine."

Zarif realized that he had gone too far, so he backtracked: "Well, we are still negotiating, so nothing is lost."

"Good, that's what I like to hear."

We had a close relationship, but he was still an official of his government, and in that position he had to push as hard as he could until he reached my limit. Since our friendship went back years, familiarity prevented us from fooling each other easily. But in a way we were on the same side, because we both wanted to close the chapter on the hostages. For him, however, I found there were personal limits. I thought it might help if he accompanied me to Beirut, but he demurred.

"Gianni, I'm not going to Beirut," he said. "I have a family."

I reminded him that I, too, had a family, to which he replied, "Possibly, but you have a far better relationship with the kidnappers than I do." He was not joking.

When I insisted, he adamantly refused to set foot anywhere in Lebanon.

Judy Karam, my assistant in New York, phoned to say that Lubrani was trying to reach me to talk about releasing more prisoners, a sign that the Israelis wanted to get back into the game. It was too late to do much good on this trip, although not too late to help them save face if I made another. Teheran had already made a strategic decision: the hostage saga would be completed without Israel. But not if I had my way. I was convinced that, in the end, everybody had to feel like a winner if we wanted a genuinely successful outcome. The UN secretary-general's role was not that of embarrassing any government but rather of helping them all if possible.

Akhtari returned from Lebanon to report that Teheran was working with Bonn; the two countries had traditionally had close relations. He said the groups wanted to see me again but warned that I was in a difficult position because I would be asking them to free hostages but offering them nothing in return. Iran was pressuring the groups to release Terry Waite and an American, but Akhtari could offer no guarantee they would respond. We continued our talks the next day, November 17.

Israeli forces had just attacked Shiite positions in southern Lebanon, which was not exactly propitious timing for me. Akhtari believed the Israelis were following American orders and asked if I could try to stop those attacks. I said that I would like all attacks to stop.

Akhtari wished me success, and that evening I was off to Beirut once again, but not before making the gesture of calling Chris Ross, the U.S. ambassador in Damascus, to advise him that an American hostage might be released soon. *The Teheran Times* reported that I was in the area and that hostages might be released; when the BBC relayed the news, it added the unwelcome compliment that every time I had gone to Beirut, someone had been freed. In the circumstances, it would be a difficult record to maintain. So the drama would play itself out as it always did. I should have known by now that everyone always asked for more, and everything still had to be settled across a table with a masked man on the other side.

I arrived in Beirut at 6 P.M. on November 17, just before dark. Things were moving fast. At 9 P.M., an Iranian Embassy car picked me up and took me across town, where I was greeted by the young diplomat Sayed Tokhteh almost as if I were heading off on a journey to an unknown and dangerous land.

"I have nothing to tell you. God be with you."

"I don't like that," I remarked. "It seems you have little hope."

"I cannot tell you anything else," he said.

So I walked out of the embassy and down the street, but the wait was unusually long—almost half an hour, a lifetime. I was very frightened because I knew I had bad news: it was my first trip to Beirut since I had "upset" the Syrians, and I had no Lebanese prisoners I could offer to release this time. I also suspected the groups had an inkling that I was bringing them nothing. I had written and typed out a full presentation from which I could read. I was asking more from them than I had ever asked of anyone, even the Iranians.

The car finally arrived and took off on a longer drive than usual. Even with my head down, I could sense the darkness; there didn't seem to be too many streetlights where we were going, which made me think we were driving out of town. The radio crackled a few words, very few and far apart. I was very nervous. It was taking too long. Was this the end of the road for me? We had changed cars only once, at the very beginning of the trip. I had time to think, too much time. We stopped, and my head was covered. Slowly I followed my guide into a building. It was not the same one as before, but then it never was. Meeting Abdullah reassured me.

When I faced Abdullah across the table to begin my presentation, I thought of the old Soviets' diplomatic techniques; they used to begin their long UN speeches by starting almost from Adam and Eve and extend their time by waiting for the interpreter to translate each passage before continuing. They could thus monopolize the floor for hours. In the Arab world, the rhetorical tradition was not too different, although it was somewhat more colorful than the Marxist dialectic.

I began my Soviet-style speech with an exegesis of the comprehensive plan going all the way back to the Israelis and their search for Arad. I told them the Israelis were very interested in reciprocating with gestures related to their own people, and I explained why the Israelis had become suspicious that they would end up with nothing. Then I warned that if the groups chose to react to the Israelis by not giving up anything, they would be acting like a child in the hands of a grown-up.

"They provoke you," I said, "and you do exactly what they expect you to do. The time has come for you to surprise the Israelis and the world by proceeding with the release of the hostages irrespective of what the others do, because you know that the release is the right thing to do. Then the pressure will not be on you anymore, but on the Israelis, who detain people without due process. When everything is completed, if I were you, I would release not only the Western hostages but the Israelis as well, because that would put you on a different level from them and let everyone know that you will do what really must be done. That would provide you with a new platform both in Lebanon and in the region, based on your own political strength."

I promised that if all hostages were released, the secretary-general and I would commit ourselves to continue to work for the release of all the detainees. Then I wound up my pitch to Abdullah and his comrades: "You will be backed by public opinion, which has sought the release of all those detained without due process. Surely this situation will improve the world's perception of Lebanon, so you will be doing a favor to your own country and helping the Shiite community because you will be seen in a positive light. This will add support to your political platform. You will have no need to resort to force."

Abdullah replied at equally ponderous length: "Only the force of God will stop us from freeing our people who are held by Israel. It is clear from what you have told us that the Israelis are sending a very simple message: they are not interested in the release of the hostages, and they are not interested in releasing our comrades. We will communicate to the Israelis in the only language that they understand—the language of force."

So much for my peaceful suggestion. But Abdullah continued, "Having said that, we will continue working with you for a solution to the hostage problem. We are going to show you our goodwill, but you must exercise pressure on the U.S. so that the Israelis understand that they have to release our people. We would have preferred to use negotiations, but the Israelis and the Americans are our enemies. They have chosen the means by which to fight this battle, and we will respond in kind. We have worked well with you. We know you by now, and we do not want to lose the opportunity to continue our dialogue. Our dialogue with you is very important for us. To show you how important it is, I want you to know that our dialogue with you is positive, but if the Israelis continue to do nothing, this will be very negative for the entire world as well as for the hostages. The Iranians have informed us that the secretary-general has obtained some guarantees about the release of our people at a later stage and that he will continue to work for that objective."

We had received no such guarantees from the Israelis, but if the Iranians had told him so, well. I was getting worried because I could not work on the basis of lies and misunderstandings and certainly not with Islamic Jihad. There were no treaties I could sign with them, and one's word was what counted, for better or worse. I had to make it clear that there were no guarantees even if it would complicate my position.

Abdullah went on, "Because of this commitment, we are going to reciprocate out of devotion to this cause. We are going to release somebody to you, but before that, we are going to talk to you in our next meeting about other matters. It is important for us to know that you will continue to work. Because of the work you have done, we will give you one hostage. And because of the work that you will do, we will give you a second hostage. One is Terry Waite and the other is Thomas Sutherland, but we need guarantees from Pérez de Cuéllar that he will continue to work for us regarding our people in prison."

Then he addressed me in a less formal tone: "I have to give you a piece of advice. If you want to solve the problem of all the other hostages, it is time for the pressure against us even by our friends to come to an end. If they continue to pressure us, there is going to be an explosion. Please tell this to the Iranians. If that pressure continues, it may have the opposite effect—there may be more hostages. We would also like a declaration from the UN that everything has proceeded well in our discussions but that unfortunately the Israelis have created difficulties because they have stopped releasing our people. We want the UN to impose upon Israel the humanitarian laws that apply to prisoners of war and to make clear that at the moment they are not following those laws."

Which was true.

"We have to continue our negotiations for the release of all the Lebanese and Palestinians in Israeli prisons," he continued. "And we insist that the International Red Cross visit the Israeli prisons and deliver them messages from their families. In the meantime, you should continue working on our comrades in European prisons. I want you to know that the recent bombing of southern Lebanon by the Israelis has also been accompanied by the taking of other prisoners and we have to bring this bombing to a stop."

I then told them that releasing their hostages was the best response to the Israeli bombardment and that we could take a public position pointing that out. He insisted on the guarantees by the secretary-general. I assured him that we would continue our work with the Israelis but that I could not help his people in Europe because they had been imprisoned legally.

At that point Abdullah stood up and walked out of the room for a conference with his comrades, who had clearly expected him to obtain UN help in Europe, especially with the Hammadis. When he returned, he said, "As of this moment they accept your word, but they want to have guarantees for the liberation of our friends."

I said, "Abdullah, guarantees are given only by God because he can do whatever he likes. What man can do is express his intentions to do the best he can. I will study how to make this announcement, but do not ask me for guarantees, because guarantees are given only by God."

He insisted on guarantees. I said I could only do my best, to which he abruptly replied, "We stop here. No more conversation. We are going to free two hostages to you."

Before I left I asked about the health of Cicippio and Steen, and of the two Germans. We had received indications that some were not well. He said nothing, went to consult, then came back and said, "You will have two people tomorrow. We will give you two more the next time, and then we will discuss what we will do with the last one."

Then he disappeared. I was taken downstairs, put into the car, and driven to where I had been picked up. I knew that I would get two hostages. The meeting had lasted for three hours.

By morning, Islamic Jihad had formally announced the release of Waite and Sutherland, but it would take hours for them to reach Damascus.

I cabled Pérez de Cuéllar, recommending that, in order to hold off the inevitable barrage of press inquiries, he should say that he was in constant touch with me following his own intensive contacts in New York and that we were "approaching the conclusion of this tragic saga and of the humanitarian problems of the region." After their release, I suggested that he express his appreciation for the cooperation of the groups in Beirut and for the help provided by Iran and Syria, and finally say, "These negotiations have been particularly difficult, and they have been resolved positively because the groups have accepted such a solution based on its merit rather than on any other consideration or quid pro quo. . . . It is hoped that not only the Westerners but also the Lebanese detainees will also be reunited with their families. The groups in Beirut have indeed made the right decision in going ahead with the release of the hostages. This is the right decision humanly, morally, and politically."

Waite and Sutherland were turned over to the Americans that evening, November 18, and the following morning I received a message from Lubrani: "Warmest congratulations to Gianni. We have followed his steps with great concern but with a lot of admiration." The key word in the message was "concern," because he realized I had achieved another release without needing his prisoners to reciprocate. He asked to meet the following week in Rome, where he knew I would be on a visit with Pérez de Cuéllar. Israel had been cut out.

Punctual as usual, Prime Minister John Major sent a letter of thanks to the secretary-general in less than twenty-four hours: "I am profoundly grateful for your success in securing the release of Terry Waite after almost five years of detention. You and your staff, in particular Giandomenico Picco, deserve special thanks. I hope that your continuing effort to secure the release of all hostages in the region will be successful. We will continue to urge on all parties the necessary flexibility and determination."

It's a pity Waite himself wasn't as diplomatic when he was handed over to his ambassador in Damascus and said, "I've been told by my kidnappers that everyone else will be out by the end of this week." Not only was this incorrect, but it put me in an even tighter bind and was inadvertently cruel to the families of the remaining hostages.

But two more people had been freed, and my record of never returning empty-handed from Beirut still held. I was worried about the difficult meeting with the kidnappers, which had ended in a cloud of uncertainty. I was also trying to bring the Israelis back into the final negotiations, because I especially wanted to show that the United Nations could be useful to them. In 1948, the United Nations had served as midwife at the birth of Israel and had negotiated an end to its war of independence. It would be a defeat for me if I could not bring it back into the circle now.

The day after the release of Waite and Sutherland, I joined the secretary-general on an official visit to Italy. We traveled to Milan, Florence, and Rome—all pleasant and anticlimactic, a world away from the fear, tension, and emotion of Abdullah and Beirut at night. But Lebanon was still with us:

There was a Lebanese sentenced to ten years in an Italian jail for possession of explosives. He would be eligible for parole in two years. That was useful information.

I talked with emissaries who had crossed the Alps from Germany to brief me on the Hammadis and ask about their own hostages.

Most important, the secretary-general and I met with the Israelis in Rome. Lubrani had come with Ori Slonim, the lawyer involved with the MIAs, and the deputy chief of military intelligence. Hostages had been released without need for any reciprocation by Israel. The Arens plan had failed completely. Iran had not only disregarded the idea of front-loading Ron Arad, it had pursued the operation with the secretary-general without even asking for an Israeli response. The intelligence assessment of the situation in Teheran had been inaccurate.

Now Lubrani was in Rome trying to recover from all that. Pérez de Cuéllar suggested the possibility of a symbolic release without any "reason" per se. In fact, the Israelis reverted to the idea of a search for Ron Arad; but this time, they accepted the concept that even at the beginning of a search Israel would make a "gesture." They were taking a page from

Lubrani's October plan. But it was too late; the damage had been done. Lubrani asked me to reconstruct a comprehensive package in which a gesture by Israel to the UN secretary-general could be factored in. That meant a release of Lebanese detainees without a stated reason. He encouraged me to discuss it with Kharrazi and sound him out on the numbers the groups would consider at the beginning of a search.

When Lubrani and I met alone, he told me that the secretary-general was on record as seeking more news about Arad. To this I replied, "Uri, I don't want news about Ron Arad. I just want him back. In fact, I want more than that." But I also said we should proceed from the secretary-general's starting point, and what they should do now was release another batch of prisoners. In other words, I advised him exactly as I had advised the groups: "Do what the other side does not expect you to do, and do it because it is the right thing to do." He replied that he was prepared to discuss the Western hostages, the Lebanese detainees, and his own missing on their own merits but needed some reciprocation if Israel were to release Lebanese prisoners.

Then he suddenly asked, "What do you think would happen if we made an independent release?" I replied that Iran would probably deliver on its side of the deal and we could push ahead on a search. All right, said Lubrani, but he wanted to make sure it would produce real information and not just conclude the deal, leaving Israel's demands quietly forgotten. So we were moving toward a compromise of sorts, where the end of the search was in the middle of what was left of the comprehensive package.

When I returned to New York to lay out to the Iranians Lubrani's offer of ten prisoners to get the last round going, Zarif brushed it aside as too little, too late. At this point, he said, such a goodwill gesture would have to involve the release of at least a hundred hostages. In bargaining terms, he confirmed in due course, that probably meant a compromise of fifty. Kharrazi also said the Israelis' opening bid would have to be much better, although he declined to discuss numbers.

When I phoned Lubrani to tell him he would have to come up with a much better number to get back in the game, he inquired slyly, "By better number, do you mean a higher number than your boss requested?"

In conversation with Lubrani in Rome, Pérez de Cuéllar had alluded to the release of only four to five prisoners; Lubrani, of course, had jumped at the idea. This time, I told Lubrani, double-digit numbers were the only ones admissible, and I cited the Iranians' figures.

Lubrani laughed. "I understand that this is a matter of appetite," he said, "but I must admit that your boss is much more discreet in his requests." I could not tell him what to do, but I could advise him of the realities of the situation: he had to put down a reasonable number for negotiations to resume, and he had to do it soon. There was no time to string it out in the hope of achieving the best deal possible. He then offered to pass on to me a letter from Sheikh Obeid to his family, which I figured I could use for the groups in Beirut.

That is, if I could get back to Beirut.

While we were discussing numbers, Zarif informed me that Iranian intelligence had heard that if I returned to Lebanon, I might be killed or kidnapped, and they took it seriously. Consequently, the Iranian government did not want me to travel to Beirut and emphatically urged that, no matter what Ambassador Ahktari would say during my next trip to Damascus, I vehemently refuse to go to Beirut.

Aside from threats against me, Zarif reported growing dissatisfaction among the groups and rumors of new kidnappings, especially of Americans. He also asked me to pass the warning to Tom Pickering, a gesture the American ambassador particularly appreciated. If the kidnappings actually resumed, it would confirm that Iran's standing with Hizbollah had fallen. Zarif, backed by Kharrazi, said the groups had promised Teheran they would provide absolutely "bulletproof" security for me, an assurance Iranian intelligence did not share.

The threat, I later learned, had come not from Abdullah and his comrades but from the Hammadis, from whom I hear occasional death threats to this day.

CHAPTER 15

Cicippio, Steen, Anderson

The Heart of a Lion

B ELIEVING THAT GOOD WORKS ARE THEIR OWN REWARD and that good news
spreads by itself, Pérez de Cuéllar had never paid much attention to
the United Nations' public relations apparatus. Now, at the last stage of
the operation, he wanted the United Nations to take a more public role
and to highlight our accomplishments, in part as a reminder to the Security Council members that the office of the secretary-general had been
transformed during his tenure. It was his swan song before his departure
from office at the end of the year.

As part of the effort, he decided that I should accept some of the requests for interviews that were flooding in. I appeared on the American
TV networks, the BBC, and other stations around the world. And to make
doubly sure that the United Nations got the credit it deserved, he also instructed me to make sure that I would be present in Damascus at the
handover of the last American hostages if I assisted in their release.

When I left for the Middle East on November 27, I was prepared to
remain in Beirut and Damascus until the first of the year if necessary.
Zarif would follow from New York shortly after me. At this point, I hoped
that the talks would move quickly so that we could meet our year-end
deadline, just five weeks away. By now the Iranian government was becoming very agitated because we were still holding off on issuing the report on Paragraph 6. My trump card was holding, and I was confident we
would secure the release of the final three American hostages, with or
without the Israelis in the game.

Still, I was trying to keep the Israelis involved, at least formally. When
we met on November 28 in Cyprus, Lubrani and his team still hoped, as

I did, that the comprehensive package could be pursued. The three remaining American hostages would be freed shortly, I felt, and Israel would benefit by concurrently releasing a group of Lebanese prisoners, even if it did it for no reason other than to make it appear part of the deal. This, in turn, would gain points for Israel in Washington. Everybody would emerge from the hostage affair looking good.

As we departed from Larnaca, it appeared possible that twenty-five Lebanese prisoners might be released in conjunction with the Americans. This time, however, the Lebanese would be freed first. This move by Israel was predicated on the assumption that negotiations on the comprehensive package would resume. The Israeli team, during our Cyprus meeting, had really done everything possible to recover from the Arens debacle. But it was too late; the political circumstances had changed.

In Cyprus, Lubrani had given me a videotape with a message from Sheikh Obeid to his family, along with a statement written on the official stationery of the Israeli government, indicating that Israel had agreed to release an undetermined number of prisoners as a gesture to the secretary-general. The message read as follows:

> Following our meeting in Rome during the 23 and 24 of November with the UN Secretary General and Mr. Picco, we would like to reiterate our full support for the Secretary General's efforts to bring his initiative concerning the release of all Western hostages and missing Israeli POWs and MIAs to a successful conclusion.
>
> We have in consequence decided to respond positively to the UN Secretary General's personal request for a special gesture on the part of Israel to bring about the release of a number of Lebanese detainees.
>
> This gesture is to be made within the framework of our understanding with the UN Secretary General and his assistant that such a gesture is to enhance their efforts to put in motion under the aegis of the Secretary General a comprehensive settlement of the problem of the Israeli MIAs and POWs and of the Western hostages within the shortest time possible. From Israel's point of view, the foremost objective of this comprehensive settlement is to receive a "sign of life" and reliable information concerning the fate of Israeli POW Ron Arad and to bring about the return to Israel of all its POWs and MIAs.

Once the details concerned in this comprehensive settlement have been worked out with Mr. Picco, by receipt of the other party's approval, Israel intends to effect the A-M [above mentioned] gesture into effect without delay.

It was evident by late November, however, that a search for Arad still had to be pursued and a comprehensive package completed, and that neither would happen until we were well into 1992. That meant it would all take place under the leadership of the new secretary-general selected by the Security Council, the Egyptian diplomat Boutros Boutros-Ghali.

When the Israelis had previously released prisoners, they had then staged a raid in south Lebanon to replenish their "inventory." This time, I told them, they would have to show restraint. I also asked for a Red Cross visit to Khiam prison and tried to ensure that the Israelis would not stall the release of the twenty-five prisoners until the result of a search for Arad was delivered to them. Lubrani said they would have to think carefully about this, but from the way we looked each other in the eyes, I knew he would not back down if he could assure his government that I was working on the cases of all the missing. So I left him with the understanding that twenty-five prisoners were in the pipeline, an important card for me.

My first meeting with Zarif in Damascus, on November 28, was for the sole purpose of once again piecing together the comprehensive package with the elements I currently had in my hands. They included an understanding with Israel not to take further prisoners from Lebanon; permission for the ICRC to visit Khiam prison; a videotape of Sheikh Obeid; and a gesture by Israel to release a number of Lebanese prisoners, all in return for a search for Ron Arad and the others.

Zarif seemed to accept, even as he complained about the number of detainees to be released, and Kharrazi, who called at the same time, gave his support for a search. Neither of them, however, could tell me how the groups in Lebanon would react to the search. On that day, I also received an understanding from Zarif that the bodies of Colonel Higgins, the American who had worked for the United Nations, and Buckley, the former CIA station chief in Beirut, would be released to me.

From Damascus, I sent the first of many messages to Lubrani that we exchanged by cryptofax via military channels during the last lap of the negotiations. I addressed him as "Interlocutor" and signed my name as

"Guest." In the code by which we communicated, Iran was "the Mother Country" and "the package" referred to the release of hostages:

> Wish to confirm that in response to my presentation, Mother Country reacted by saying that they undertook to help me with the comprehensive package which, of course, includes search from beginning to end. Groups, of course, will prefer to negotiate before agreeing to this package. This comes from K [Kharrazi]. I wonder if this would facilitate implementation of your gesture. From where I stand, it would help all of us much. It seems to me that even irrespective of above, it would be in your interest to consider a gesture now, for I may soon be receiving a package. You may remember my reasoning when we met on island. Looking forward to hearing from you. Signed, Guest.

I went to bed early, thoroughly exhausted. In thirty-six hours, I had flown from New York to London to Damascus to Cyprus and back to Damascus. At ten minutes to midnight, I was awakened from a deep slumber by a call from Zarif. "There are some complications," he said in the time-honored phrase that meant trouble.

Half an hour later, we met at his embassy. The groups had sent word that if I did not meet with them, there would be no releases. He reiterated the dangers and warned me that when I met with Akhtari the following morning, I should continue to stress that I would not go to Beirut. I then remarked to Zarif that if he came with me, I would be safe. Once again, he refused. Before I climbed back into bed at 2:15 A.M., I wrote in my notebook, "So much for everything being on automatic pilot."

Zarif joined me when I met Akhtari the following morning. As usual with the ambassador, the conversation began with an exchange of pleasantries, in this case about the latest hostage release. I then walked him through the package so that there would be no misunderstandings: Israel's prisoner releases, the United Nations' role as mediator in dealing with the Israeli missing, the secretary-general's efforts to help free all Lebanese detainees, the groups' role in helping find the Israeli missing, the secretary-general's role in investigating Israel's treatment of its prisoners with the help of the Red Cross and Amnesty International, and finally the Israeli videotape carrying a message from Sheikh Obeid to his family. These were the main points, but what I told him was far more elaborate and detailed than that. I sugarcoated it as much as I could to gain his cooperation and influence in Beirut.

At first, Akhtari reacted as if Israel had not modified its position at all—as if there would be no up-front release of twenty-five detainees. As far as he was concerned, the case of the Israelis was closed and they were no longer part of the operation, since Western hostages were being released without even the slightest gesture from them. But then he acknowledged that the secretary-general had received new assurances from Israel and, as a result, said that the groups should be told.

I asked him to try to persuade the groups' representatives to confer with me in Damascus. He said that it would be very difficult. The Iranians were usually very prudent when it came to dealing with the Lebanese, knowing that it required "the heart of a lion," but he was certain that Allah would help me.

In plain language, he stated that the groups no longer trusted Iran and would not accept it as intermediary. Akhtari said they wanted to deal with me directly because I had displayed a lion's heart.

Akhtari suggested, for my own safety, that I postpone my meeting in Beirut until Israel released its first batch of twenty-five hostages, since the groups' main worry was that Israel would renege on its promise. It would be even better, he said, if the release were to include some of the more important prisoners that the groups wanted released.

But the meeting ended on an ambiguous and even threatening note: Akhtari said that Iran, and in particular its president, had given clear instructions to resolve the issue of the hostages and everything attendant to it. He sincerely hoped that the groups would help on the basis of what I had to offer. I replied that with due respect for what he was saying, I had also received very strict instructions from the secretary-general to steer clear of Beirut. The sabers came out, and we fenced. I reiterated my preference for Damascus and the secretary-general's insistence that I avoid Beirut. Akhtari's parry: If the Israelis could release *some* of the prisoners to help pave the way for a comprehensive plan, he would then be able to reassure the secretary-general as to my safety in Lebanon. In other words, if the Israelis did not deliver, my security would be at stake.

"God willing," he said with an air of optimism, "this could be resolved by tomorrow evening."

Things had now come to pass in a way I had foreseen. I was in the unenviable position of risking my life to secure the release of the final three hostages. Anyone who boasts that he is without fear in such a situation is a liar or a fool. My friend Javad Zarif, with whom I had worked so long on so many matters, had warned me about the grave dangers of going to Beirut. Meanwhile, Ambassador Akhtari, who had been of enormous help but was essentially a professional doing a job to get his country out of a mess, was looking for a way to get me to Beirut with some guarantee for my security.

I may have had the heart of a lion, but I did not have the protective metal skin of a tank. It was my call. I could not pick up the phone and ask Pérez de Cuéllar what to do, for he would always advise me to put my safety first. So at 11 P.M., I had another meeting with Zarif, during which we went through some mutual theatrics. I told him I could probably convince Lubrani to release at least some of the twenty-five beforehand. Zarif could not believe that we had the gall to expect Iran's full commitment to a comprehensive plan when we were not even prepared to release all twenty-five at once.

The Iranians had already written off Israel in the deal but, having realized that Tel Aviv wanted in again, were trying to squeeze as much out of it as they could. On the other hand, Lubrani needed some commitment to a complete search for Ron Arad, which was the bottom line of the comprehensive package. We, being in the middle, knew that we would get the last hostages in exchange for the report on Paragraph 6, but we also wanted to help the Israelis resolve the cases of their missing. I sincerely believed that Iran would help me with the search for Ron Arad, so I tried to obtain confirmation of it from Zarif and from Kharrazi in New York.

November 29 was spent in meetings with Zarif, on phone calls with Kharrazi, and in cryptofax conversation with Lubrani; at the same time, I was holding off Akhtari about a decision to go to Beirut. I had ethical, political, and practical concerns to tackle that day. Decisions needed making, and there were no colleagues around with whom to discuss them, no superior who could give me wise advice, and, most of all, no time. The pressure, the adrenaline, and my desire to see the hostages released as soon as possible were not the best advisers.

One of my several messages to Lubrani that November 29:

Scenario of comprehensive will be discussed when I return to my headquarters mid-week and sit down with K [Kharrazi] in New York to discuss the comprehensive. As for the timing, I just spoke to K who said that implementation was expected under the present UN administration. K insisted that the search would be a genuine search and that they could not say what the result would be.

I called Kharrazi in New York to ensure his support of what I had written, and four hours later, I sent another message to Lubrani:

Have just received further declaration of assistance toward comprehensive by Mother Country. They sincerely hope you can tell me that you will make the gesture to Secretary General. It will help me more than you know. If this happens in the next two days, you will gain no matter what. At worst, delivery of package will be credited to you. At best, you will facilitate work on the comprehensive. Hope to hear from you soon. Next few hours crucial for me. Regards, Guest.

At 9 P.M., I received Lubrani's reply. It was long and suggested that "the Secretary General and yourself together with us are being taken for a ride" and "that the requested gesture by the Secretary General will turn out to be another successful act of extortion on the part of the other party." But it reposed final trust in me—"your personal sense and gut feelings for what is presently required"—and in the end conceded what I wanted: "We have decided to enable you to use the up-front gesture, an additional release of twenty-five detainees at a mutually determined point in time, toward the middle of next week."

So I had the twenty-five prisoners in my hand at last but could play them only in the middle of the following week. I messaged back that I needed them, and had asked for their release, within forty-eight hours.

Within minutes I got another response from "Interlocutor": "Due to logistics, it will not be possible to release any detainees before 1500 local time Sunday." It was now late Friday evening. Sunday was good timing for me.

"Guest" replied almost immediately: "Thank you for the useful answer. I have taken careful note of your communication regarding the time of release, and am most grateful. Further message and substance will follow in a few hours."

But I did not need to wait. At 7 A.M. Saturday, I received yet another message from Tel Aviv:

Thank you for your message received at 0130 local time. 1) The number will be 25 as initially mentioned. 2) We will let you know as soon as possible of the exact time of release. 3) Keep us informed about developments at your end, in particular, where and when details of "comprehensive" may be finalized. 4) I appreciate your efforts and wish you great luck in your next move.

At the end of the day, I replied:

1) I wish to inform you that I've now received from Mother Country: a) Commitment to work on comprehensive, b) Commitment to start working mid-week. c) Commitment to implement in December. They feel that thus they have responded in full to your request through me for the up-front gesture. Since they took that position I would have to count on your figure as given to me previously. To change now would appear to be going back on our word. I would count on your gesture materializing on Sunday afternoon. I expect package around same time, though I cannot predict with exactitude. I've done my best to proceed with everybody working together.

Back at the Iranian Embassy, I informed Akhtari of how I had brought the Israelis around to release twenty-five prisoners up front as a gesture to the secretary-general. He thanked me and said he hoped I could wrap everything up in one last meeting; the groups said it would probably be a long one to iron out all details, so I would not need to risk returning. Very considerate of them, I thought. But we were not going to meet in Beirut. He had persuaded the groups to meet me halfway. The encounter would be outside Damascus. I was perplexed. I could not decline since they had acceded to my request to meet somewhere other than Beirut, but the words "outside Damascus" and "halfway" did not quite compute for me.

As I walked downstairs from the ambassador's office toward my waiting car at about 10 P.M., Akhtari stopped me, asked me to wait in another room for a moment, then came in and asked, "Do you mind going now?"

"Where?"

"For your meeting with the groups."

He said it was a good time to go. I at least wanted to tell my UN driver that I was disappearing again, but this was Akhtari's move and he had his own way of operating. However, I insisted because I wanted to leave all my papers with the driver and tell him personally about my unexpected trip, which he needed to pass on to my two UN colleagues in Damascus.

I went to my driver and told him, "I will be going on a trip. Take my papers to Bjornsson and my documents [except my UN identification] and tell him just what I told you." I then asked him to leave so that the exit from the gate of the embassy would be clear.

Reentering the embassy compound, I found a car with one rear door open waiting for me between the garage and the gate. The driver was alone, and he asked me to lie facedown and not to look at anything. We left in a westerly direction out of town. I could tell from the turns the driver took that we were driving in the direction of Lebanon.

After about forty minutes the car stopped, the door opened, and I was dropped in the middle of nowhere. A few minutes later, a car that seemed familiar approached. My first thought was: Why is the Jihad here in the middle of Syria? We were on the shoulder of a road in the countryside, surrounded by fields, and a masked person asked me to walk into the fields and take off my jacket and tie. He handed me a windbreaker, a cap, and large dark glasses painted black on the inside. Then we walked back to the car. He asked me to sit, not lie, on the backseat behind the driver, who had no mask. Another person was on the backseat with me. A voice said, "Please, please, for everybody's sake, don't move, and do exactly what we tell you. And most of all, perhaps it is better if you close your eyes."

Everything was new this time. I had no idea where I was or where we were headed, and to say that I felt insecure would be an understatement. I did not close my eyes and got a ferocious headache from staring at the inside of the painted glasses. They had dressed me inconspicuously because we were going to cross the border, and I could hardly have been lying in my usual position without arousing the suspicion of border guards. The purpose was to create the image of a high-ranking member of Hizbollah or perhaps the Revolutionary Guards. When we arrived at a checkpoint (I never saw which one), I could feel the tension in the car. My handlers told me to sit still and not to turn my head. I heard voices close by; then a flashlight from outside was shone through the dark glass of the car. What anybody could see from the outside was the profile of a man dressed like many others who must have gone through Zebdani, the Syrian village on the Lebanese border where the Revolutionary Guards were said to have their own border checkpoint. We drove on.

I could tell we had entered a town from the noises, which differed markedly from the rural sounds and night silence of the region. The car stopped in front of a multistory building. I walked up five flights to enter an apartment draped with the traditional white sheets. Our meeting room was large, with all the furniture piled to one side and covered with sheets, giving it the appearance of a snow-covered mountain. On the other side of the room stood the regular small table and two chairs. After I sat down, the hooded Abdullah took off my glasses.

"Why did you doubt us?" he asked.

"Abdullah, I did not doubt you. I doubted those I didn't know. If it was up to you and me, there would not be a problem."

"You know that we wouldn't let anything happen to you in Lebanon. No one would touch you in Lebanon."

"That's good to know. I'm glad to hear that."

He said security was a fake issue because they needed me to continue working for the freedom of the Lebanese in Khiam prison. But he also complained that my refusal to go to Beirut had required him to take extra risks and to make quite a few arrangements. He did concede that some people who opposed an end to the process wanted me dead, but he said that one of the unfortunate consequences of meeting in this particular place was that it was more dangerous for him. Furthermore, the groups had a present for me in Beirut that they could not carry to this meeting place.

I thanked him for the release of Waite and Sutherland and went over the entire list of issues yet to be resolved: three Americans, two Germans, the missing Israelis, the Lebanese in Khiam, the bodies of Higgins and Buckley. We moved to the gesture that Israel was ready to make by releasing twenty-five detainees from Khiam and the acceptance by Israel of ICRC visits to Lebanese prisoners if reciprocated by visits to the Israelis. Then it was on to the new effort by the secretary-general for a comprehensive package, including, of course, the search for Ron Arad. I went over the plan. I reminded him of his repeated expressions of support for the package and told him our meeting would be useful only if this support continued. He said the groups would do their part, and so would Hizbollah. I told him about the tape of Sheikh Obeid, which I explained was still in my office in Damascus because I had been whisked here without warning and had had no time to collect it for him. He was disappointed by that. Then he left the room.

When he returned, he complimented me on my efforts and announced that the groups had decided they could deal only with the remaining American hostages; for everything else I would have to address the Hizbollah leaders and the Iranians. The groups themselves still held three hostages, and Abdullah said they considered my work good enough to give me all three. One was held by the Revolutionary Justice Organization, one by Islamic Jihad, one by Jihad Islamic Palestine.

Abdullah said that delivering anyone other than the three Americans was beyond their power, and that included the two Germans held by the Hammadis, to say nothing of Ron Arad and the other missing Israelis. Trying to intercede for the Hammadis, he asked if I thought it possible for Mohammed Ali Hammadi to be pardoned under German law. I told him it was most unlikely.

This had no effect on his next announcement: "Tonight we have decided to make a public statement in total accord with Picco and announce that there is a clear understanding of what will happen and when." He proposed a declaration saying that the secretary-general and I had guaranteed to continue working for the release of the Lebanese prisoners and that the groups would not search for the missing Israelis until they knew the Israelis were doing something to reciprocate. He asked me whether I agreed.

I replied that I could promise only that the secretary-general would do his best, and I insisted that there be no reference to the number of Israeli releases in their plans because a specific figure might provoke a change of heart by the Israelis. He then said what I had been waiting for: in recognition of the work done by the secretary-general and myself in the past and what they expected of us in the future, they would release the remaining American hostages in the following sequence: Cicippio on Monday, Steen on Tuesday, Anderson on Wednesday. In response to their press release, they expected a statement from the United Nations recognizing their contribution to the solution of the hostage problem and indicating the commitment of the secretary-general to continue working for the release of the Lebanese prisoners.

Abdullah also asked me to refer to the Lebanese prisoners in Europe in the hope that it would assist in obtaining the Hammadis' release. Out of the question, I said. In Middle Eastern fashion, he leaned on me to obtain more releases from Israel, "even one or two more." He still wanted a larger UN commitment to work for the release of his comrades. I repeated the limits of what I could do.

He again left the room to confer with his comrades. When he returned, he insisted that there was need for a guarantee by the secretary-general to free more of his friends from Israeli hands and that it was the condition for the three hostages. Having dangled what I could get in front of me, he snatched it away.

Abdullah's voice was low, somber, and authoritative, and he always negotiated with confidence. But this time I had nothing more to negotiate. I said that we had come to the end of the road and that what we had previously agreed on should be enough. He was clearly under pressure from his comrades. But after we tossed the ball back and forth for a bit, he agreed with me. I would receive the three hostages but nothing more from him—not the search for the Israelis, not the bodies of the Americans, not the Germans. Our negotiations, he said, were finished: "This is our last meeting, but one day I will write you a personal letter. And after that, we'll probably meet in the next world—if there is one. Then, at that time, I will tell you the real story of the Western hostages."

He then took my hand in his two hands to say good-bye, and I tried to read his future in his eyes. I knew he would spend the rest of his life on the run because neither Israeli nor Western intelligence would forgo opportunities to look for him and his comrades. As he walked away, I could see that he was slipping his mask off. He gave me a parting compliment, which I didn't quite know how to take: "Actually, you are the only person who could be an ambassador for us." I never saw Abdullah again.

Who was he? Western and Israeli intelligence believe he was Imad Moughniya, a young man from a Shiite family in the south of Lebanon who had joined Hizbollah at a very early age. Moughniya had worked with the Hammadi clan as a Hizbollah security man before they started seizing hostages. I heard the name mentioned many times in Lebanon. Others said that my masked interlocutor could have been Mustafa Badruddin, the brother-in-law of Moughniya who had been one of the Dawa Seventeen.

I could recognize Abdullah by his voice and other mannerisms, and I knew for sure that he was always the same person I spoke with right through to the end. By saying to me that he would tell me the "real" story of the hostages, he hinted that he was aware of the entire affair, which Badruddin could not have known because he had spent seven years in Kuwaiti jails. I have no idea where the man who called himself Abdullah lives now, but my suspicion is that this fervent, misguided Lebanese patriot was likely condemned to live out his days in Iran under its protection.

The crimes committed by the terrorist groups grew out of the murderous emotions of a fifteen-year civil war during which alliances and enemies changed continually. Their world seemed to go berserk, and they with it. They were Shiite Muslims coming of age in a country that had given them nothing for centuries, ignoring them in the traditional division of power among their Sunni Muslim cousins, the Christians, and the Druze tribal leaders. The Lebanese civil war shattered this long-standing arrangement, and the result was chaos in which all the old ways vanished. Moughniya's generation was raised without rules in this war-torn land, a country in which they had lived in deprivation since childhood. Most of their families did not even have running water in their homes. Their religious leaders taught them to fight back. They were told they faced a powerful enemy, and they saw that enemy themselves: the Israeli Army in Beirut in 1982. Hizbollah, which saw itself literally as the Party of God, formed a fighting force and by 1986 had achieved what no one else in Lebanon ever had—the expulsion of a multinational force led by Americans and the withdrawal of the Israelis from Beirut.

We returned as we had come, although we passed the checkpoint very quickly. We changed cars again, my jacket was returned, and they sped away. I had to wait alone for about fifteen minutes in the middle of the dark countryside until a car came to pick me up, a different one from the car that had brought me from Damascus. Without anything being said, I got in and lay facedown on the backseat. I had no idea who had come to get me, but in my exhaustion I let down my guard and decided that if I had made it this far I would make it back safely. I had a fleeting thought that since this was probably my last meeting with the kidnappers, it was also the last opportunity for opponents of the groups orchestrating the releases to snatch me as the last hostage.

The driver finally stopped and grunted, "Door." I looked up and saw I was in front of the UN building in Damascus.

I sent several messages before falling into bed. Pérez de Cuéllar got the first word that the hostages would be freed. Then it was "Interlocutor": "Just finished my work with Abdullah. They reaffirmed interest in comprehensive solution. Your gestures are received very well and expected for Sunday. Please note that in the statement to be released in Beirut they will refer to comprehensive and to your gesture to the Secretary General. Package due on Monday." And finally I messaged Judith Karam to call the AP's Heinzerling and Foley and tell them, "Please come for coffee immediately." They did, stopping in Cyprus to pick up Anderson's wife, Madeleine, and their seven-year-old daughter, whom Terry had never seen since she had been born shortly after his abduction.

On Sunday, as promised, the Israelis released twenty-five prisoners, including three women, and all the appropriate press statements were issued giving the United Nations and Israel credit. The same day, I called on Farouk al-Shaara, the foreign minister of Syria—my first contact with a high-level official in Assad's government. That meeting had been prompted by the American and Iranian ambassadors, who separately had let the Syrian authorities know that Pérez de Cuéllar would appreciate my presence when the hostages were turned over in Damascus. At the end of our meeting, with great elegance, Shaara asked me to be present if and when the next releases took place.

They began the next day, as promised. Cicippio was released on Monday morning, December 2, to the Syrians in Beirut, then brought quickly to Damascus. As he subsequently recounted in his book, *Chains to Roses*, his final ordeal was not without drama. He was sealed in a box, shipped out of his captivity as a package, and "dropped off" at Syrian intelligence.

When I met with Cicippio, we learned of the terrible conditions under which he had been kept. A frail man with a kind heart and gentle demeanor, he told us that he had been left outside on a balcony for one entire winter and had contracted bronchitis. He had spent five years in chains with no word from the outside world or from his family, not even news of the recent death of his son. His chains, he said, had been only thirty inches long.

Joseph Cicippio loved Lebanon and his work as a senior administrator at the American University. Despite the terrible torture during his captivity and the harsh conditions, he retained his equanimity; I did not see any anger in him. His joy at being freed was just too strong.

When the ceremony ended, Cicippio and Chris Ross, the U.S. ambassador to Syria, left first. A number of journalists surrounded me, but I said, "Picco doesn't talk." Then I went back to my office, because even while waiting for the final releases of Steen and Anderson the next day, I had much to do.

At the office, I messaged Uri Lubrani to ask General Antoine Lahad, the Lebanese pro-Israeli general in southern Lebanon, to release one or two of the Lebanese he was holding; in exchange, I would try to arrange for an ICRC visit to Lahad's own men imprisoned by Hizbollah. Within a few hours, Lubrani informed me with some regret that he had "just had the most acrimonious exchange with General Lahad who claims that we are softies and do not know with what kind of hoodlums and extortionists we are dealing, and that any further gestures on his part are totally out of the question."

My objective at the closing stage of the operation was to make sure that there would be a sequel to the last releases so that the comprehensive approach would be kept alive. But I realized I had pushed Lubrani beyond his limit. That evening I decided to take a different tack and wrote a personal letter to Abdullah. I explained to him that in my view any further requests of the Israelis would be hopeless and that it was time to conclude this chapter of the Western hostages without further conditions. "Let me tell you as your ambassador that we are heading toward a dead end," I said. "We need to return to the main highway." Under the terms of my plan, the groups were still expecting something from the Israelis in exchange for Cicippio. I wanted them to release the two American hostages. I received word back from Abdullah that the releases of

Steen and Anderson would proceed as scheduled and that no other requests would be made to me.

The next morning, Alann Steen was released on schedule. It was December 3. I went to the ministry to participate in the ceremony with Syrian Deputy Foreign Minister Nasser Khouldour Shakour, the very same person who in the past month had actually asked me if I had ever visited the Middle East before. This time he referred in complimentary terms both to me and to my boss, whom he misidentified as Boutros Boutros-Ghali.

Steen appeared weak and in pain, his voice barely audible. He was only fifty-two, but he, too, had suffered greatly during his four years in captivity and looked much older. I understood at the time that this quiet college professor had been beaten severely.

We were now waiting for Terry Anderson, who had appeared in more of the videotapes recorded by the kidnappers than any other hostage and thus had the greatest worldwide TV exposure. He was also a newsman, which made him the most important hostage in political terms. Journalists who had not come to Damascus the previous day had now arrived to witness the release of one of their own. Reporters and cameramen had been camping outside the UN office, the American Embassy, and the Syrian Foreign Ministry since early morning.

I had spent the night in the office to be sure I could be reached if anything went wrong. Having witnessed how many things had gone wrong in the previous months, I was concerned that the release of Anderson could have "complications." Abdullah had kept his word with the releases of Steen and Cicippio, but in the Middle East nothing is certain until it happens.

At 7 A.M. on December 4, Zarif told me he had heard that Anderson would be freed in an hour. Three hours passed with no sign of Anderson, and suddenly the story of the delay took on a life of its own: he would be released any second, he wouldn't be released for hours, he might not be released at all. At 10 A.M., I asked Zarif, but he had no idea what was happening and asked me if I had received any messages. At noon, the Syrian Foreign Ministry advised us to be ready at 8 P.M. Then it told journalists to come to the ministry at 3 P.M. At about the same time, Islamic Jihad released a tape of Anderson in Beirut to the foreign press. At 3:10 P.M., Syrian Foreign Minister Shaara told the U.S. ambassador to arrive at midnight. It seemed that the delay was due to heavy snow on the road

over the mountains between Beirut and Damascus. At 4 P.M., Zarif called
to tell me that the situation was tense and the weather bad. Ross called
me for information; I had to tell him I had none. Half an hour later, Anderson's tape was played by the media.

For several hours Zarif, Ross, the Syrians, and I exchanged calls,
swapping whatever information we had. Pérez de Cuéllar, besieged by
journalists at the United Nations as he arrived for work, called around
lunchtime in New York, midevening in Damascus. I did not want to create undue concern for Pérez de Cuéllar, nor did I want him to hint to the
journalists in New York that there might be problems. In subsequent calls
to and from New York, I blamed the delay on the heavy snow in the
mountains between Beirut and Damascus. If Anderson had been released
in Beirut and driven to Damascus, clearly bad weather could be a justifi-
able excuse. In fact, Anderson was already in the Bekaa Valley, where there
was no snow.

The snow helped all of us keep the media satisfied, but we were extremely worried: we simply could not make sense of what was going on.
What had happened was weird—and typical of how goofy things in the
Mideast can become. It seemed that a German reporter in Teheran had
been misinformed by a low-level official that the two German hostages
were also to be released on December 4. He had flashed the news, which
had made the Hammadi clan furious with the Iranians and Hizbollah,
which had then delayed the Anderson release. Teheran had quickly denied
the story, but the damage had been done, and Anderson was kept waiting
from the early morning of December 4 until the evening while the Hammadis and the groups wrangled among themselves.

I was frightened that the kidnappers would find some excuse to hold
on to the last American hostage to protect themselves. But they didn't;
Ross and I were finally called to the Syrian Foreign Ministry late that
night to meet with Terry Anderson. He walked up to me and said, "My
God, I really want to kiss you. You gave us hope." Terry and some of the
other hostages who had had access to a radio in their last year of captivity had heard my name on the BBC World Service, which had covered our
operations closely.

It was a great moment in my life. Terry Anderson had been the absent
companion of my thoughts for four years, and now a man I had never
seen pulled me close and hugged me. I was shaking with emotion. For
the cameras I delivered a short statement: "Mr. Anderson, it is with great

satisfaction and joy that I am conveying to you Mr. Pérez de Cuéllar's warmest welcome to freedom. This could not have been achieved without the cooperation of Syria and Iran. Much has been done to solve the humanitarian problem of the hostages and others, including those detained without due process in Lebanon. Much, however, remains to be done as we rejoice tonight for the developments of the last four days. I pledge the commitment of the Secretary General and his staff to pursue the effort aimed at closing this sad chapter. Your freedom, Mr. Anderson, is a victory for all."

I spoke as briefly as possible, making sure that my diplomatic bases were covered because that was part of my job, but mainly trying not to keep Anderson waiting to be reunited with his wife and daughter any longer. As I left the building, I was swamped by journalists who wanted to congratulate me. That night I wrote in my diary, "Much has been done but much remains to be done. The hostages have been released. But I must say that the thanks that Terry Anderson gave me are more than I could have imagined."

CHAPTER 16

Those Beyond Reach

*L*IFE USUALLY GOES IN ONE DIRECTION after such an emotional climax, and that's downhill. The freed hostages now were deservedly international celebrities, Anderson above all. With less than one month remaining in Pérez de Cuéllar's mandate, I had to continue my efforts, but I had little hope: we had the fate of the missing Israeli military men, the return of the bodies of the Americans Higgins and Buckley, the freedom of the two German hostages, the fate of Alec Collett, the Lebanese detainee in Khiam, and four Iranians.

After Terry Anderson's release I remained in Damascus only a few hours. A Lufthansa flight took me to Frankfurt in the early morning of December 5, the euphoria from the previous day already fading. Zarif was on the same flight, and we talked a lot about the work yet to be done. In Frankfurt, I was received by Ambassador Reinhard Schlagenweit, who took me by helicopter to Bonn for a meeting with Foreign Minister Genscher. My role was to provide political support to the German government at that moment, when their two nationals were the only Westerners still being held hostage in Lebanon. A few hours later, I was taken back to Frankfurt Airport, where I met Uri Lubrani and his team.

The Israeli government was concerned that it had still received little in return for the gestures it had made. Lubrani and his team had put heavy pressure on me and the secretary-general, reminding us that our commitments and responsibilities covered the Israeli MIAs every bit as much as the Western hostages. "It is now time to say to the Iranians that the resolution of the Ron Arad case and the return of the two bodies, which was confirmed in September, is a top priority," said Lubrani. One of his colleagues put it more bluntly: "You have been cheated."

The Israelis rightly felt they had made more than enough unreciprocated gestures; now it was the Iranians' turn. If the Iranians could find Arad and identify the bodies of the other missing, Lubrani promised, the Israelis would empty the jails of Lebanese detainees. They were now ready to agree to any settlement that would see the resolution of the Arad case at "the beginning, the middle, or the end." They even offered to let me visit Sheikh Obeid in prison. The meeting was painful: it was clear to one and all that the engine driving the entire operation had begun to stall now that Terry Anderson was free.

They took me to a room at the airport Sheraton to meet Ron Arad's wife and his little daughter, Youval. It was heartbreaking. I knew what they wanted, but I was helpless—unable to produce the information they sought, unable to fully understand their terrible grief. The little girl gave me a drawing she had done on hotel stationery that depicted a big menorah on one side and the walls of the city of Jerusalem on the other. It was addressed to me from Youval "with hope."

Back in New York the next day, I heard from Lubrani again. This time he warned me that Israel was ready to go public and accuse the United Nations of having been duped. He urged me to go to Teheran to try to speed up the search for Arad and said that, in any case, the pro-Israeli lobby in Washington might turn against the United Nations. This was meant not as a threat, he insisted, merely as a fact of life. The next play in this game of political hardball was an Israeli warning to be relayed to the Beirut terrorists: they would not get Sheikh Obeid back unless Tel Aviv got Arad.

To make my life more exciting, President Bush, normally an astute diplomat, let slip in a speech welcoming the release of the hostages that the United States might consider retaliating against the Beirut terrorists. It was the wrong comment at the wrong time, given Israel's continuing need to engage either the groups or Iran in further indirect negotiations. Kharrazi and Zarif wasted no time in telling the secretary-general that they were appalled by Bush's remark. Zarif warned that such statements could only help promote a new wave of hostage taking by the terrorists to protect themselves.

A story also appeared in *The Wall Street Journal* about that time, reporting that the FBI would pursue the kidnappers of the Americans and pros ecute them in U.S. courts. Lubrani was as appalled as the Iranians, knowing as he did that this was no way to coax information out of Lebanon. We essentially shared their view and suggested as much to the American government. Its reply to our démarche was that the reports "did not reflect any current official operational activity." Later in the month, Defense Secretary Richard Cheney said that the kidnappers ought to be prosecuted. This brought Zarif to my office, warning of increasingly poor prospects of obtaining information about Arad.

But it was also becoming clear that Washington had come to respect our work. On December 10, the secretary-general received a "Dear Javier" letter from Jim Baker praising the United Nations for its efforts to free the hostages. "Our joy is only tempered by what still must be done," he said, referring to the Germans, the Israelis, and the bodies of the American hostages. Baker than added by hand, "You and Mr. Picco have done a magnificent job, history will so record." We had apparently earned the secretary's confidence at last.

Two days later, Pérez de Cuéllar and I were on the shuttle to Washington for a White House ceremony we had learned about less than a week earlier. In the car to the presidential mansion, I was told for the first time that I was about to be awarded a medal; until then, I had thought I was simply accompanying my boss. We were received with military honors and ushered into the Oval Office. There we met with Bush, Baker, Scowcroft, and five of the liberated hostages. It was unexpected recognition, prompted, I was to learn later, by a request by Terry Anderson to the president. Bush praised Pérez de Cuéllar for his leadership of the United Nations over the past decade and for his many achievements, capped most fittingly at the end of his mandate by the release of the kidnapped Americans. The president's comments to me during the presentation were very flattering as well, but I was embarrassed to be called a hero in front of Anderson, Steen, and the others, who had endured so much hardship for so long. Indeed, the warmth, kindness, and sympathy shown by the hostages and their families overwhelmed me.

The ritual pictures were taken with the hostages, and in due course we found ourselves before the press to be decorated. Pérez de Cuéllar received the Medal of Freedom, and I received the Presidential Special Award for Exceptional Service. I was honored that the medal was placed around my neck by Mrs. Bush. We were flown back to New York in much grander style aboard a military jet.

For us, the day was significant for another reason as well: in New York, the secretary-general's office released Pérez de Cuéllar's Paragraph 6 report on the origin of the war between Iran and Iraq. It took guts. There was little doubt that Iraq had started the conflict, but the argument could have been made that the report was a straight quid pro quo: Iranian support for the hostage-release operation in return for an official document labeling Iraq the aggressor. The fact was, however, that the context of the report had nothing to do with its findings. Well-respected academics had concluded formally and in great detail what everyone in international affairs had known for years. If there was a deal, it was to state the truth in exchange for the freedom of the hostages, both of which were the right things to do, whether in tandem or separately.

The other bone of contention was whether the report could have bought not only the Western hostages but also Ron Arad and the other Israeli MIAs—an argument-cum-accusation leveled at us by Uri Lubrani and his team. I had struggled with this issue personally before the Israelis raised it. Could we have linked the entire operation to Arad? Could we have risked linking the freedom of the hostages to one MIA? But by early September, we were already committed to the Iranian government: How could we even contemplate breaking the word of the United Nations' highest official? Second, we did not believe that incoming Secretary-General Boutros Boutros-Ghali would share our commitment: Would an Egyptian national, even one in the top spot at the United Nations, issue a report critical of a major Arab country? Delaying the report, we thought, might mean that it never got released at all.

The report itself was clear on the central point: "Accordingly the outstanding event under the violations referred to in paragraph 5 above is the attack of 22 September 1980 against Iran, which cannot be justified under the Charter of the United Nations, any recognized rules and principles of international law or any principles of international morality and entails the responsibility for the conflict."*

*From Paragraph 6 of UN document S/23273, "Further Report of the Secretary General on the Implementation of Security Council Resolution 598, 1987."

It was front-page news in Teheran, sent Iraq to the bicarbonate of soda, but went largely unnoticed elsewhere in the Middle East. Zarif expressed Iran's thanks and appreciation to the secretary-general and said the release of the reports would speed the return of the bodies of Higgins and Buckley. As usual, his timing was off.

In the meantime, I resumed a conversation I had had with Brent Scowcroft at the White House the previous week about what the Iranians could expect in the way of presidential goodwill now that the American hostages were all free. An arbitration panel at The Hague had been wrestling with American and Iranian claims against each other for years, and a number of compensation payments had been made. In late November, the Bush administration had agreed to a repayment to Iran of $270 million of its own money that the former shah had paid for goods before their actual delivery took place. If that was supposed to be a sign of goodwill, Iran certainly did not see it as such, and in fact the administration insisted it had nothing to do with Iran's role in liberating the hostages.

I asked Scowcroft for details of embargoes on American exports to Iran. My idea was that if Iran could help solve the Arad case and its role could be publicly demonstrated to the Americans, the embargoes could be relaxed. Scowcroft said that solving the Arad case would surely help. Since Pérez de Cuéllar had asked me to go to Iran to seek Rafsanjani's help on the various outstanding cases, I would include the embargo proposition in my portfolio.

So I left on December 16 for Teheran and Damascus, attempting to finish up our business during the final fortnight of Pérez de Cuéllar's term or at least get answers to several interrelated questions: Would the Iranians continue to work toward the conclusion of our operations as they had promised, including the release of the bodies of Higgins and Buckley? Would the Americans signal their goodwill on behalf of the Israelis? Would that prompt the Iranians to help in somehow loosening the Hammadis' grip on the last two German hostages?

On a stopover in Frankfurt, I picked up what I thought might be a worthwhile chip. Reinhard Schlagenweit, the German diplomat handling the hostage dossier, gave me a statement to pass on to the Hammadi clan in Lebanon: The two jailed brothers would be permitted to receive visits from members of the family, individual visits could take place without a third person present, and the German authorities would favorably consider allowing them to serve their sentences in the same prison.

I arrived at my Teheran hotel at 5:45 A.M. on December 18 and was received by Rafsanjani by midday. He was accompanied by Mahmoud Vaezi of the Foreign Ministry. I presented a letter from Pérez de Cuéllar asking for help in finding the missing Israelis and told him how personally grateful I was to all the Iranians who had helped me. Rafsanjani said he had instructed Vaezi and Kharrazi to continue their efforts and had sent a special envoy to Lebanon to work for the release of the German hostages, but the Germans would also have to make some gestures.

I tried to link the possible release of Sheikh Obeid to news about Arad and told Rafsanjani that the Israelis would empty their prisons if the Arad case were solved. He said the releases should resume no matter what and that Iran had already done more to help find Arad than I could possibly imagine. "What makes this case complicated is the fact that the people originally involved have disappeared and there seems to be no way to trace information," Rafsanjani insisted. "However, the government of Iran will continue its efforts to resolve this matter because it is interested in getting all Lebanese detained by Israel released."

Finally he asked me about my professional plans. I answered, "My future is in the hands of God, and then the secretary-general." I subsequently met with Vaezi and Kharrazi on every possible remaining issue that I could close, and there were many. In the end, Vaezi gave me a tentative schedule of my meetings in Damascus on the Ron Arad case and other matters: December 19, meet with Akhtari; December 20, meet with Abdel Hadi Hammadi; December 21, meet with "others" about Ron Arad; December 22, meet with Hizbollah about the release of the two American bodies, as well as with another "unspecified" group in Beirut.

It would have been a busy program had it actually taken place. But by the time I arrived in Damascus, events had taken a turn for the worse: Israeli troops had just raided Hizbollah bases in south Lebanon north of the Security Zone and kidnapped three Lebanese. This, of course, raised doubts that I could deliver anything on behalf of the Israelis.

The Germans then delivered another blow. Having just briefed Vaezi on Bonn's message to the Hammadi clan, I learned that the German Justice Ministry had vetoed any relaxation of the prison rules for the brothers—not because the ministry objected per se but because the proposals Schlagenweit had given me also included a final request to release them early as permitted by law. The Justice Ministry refused even to address a request about the length of their sentences.

My diary reflected my sense of discouragement. Entry for December 19: "I have pushed the Iranians as far as Ron Arad was concerned, in every possible way. Even Cyrus Nasseri, who had just been visiting Iran for two days, got my point. They now know that I can no longer help them in Washington . . . and they have begun to doubt the fact that I actually still believe them and have told me as much. They said, 'We are getting signals from you that you think that we are lying to you.' "

In Damascus on December 20, I had no more cards to play. In my diary I was acutely aware of the looming deadline: "Time is running out. Only a miracle can move the whole case. However, after this morning's kidnapping by Israel in South Lebanon, I will need a double miracle."

When Zarif finally arrived in Damascus, he was surprised that I still had not received the bodies of Higgins and Buckley. Upset, I recalled the words of his president on September 11, when Rafsanjani had told the secretary-general that he would assist in their return. But then, nothing else seemed to be working either. By the end of the day on December 21, none of my meetings with Akhtari, Abdel Hadi Hammadi, or the "others" had taken place. The Iranian Embassy was doing its best to arrange them, but clearly nothing was happening. Ever since the release of Terry Anderson, the situation in Lebanon had become tense; there were those who had opposed the releases, and they found in the lack of reciprocation proof of their position. Meantime, the groups that had released the hostages were becoming concerned about their own security. The public talk in Washington about going after "terrorists" had only increased their fears. All this had fueled tensions between the groups in Lebanon and Teheran, which also affected me, since the Iranian Embassy in Damascus said that new threats against my life had been picked up by its people in Beirut.

As we headed toward Christmas and the midwinter hiatus in official activity, even in the Middle East, I called Pérez de Cuéllar and told him things looked bleak. The projected meetings had fallen through. Akhtari was ill, they had said, and Abdel Hadi Hammadi, the head of the clan, would meet me only in Beirut. Even the Iranians had vetoed that because it was obvious he wanted me in Beirut to kidnap me, or worse. I had to tell Zarif in a very strained meeting that we felt Iran had let us down; he replied that Iran feared we were only helping the Israelis, who were not keeping their word.

Three days before Christmas, Zarif told me Higgins's body would be released, but he did not know when or where. I alerted Jens Nielsen, the Danish major at OGB who had been so crucial to my work, and he located it twenty-four hours later; it had been wrapped in a black plastic trash bag and dumped beside a mosque near a south Beirut hospital. The hospital staff had placed it in the morgue and was about to dispose of it when the resourceful major turned up. Higgins's body had been refrigerated since his murder in 1988, so he could be identified quickly.

As the Western hostage affair was coming to a close, my own government became more eager to get information about Alberto Molinari, an Italian businessman who had lived most of his life in Beirut and had become a victim of intra-Lebanese feuding during the civil war. My hope of obtaining forensic proof of his death had not been fulfilled, even though I had raised the issue with the Iranians. But the Italian authorities weren't giving up: they sent a plane to Damascus so that at the end of my stay I could fly to Rome and meet with officials on the case. But the plane would have to wait. Before leaving Syria, I needed to attend to several important matters on a human level. I wrote two letters—one to Abdullah, one to Abdel Hadi Hammadi—conveying my personal commitment to resolving all the cases of the MIAs and POWs in the area; each of them, I hoped, would work for the same objectives.

I also messaged Lubrani, summarizing my meetings and my difficulties, most notably the Israeli raid and kidnapping of three Lebanese two days earlier that had been most unhelpful, and conveying my profound sorrow that I had not been successful in helping Mrs. Arad. I promised him that somehow I would continue the search. He thanked me and sent holiday greetings to me and my family, a bittersweet message trying to maintain human relations despite our mutual disappointment.

Finally, just before my departure, I managed to obtain a videotape of the two German hostages. It was the first proof of life that their governments and their families had seen in many, many months.

The Italians flew me to Rome very early on Christmas Eve to talk about Molinari, but I stayed only a few hours before heading home to New York; I got there just as Christmas Eve was turning into Christmas Day.

It was Christmas Day plus one before Buckley's remains turned up. Once again, the body had been dumped on the street, and once again Major Nielsen located it, using his extensive network of Arabic-speaking contacts. For this and much else, I later made it my business to ensure that a letter of commendation for Nielsen went to the chief of staff of the Danish Army over the secretary-general's name. I also contacted the Canadian, Icelandic, and Finnish governments through their UN missions to request that they give official recognition to their people in Damascus and Beirut for the help I had received. Loyalty runs both ways, and it's a terrible mistake to forget people who help you.

There was a round of messages and exchanges during the final week of the most tumultuous year of my life as the Iranian and German governments and I tried to engineer the release of the German hostages before Pérez de Cuéllar moved off the stage. It came to naught: Abdel Hadi Hammadi flatly refused to set them free. It was 12:15 A.M. in New York on January 1, 1992, when I concluded my last communication with the government of Iran for the year just past.

Later that day, Javier Pérez de Cuéllar formally ended his ten-year run as secretary-general of the United Nations, yielding his gavel to Boutros Boutros-Ghali (but not before delivering, after midnight on December 31, an agreement to end the civil war in El Salvador). A very fitting closure. I was losing a boss whose diplomatic skills and personal confidence had made my great political adventure possible. Our personal relationship had far transcended our official one. I still had more to achieve. Even though work remained, I felt that a chapter of my life was closing. My emotions had been on fast-forward for the better part of two years, ranging from the great sadness of admitting failure to Mrs. Arad to the intense gratification I had felt upon looking into the faces of the hostages on their release. It was something I had never experienced before or probably ever would again.

I had no idea what would happen next in my UN career, except that I wanted it to continue when this was over. The office of the secretary-general had achieved an unprecedented level of importance and effectiveness in helping governments and peoples. Our mission was to transcend politics, to give the United Nations a human face when it dealt with the critical issues. The United Nations under Pérez de Cuéllar had enabled me, as well as others in his office of unarmed commandos, to assist in bringing an end to wars, saving lives, and securing the liberty of individuals. We had achieved a new role for the secretary-general—peacemaker, not just peacekeeper—and I hoped the new administration of Boutros Boutros-Ghali would not only husband what we had wrought but build on it as well.

But before I could move forward to a new agenda in 1992, the old one still beckoned. I had made it clear to everyone involved that I was committed to my Lebanon mission, and I hoped to be given the leeway to complete it. I would make one last trip into the lion's den.

CHAPTER 17

The Last Hostage

✍

M Y NEW BOSS WASTED NO TIME in imparting a new perspective on the matter of the hostages. On January 2, 1992, at 10:30 A.M., I had my first one-on-one meeting with Secretary-General Boutros Boutros-Ghali; he had been in office one hour. I presented to him the various dossiers I was working on, including an update on the hostage file. He said that resolving the outstanding problems would generate little public interest in the press or elsewhere and that the issue as a whole no longer had as much "return" as before now that the American nationals had been freed! It was an ominous beginning to what would become a very difficult relationship.

Since he did not tell me directly to stop working on the remaining issues, I would continue to work toward the release of the German hostages, making plans to seek continued Iranian support from Foreign Minister Velayati and to meet with the Germans in Bonn. But there was more to come at that first meeting. His first suggestion for resolving the German hostage dilemma was ethically worrisome to me: he instructed me to propose that the Germans shift the Hammadi prisoners to a form of house arrest usually reserved for white-collar criminals. I was outraged. Mohammed Ali Hammadi had been sentenced to serve fifteen years in prison because of the assassination of an American citizen during the hijacking of an American airplane in 1985. He could be considered for early release after thirteen years, or by the year 2000. Further, German legislation did not allow for house arrest in such crimes. It would take no more than a few hours for the Germans to dispose of the idea.

I returned to my office, disillusioned. Boutros-Ghali was seen to be an intellectual, a man somehow above politics. But to me the reality was quite the contrary: he had too much politics in his bones. Although he had campaigned for the office and had been elected on the promise of serving as secretary-general for only one five-year term, "this man will be running for a second term, and we are leaving the UN," I said to my family later that day. That decision, in turn, put an even higher premium on my finishing up my last important assignment at the United Nations as quickly as possible.

I moved quickly to regain the momentum. Judy Karam and I had a long discussion with Lubrani and his two negotiating partners, who insisted that I press for a meeting with Azkari, the Iranian Revolutionary Guard leader in the Bekaa Valley. They thought Arad might be held in Syria at an Iranian Revolutionary Guard base just inside the border that had some kind of immunity from Syrian sovereignty. I, in turn, suggested that they offer to return the plane in which the Syrian pilot had defected since they could not offer to exchange the pilot himself. But when I offered to meet Sheikh Obeid in prison, Lubrani said, "The chapter with Hizbollah is finished as far as these missing people are concerned. What we need now does not come from Hizbollah."

On January 7, I flew to Frankfurt. Fog grounded the government helicopters to Bonn, so we sped along the autobahn in a motorcade of three Mercedes limousines at about 130 miles an hour. The press was invited so the government could demonstrate that the process was continuing. I invented all sorts of possibilities—eleven of them, to be exact, and all within the law—to discuss with the Germans. They ranged from allowing the Hammadi brothers to play soccer together to the most ingenious, I thought, which would be a program of artificial insemination for their wives, since one of the Hammadis' complaints was that an Arab husband without children was a man held in contempt.

German Foreign Minister Genscher wrote the new secretary-general on January 10, appealing to him "to continue this noble tradition and to apply your personal reputation and the high authority of your office to this humanitarian task. There can be no return to normality in Lebanon as long as hostages like the two Germans are held there." He was absolutely correct. Even the president of Lebanon recognized that his country would remain an international pariah until all hostages were freed. Why Boutros-Ghali, a scholar of the Middle East and himself an Egyptian, had to be reminded of this by a German politician was beyond me.

Late that day, I went on to Vienna to meet Velayati, which raised an unexpected complication: the Germans had publicized my prospective meeting with the Iranian foreign minister, and this close connection was too much for Iran. I conferred instead with Vaezi, who said the best thing I could do would be to go to Damascus and meet the leaders of the Hammadi clan. He said the Iranians realized there was no hope of early release for Mohammed Ali Hammadi so they were concentrating their efforts on his younger brother, Abbas, whose crime was "only" smuggling explosives. The Iranians wanted him released as soon as the law permitted.

But all this diplomatic activity and invention guaranteed nothing. The Iranians finally admitted that it would be very difficult for them to arrange a meeting for me with Azkari, even though he was an Iranian. I had to assume that his "ayatollah of reference"—the one to whom he looked for guidance—did not approve of further meetings taking place. Nevertheless, the Iranians wanted me to go to Damascus to meet at least with the Hammadis, a meeting the Germans supported as well.

The reason for meeting with them in Damascus and not in Beirut is that the Iranians had heard reports that Abdel Hadi Hammadi wanted me dead because he saw me as an opponent of a straight swap between his two brothers and the German hostages. Until that time, Abdel Hadi Hammadi had refused to meet with me in Damascus.

Meanwhile, the German Foreign Ministry came up with an ingenious idea—probably too ingenious. They proposed that the Iranian mullahs declare a fatwa against the Hammadi clan, the same kind of decree the Ayatollah Khomeini had issued against the writer Salman Rushdie. The only problem with that, we soon realized, was that the Hammadis were perfectly capable of retaliating by killing one of their German hostages, maybe both.

In pressing me to go to Damascus, the Germans did so in a manner that taught us all something about the increasingly pharaonic nature of Boutros-Ghali's administration. In mid-February, Hans-Joachim Vergau, deputy chief of the German Mission to the United Nations, who was sitting in for his absent ambassador, received instructions from Bonn to discuss the hostages with the secretary-general. His instructions specified that he was to ask that I be sent to the Middle East. I passed on Vergau's request to be received by the secretary-general. For a week there was no response. Boutros-Ghali finally replied that he did not receive ordinary diplomats—ambassadors, perhaps, but not very often, and certainly nothing below that.

When the Iranians met Boutros-Ghali, I was not present. Neither was I briefed by the secretary-general. I *was* briefed by Kharrazi, who told me that the secretary-general had not reacted in any way when the Iranian ambassador had told him that his country was prepared to continue working for the hostages' release. He had let the issue pass without comment, and Kharrazi had remarked on this both to his government and to the Germans. I tried to defend the secretary-general as a matter of duty and said that while he might not see the issue as a high priority, he was very much available, and in any case I had been pursuing it actively with his full knowledge. But Kharrazi wondered why his government should stick its neck out if it did not know where Boutros-Ghali stood.

When I brought these comments to Boutros-Ghali's notice, he told me to tell Kharrazi that I was fully authorized to pursue my discussions with the Iranians and that he had remained silent during their meeting because he had been pressed for time. He added that he was even interested in visiting Teheran soon and that he was ready to intervene whenever the Iranian government asked him.

By this time, my movements had begun to be heavily circumscribed. Boutros-Ghali ordered all senior officials like myself to obtain written approval from him for any travel, not only outside the United States but within it as well. I submitted travel requests but received no replies. I could no longer just walk into the secretary-general's office for a chat, but I succeeded in obtaining an audience with him to explain that the Germans and the Iranians wanted me to go to Damascus to arrange a meeting with the Hammadis.

"But, Mr. Picco," Boutros-Ghali said with a straight face, "I can receive the Hammadis myself. Why do you have to go to Damascus? I can talk to them myself in New York."

I repeated my request three times. He insisted that the Hammadis could simply come to New York. I tried to explain reality to him as gently as possible: "They hardly go to Damascus, and once in a while to Teheran. A trip to New York would be a bit audacious for them." The Hammadis were the security apparatus of Hizbollah, and Abdel Hadi, in particular, had been with Imad Moughniya at the very core of hostage taking in Lebanon. Together they headed the Special Security Apparatus (SSA) of Hizbollah.

I was astonished by his lack of knowledge and his expectation that people involved in terrorist operations could easily travel outside Lebanon, even to the United States. I asked if he would mind if I told Genscher that he was prepared to receive the Hammadis in New York. He said I should tell the Germans exactly that. The Germans were amused and too well mannered to show it, but Zarif showed less restraint when I told him.

Boutros-Ghali was displeased by the amount of publicity I was receiving. Jean-Claude Aimé was appointed *chef de cabinet,* and he had no choice but to enforce tighter control over my movements. The press soon began to report that the hostage process was collapsing. They did not know the half of it.

I tried to use the press to spread the word that the fight for the hostages was not over. My faithful helpers at OGB in Beirut messaged me that hostage kidnappings might resume, based on what their operatives were hearing in the streets. Some Beirut newspapers reported that the Hizbollah hard line was now arguing that releasing the hostages had been a mistake because Israel would not dare to attack Hizbollah if they were still held captive.

By mid-January, Lubrani and his team were in New York. He was now the chief Israeli negotiator with Lebanon on matters having to do with the Mideast peace process, so he was taking advantage of his new position to pursue every possible channel with his Lebanese counterpart. He also discussed with me the prospect of somehow packaging the German case and Ron Arad. For my part, I was still hoping to speak to Azkari and to Mustafa Durani, allegedly the last person to have handled Arad. The Israelis maintained that Arad had probably been taken to Teheran for interrogation. I had doubts that the Iranian authorities would expose themselves at that level even if they were involved. But if the Israelis were right, the chances of seeing Arad alive again were very small indeed.

Meanwhile, Iran bashing in the American press had started afresh. On January 21, 1992, I paid my first visit of the new year to General Scowcroft. He implied that perhaps something could be done about compensation for the Iranian Airbus that had been shot down in 1988, or in one area of the sanctions, but he could not communicate anything more until the following month. Iran's request to be removed from the U.S. list of terrorist states was, of course, out of the question.

The German justice minister, Klaus Kinkel, who would later become foreign minister, visited Teheran on February 3 and was asked by Rafsanjani why I was not in Damascus. But every piece of the puzzle seemed to become more and more complicated. Rafsanjani had told Kinkel that he was now expecting something: a gesture from the Americans on the interest accrued on the assets frozen since 1981, which in his view had now mushroomed to $10 billion.

That same day, I learned from Zarif that the forensic evidence on Molinari's death was now with Ambassador Akhtari, but for some reason that was inexplicable, even to Zarif, he did not want to give it up. The table was becoming cluttered again, and grapeshot was in the air.

On February 12, British foreign correspondent Robert Fisk wrote a critical piece on the stalemate in hostage negotiations for his newspaper, The Independent. Fisk was highly respected for his seasoned and accurate reporting on Beirut, as well as for his book on Lebanon, Pity the Nation. His article, which included references to the death threats against me by the Hammadi family, did not go unnoticed in international circles. The operation was fraying at the edges—in public.

Four days later, an Israeli missile killed Sheikh Abbas Mussawi, secretary-general of Hizbollah and a relative moderate in the party, and his family while they were riding in their car in south Lebanon. It could not have come at a worse time. Needless to say, the pro-Iranian groups were up in arms, hardly in a mood to negotiate—and here I was, making plans to go to Damascus.

My time for this operation was almost up, which posed problems. On the one hand, I could not make promises or offer my word if I would not be around to deliver; on the other, any indication that I was on the way out would increase my personal risk in Beirut, since speculation about my departure would erode my credibility and perhaps justify action against me. In any event, I spoke to no one—not even my assistant, Judith Karam—about my plans to leave the United Nations. At the same time, to be literally correct, I began speaking as if the commitments I was making were coming from the United Nations rather than from me personally. Alternatively, I would pledge my support "in whatever capacity I may find myself." I could not say I was leaving the United Nations, but I tried hard not to mislead anyone.

By late February, I was once again trying to craft a package tying together the German hostages, Arad, and the Lebanese detainees. My plan was to persuade the Israelis to do something for which the Germans could then take credit and use that as a lever to help free their hostages. The Israelis, in turn, could also use it to spark the search for Arad. The idea was for all sides to work together in private so that they could appear victorious in public—a win-win game. My role, apart from assembling the package out of sight, was to serve as guarantor for the Hammadi brothers' prison conditions in Germany.

The problem with my diplomatic construct was that the players were not eager to provide the raw materials. The Israelis would release no more prisoners unconditionally. The Iranians, meanwhile, had developed excellent economic and political relations with Germany and could see no reason to draw in the Israelis, whose missing men were no concern of theirs. As early as January, Velayati began saying in public that it was time for the German hostages to go home, that Iran was doing its best, and that the whole thing would be wrapped up in a month. The Iranians actually wanted to help the Germans—and they proved it after the Israelis assassinated Mussawi.

The Hizbollah leader had been replaced by Sheikh Hassan Nasserallah, and in less than a fortnight after his installation, he said his predecessor's killing should not affect the operation to free the German hostages. This was a clear sign of Iranian influence. "We have heard that Picco will be coming to the region," Nasserallah added. "I think our brothers will not mind meeting him and listening to what he has to say or seeing what he brings. In light of this, Hizbollah will decide whether to respond positively."

As agreed in late January, I met with Scowcroft on February 25. (By that time, Boutros-Ghali had named me assistant secretary-general for political affairs and ensconced me in a huge office on the thirty-fifth floor—the same floor, ironically, where I had begun my UN career nearly twenty years earlier.)

There were two items on the agenda: Scowcroft's evaluation of the death of Mussawi and his family and "goodwill begets goodwill." On the first point, he said he thought perhaps the Israelis had received a strong indication that Arad was dead, then retaliated by killing Mussawi. On the second, he hinted at the possibility of allowing the sale of some civilian aircraft to Iran. He also suggested that there was some hope for relaxing, to a small degree, some of the sanctions against Iran. But again, he asked for one more month.

Lubrani and his team, including the deputy chief of military intelligence, came to see me on February 28. Ori Slonim, a key team member, had resigned and returned to his law practice. Judy Karam sat in on the meeting. We were all pessimistic. Arguing for an Israeli move on the detainees, I told him that my objective was not just to liberate people but to contribute to the deradicalization of Lebanon, and someone had to take the first step in breaking the cycle of violence. Not only did I believe this profoundly, but I had nothing else in my hand to help him. I argued that a stable Lebanon would eventually benefit Israel. In addition, the Lebanese government had set up a committee of ministers from all sects to work for the Germans' release.

But Lubrani insisted that I try to meet Durani, the Lebanese security officer in the Bekaa Valley, and Azkari, the Iranian Revolutionary Guard leader, the last two people known to have seen Arad alive. The Israelis had begun to realize that things were slipping out of our hands.

On March 5, Lubrani was back in New York, and this time he was accompanied by another general so secret they would not reveal his name. We explored all the possibilities on Arad. The general said he thought the Germans would soon be released. Once they were free, the Israelis knew they would definitely be out of the game. As a result, I was still trying to suggest a surprise move by the Israelis that could break the stalemate and perhaps get them something in return. Surprises in the Middle East, I knew, are used by politicians to move impossible situations forward.

The general was up to speed on the continuing diplomacy. He knew a great deal about the Iranian and German exchanges, but he could see that Israel needed to come up with its own card and pressed for my meeting with Durani and Azkari. The general was sure that Durani had information, and so were the Iranians. (In fact, it is clear now that Durani did not. The Israelis kidnapped him two years later and tried to get him to talk in exchange for his freedom. At this writing, four years after that, he is still in an Israeli jail, but no progress has been made on the Arad case.)

But "complications" were always abundant in this difficult journey. Germany's support for a resolution on human rights in Iran at the UN

Human Rights Commission in Geneva prompted a declaration by Iran on March 6 that it was no longer prepared to cooperate with Germany on the hostage cases. It would be a short-lived position.

I left for Germany on March 7 to discuss my proposals about relaxing the Hammadi brothers' prison conditions. I came up with an idea to increase pressure on the Hammadi family. The Germans had already persuaded their partners in the European Community to block reconstruction funds for Lebanon, and I suggested that they isolate Lebanon even further by making the Hammadis appear an obstacle to its reentry into the community of nations. The Germans agreed, so now I had another card in my hand.

Lubrani called me in Frankfurt to say that his boss wanted to see me as soon as possible. I agreed to go to Tel Aviv but warned him that the operation would be set back if I returned empty-handed. I also said my trip had to be kept secret. At Ben-Gurion International Airport the plane stopped on the tarmac to discharge me into a waiting van, which whisked me away. I was taken to a nondescript office building and into a long, narrow room in which ten generals were sitting in an oval of chairs. Among them was Ehud Barak, chief of staff of the Israeli armed forces. I had the impression that I was facing a court of final military appeals. The meeting lasted two and a half hours and was exhausting because I could not wring a single concession out of them. Actually, they insisted that the Iranians and Germans were about to conclude their deal and that I was no longer needed for that operation. They were wrong on both counts.

The heart of our discussion was that they would allow me to visit Sheikh Obeid only after I got confirmation of my meeting with Azkari and Durani. I said that I was less interested in visiting their prisoners than in starting an exchange of messages between the prisoners and their families via the Red Cross. Until I got confirmation of my meeting, they refused to promise even that, although such exchanges are permitted by international law.

In fact, approval of the exchange of messages was really my fallback position in case the Iranians were unable to arrange the meeting with Durani and Azkari. Even though things often fall apart, the key to success is working at them hard enough and persistently enough to obtain something eventually. As I learned from the hostages themselves after their release, the process itself had given them hope and helped keep their spirits from ebbing away. The alternative is to do nothing, which means simply reacting to what others do. Anyone who does not try to lead the game quickly becomes irrelevant.

I could see myself sneaking out of Israel with nothing to show for my trip, so I decided to try one more time and asked for another meeting with Barak on the following day. I prepared a six-point plan for Israel to start obtaining what it sought:

1. Agreement for me to meet Sheikh Obeid in Khiam prison.
2. Arrangement for Sheikh Obeid's family to visit him.
3. Agreement for me to meet Durani and Azkari.
4. Meeting with Durani and Azkari.
5. Visit by the International Red Cross to Khiam and to prisons in Israel.
6. Return of the body of one of the dead Israelis and release of an unspecified number of Lebanese prisoners.

When I met Barak, he asked me if I thought the plan would work. I said, "*Inshallah*," Arabic for "God willing."

Back in New York on March 15, I contacted the Iranians and told them that if they could arrange a meeting with Durani and Azkari, things would come from the Israelis, although I declined to say what. We all should do things based on their merits, I added, and it was common humanity for them to help the Israelis learn Arad's fate.

On March 17, President Rafsanjani instructed the Iranian Mission in New York to "reactivate Picco," which meant that they would soon ask me to return to Damascus.

But by this time, Zarif and Kharrazi were not especially worried about the Israelis. They began pressing me to learn what goodwill gesture they could expect from the Americans for having helped deliver their hostages. I was getting hints from Scowcroft that they could expect very little, but I was hoping against hope that these hints were wrong. I had intense brainstorming sessions with Zarif and Kharrazi, and by April 20 we decided I should write another letter to the Hammadis explaining precisely how I could help them with the Germans. Basically, it would say that I would continue to ensure that their sons and brothers would be treated well in prison.

Meanwhile, on my return, Boutros Boutros-Ghali informed me through an under secretary who was also my boss, Vladimir Petrovsky, that I had a new assignment. I was appointed chief negotiator in the deal being brokered by the United Nations for Iraq to exchange oil for food as a modification of the Gulf War sanctions. I succeeded Kofi Annan in that post. The job was important, but it was strange that the secretary-general had not discussed the appointment with me before making it, especially given my other responsibilities. Then again, his management style was a far cry from his predecessor's.

On the same day, I received a brief excerpt from the secretary-general's office of the official notes of his meeting with the German ambassador, Detlev Garf zu Rantza. The passage read, "The Ambassador expressed his government's appreciation for Mr. Picco's assistance with regard to the German hostages in Lebanon. The government has great esteem for Mr. Picco's modest and silent approach and was aware that his activities entailed personal risk. The government hoped that he would be able to come closer to a solution." According to the excerpt, the secretary-general replied that he attached great importance to quiet diplomacy and noted that, as a minister of his own government, he had been able to pursue contacts with top officials of South Africa for three years before the newspapers printed anything. Unfortunately, Boutros-Ghali continued, "it is difficult to pursue quiet diplomacy within the United Nations building."

A few days later, Lubrani called to report that a member of the Israeli Parliament had just met with Boutros-Ghali, who insisted he was working quietly on the Arad case and had sent three emissaries to the Middle East to solve it. Lubrani wanted to know what was going on, and so did I. When I asked Boutros-Ghali, he denied he had ever said any such thing.

For me, this had now become a matter of conscience. I was determined to leave the United Nations and had accepted a job with a multinational company. The company promised to make no announcement until I resigned, because if the news came out and I had to go back to Beirut once more, I would never have gotten out alive. I wanted to prove to myself beyond a reasonable doubt that I had exhausted all possibilities of assisting the hostages and the MIAs, and I also promised myself that I would not leave as long as I felt I could still help.

Three months had passed with no concrete progress in resolving the remaining part of the hostage affair. I had to work with what I had, which was very little. The Israelis were ready to release more prisoners and to allow me to visit their prisons, but only if I met with Durani and Azkari on the Arad case. The Iranians wanted something for the Shiite groups in Lebanon as well as more news on the fate of their four diplomats who had disappeared in Beirut a decade earlier; they also wanted the release of the German hostages, Thomas Kemptner and Heinrich Struebig, who had been kidnapped in May 1989. The Hammadi clan in Lebanon insisted on a straight swap: the brothers held in Germany for Kemptner and Struebig. The Germans said the best they could do was to improve the treatment of the jailed prisoners—based, of course, on their laws. The only positive aspect of all this was Teheran's agreement that a straight swap was not going to happen.

I had one hope, which was that the response to the release of the American hostages, namely the goodwill gesture President Bush had suggested on January 20, 1989, would be given to me soon and I could use it to put together another package with the remaining fragments I had left. But on April 2, Scowcroft telephoned and said that Washington was unlikely to lift the economic sanctions because Iran had turned to terrorism abroad, even in the United States. He then asked me to meet with him the following week. According to the new restrictions imposed by Boutros-Ghali on high-level officials, I filed my travel plans with the chief of staff, Jean-Claude Aimé, to get permission. I specifically requested the Washington trip to see the national security adviser to the president of the United States. No member of the Secretariat was in touch with him, neither in the past nor the present. Such high-level contacts could not but have strengthened the office of the secretary-general. In this specific case, it was simply necessary in the ongoing operation. No reply came until April 9, the day before my scheduled meeting with Scowcroft.

But at 11 P.M., a senior official, Alvaro de Soto, telephoned me at home and apologetically explained that permission had in fact not been given. My patience with the chief of staff and Boutros-Ghali was wearing very thin. I was trying to save lives, and they were playing petty bureaucratic games. Accordingly, I told de Soto, who had also served under Pérez de Cuéllar for ten years, that he had two choices—either to pretend this call did not happen and call back in half an hour or simply to report that he had tried to reach me in vain. When the phone rang thirty minutes later, I didn't answer.

The following morning I took the 7:30 shuttle to Washington; formally, it would be a half day of sick leave, the first in my entire UN career. I had real reason to feel sick soon enough: when I arrived at his office, Scowcroft wasted no time explaining that there would be "no goodwill to beget goodwill." I was flabbergasted. I had worked for three and a half years on the assumption that the expression "Goodwill begets goodwill" was the engine of the entire operation. What's more, when repeatedly asked by high Iranian officials for further explanation, I had made it clear that these words should be enough until they became reality.

The general argued that the Iranians were conducting terrorism around the world. In particular, there was the case of an Iranian national who had just been killed in Connecticut in an apparent case of mistaken identity with an Iranian dissident. Other terrorist operations, according to the general, were being prepared in Europe and elsewhere in retribution for the assassination of Hizbollah leader Abbas Mussawi. Finally, Scowcroft mentioned Iran's nuclear program as yet another reason for nullifying the promise of a goodwill gesture. In a flash, I now found myself in the position of having unwittingly lied to my Iranian interlocutors for almost four years.

As I departed, Scowcroft thanked me for what we had achieved but apologized that he could not help me anymore. Within two weeks, the press would report that U.S. officials had uncovered "strong indications" that Iranian diplomats had helped plan the March 17 bombing of the Israeli Embassy in Buenos Aires. And six weeks after that, a Berlin discotheque called the Mykonos was blown up by Iranian agents because the Iranian Kurdish opposition congregated there.

To my knowledge, the 1992 terrorist attack in Berlin was the last operation directly connected to Iranian officials. But none of this was known to me when my house of cards collapsed with two Germans still in captivity, many Lebanese detained without due process, and the Israeli MIAs still unaccounted for. Two days after seeing Scowcroft, in a meeting with Ambassador Kharrazi, I indicated that perhaps it would be best if the entire hostage matter were to come to an end without any more quids pro quos, real or imagined. I also added that my time was running very short. Kharrazi may have understood that my relations with Boutros-Ghali had gone from bad to worse and that I might be moved to a different assignment, so he asked me to go to Teheran and Damascus as quickly as possible. But he still offered little hope that I could meet Durani and Azkari.

Boutros Boutros-Ghali had been a very close friend of the shah of Iran. He had even hosted the former Iranian leader at his villa in Egypt after the shah had left Teheran. In April 1992, he visited Iran with his wife, a trip tied in with a visit to Pakistan. He never knew that his trip to Teheran had been the subject of several discussions between Ambassador Kharrazi and myself. I had suggested that to underscore Iran's great hospitality, Mrs. Ghali should be received by Mrs. Rafsanjani. The Iranian president's wife never appeared in public at these kinds of functions, and it would be a significant gesture to have her entertain Mrs. Ghali personally as a sign of respect for the secretary-general's office. Mrs. Ghali was Jewish to boot, which would only add to the drama and symbolism of being entertained by the Muslim Mrs. Rafsanjani.

And that's the way it turned out, with Mrs. Ghali the first and last wife of a foreign dignitary ever to be entertained by Mrs. Rafsanjani. When he returned, Boutros-Ghali boasted to me about the importance of his visit because of the unprecedented gesture toward his wife. He never learned how I had arranged it all by drawing on my line of credit with the Iranians.

But this was nothing compared with the damage he created during his visit to Teheran, undoing months of diplomatic preparation in one stroke. By then, I had been dealing with the Iranian government for nearly a decade. I was never asked to prepare a briefing for his trip, but I knew that the hostage issue would come up in his conversations. To avoid crossing wires, I needed to alert him to the state of the negotiations. Knowing that at best he would skim over them, I simply wrote three lines, essentially saying that Rafsanjani had agreed with me that a straight swap of the German hostages for the Hammadi brothers could not happen.

The message was sent to Boutros-Ghali in Pakistan. The meeting took place in Teheran on April 26. Amazingly, he told Rafsanjani that he would recommend a swap of the two German hostages for the imprisoned Hammadi brothers. Zarif later reported to me that Rafsanjani had been ecstatic; the president wondered why I had told him such an exchange could not be done when my boss was saying it could. After the meeting, Boutros-Ghali called German Foreign Minister Hans-Dietrich Genscher to tell him about the deal; Genscher was livid, as I soon found out from the minister himself and from other German diplomats. Germany, Genscher told the secretary-general, could and would do no such thing.

On April 30, Boutros-Ghali returned to New York and called me into his office with Vladimir Petrovsky, under secretary for political affairs and my direct superior, to complain that we had persuaded him to visit Teheran. But at the conclusion of his tirade against us, he boasted that the visit had been a great success because he had made a three-point agreement with Rafsanjani for the release of the Germans. First the German hostages would be liberated; then we would contact the Hammadi family in Beirut; then the German government would reopen the case against the Hammadis. "I have spoken to Mr. Genscher, who has accepted the plan, except for point three. But since I had already promised point three to Rafsanjani, I could not go back." Amazing!

Petrovsky, a veteran of the Soviet diplomatic service, was a good friend and a fine human being, and would have performed acrobatics to help me if he could. But he had no choice but to agree with his boss. I said, "Excuse me, sir, if Mr. Genscher does not accept point three, there is no agreement."

Boutros-Ghali replied dismissively. "Basically, Rafsanjani has agreed to release the Germans."

"But, Mr. Secretary-General, he isn't holding the Germans. How can he release them? If it had been up to him, they would have been freed three months ago. And even if he did have them, the quid pro quo you promised cannot be delivered."

"Well, go to Damascus and fix it," he replied.

As I suspected, following the brilliant meeting between Boutros-Ghali and Rafsanjani, an Iranian envoy had gone to Lebanon to inform the Hammadis of the offer made by the new secretary-general of the United Nations. Ambassador Kharrazi told me this on May 6, adding that my meeting with Abdel Hadi Hammadi was now being discussed. He also suggested that since a new foreign minister was taking over in Bonn, I should probably stop in Germany on my way to Damascus. This made sense, especially since Klaus Kinkel had been minister of justice until then and was familiar with the case, and the Germans agreed. But

Boutros-Ghali had cleared me only for travel to Damascus, and the word through Petrovsky was that he saw no reason for me to visit Germany since he had already dealt with the Bonn government. Lubrani, meantime, was asking for a meeting in Europe as well. I had only one option: I got my authorized ticket to Damascus, with a stopover in Frankfurt.

My meeting with Kinkel did not reveal any new German position. He had promised the American government that the Hammadi brothers would not be exchanged for the German hostages. He told me he had met with Abdel Hadi Hammadi, whom he described as particularly cruel. "I spoke to the man myself a few times," Kinkel explained. "He is a small man physically, and he even has small hands, but you can see how cruel he is. On the legal front, there will be no change whatsoever. There is no possibility of an early release." He added that he had also explained this to Rafsanjani a few weeks earlier, and Rafsanjani had said that the only people who could influence the Hammadis were the religious leaders, not political leaders. Kinkel seemed highly pessimistic about the release of the German hostages. The German government, he said, could not budge on the sentence because "the gravity of the crime is just too outrageous."

So much for Boutros-Ghali's deal to free the German hostages! I saw Lubrani at Frankfurt Airport, and the first thing he asked me was whether the secretary-general had discussed Arad on his visit to Teheran. "My dear Uri," I replied, "I don't know the answer to your question. He has not mentioned it to me, and neither have the Iranians." Lubrani said nothing, and we continued our discussion. With disappointment written all over his face, he finally told me, "You're going to Damascus only for the Germans. Our case is forgotten." The case was not forgotten; I had just been unable to get anything on the search for Ron Arad from the other side.

I was in Damascus on May 22, and the back-and-forth with Ambassador Akhtari and the Iranian Embassy became even more frantic because the Israelis had resumed bombing in south Lebanon. The situation had become so tense that Foreign Minister Velayati had gone to Beirut for the first time, at great personal risk, apparently to confront the Hammadis. However, his visit had produced no concrete results, and he had returned to Teheran empty-handed.

I spoke to Akhtari after Velayati's arrival in Beirut. "You have to know that the Hammadis have come here to try to intimidate me and my people," Akhtari said, "and they told me that if you go to Beirut, the least

they would do is capture you, so we are still hoping to have a contact between you and the family in Damascus. Things are very difficult." I spent
the next day at the UN office in Damascus trying to devise new options.
I left very late, and as I walked past the Iranian Embassy I saw a stream of
parked cars with Lebanese license plates—big Mercedeses with tinted
windows. I suspected a meeting with Hizbollah or a similar group was
taking place, and as I walked past, I felt a flashback of anxiety, reminding
me of my nights in Beirut. I spotted a young man walking out of the embassy toward the cars and immediately recognized him as a member of
Hizbollah by his informal uniform: a beard, a gray, long-sleeved collar-
less shirt buttoned to the top, and black trousers.

On May 27, in another late-night meeting with Akhtari, he confronted me with more problems in Beirut. I was still trying to obtain the
forensic information about the Italian hostage Molinari, which he again
refused to give me, and to arrange meetings with Abdel Hadi Hammadi
and Azkari. On May 29, he said the meeting with the Hammadis could
take place only in seven days. I was furious and phoned Zarif in New York
to vent my frustrations.

When I met Akhtari the next day, I told him that I would stay in Damascus only one more day and that he must persuade the Hammadis to release
one German quickly. When that was done, I would return to Damascus in
a few days to meet with them. I then warned Akhtari that if this were not
possible, I would have to inform the secretary-general that I had to abandon my efforts. He again repeated that the Hammadis were not under his
control, but perhaps if I met with the other groups, they might put pressure on the Hammadi clan to release the Germans unconditionally.

I cabled Petrovsky and Boutros-Ghali, informing them that things in
Damascus were moving more slowly than expected and that I was planning to shift to another location: Beirut. Up to that point, there had not
been one word of compassion for the two German hostages or the Israeli
MIAs from the thirty-eighth floor of the UN Building. The transition to a
less kind, less gentle United Nations had been completed.

On May 31, Zarif called to say that Akhtari finally seemed to realize I
was not bluffing. The previous day, I had proposed a two-stage release of
the Germans, to start in early June. I had received two letters written by
the German hostages for their families and had delivered them to the
German Embassy in Damascus. (Reciprocal letters from the Hammadi

brothers were conveyed a few days later.) At the German Embassy, I asked about rumors I had heard that another channel was also being used. Within a half hour, Bonn replied that I was the only channel. Things were starting to move.

I left for Europe for two days to await my meeting with Hammadi. Velayati, the Iranian foreign minister, was due back in Damascus on June 1. I cabled New York to let them know but warned that the Hammadis were still sticking to a hard line and not to expect a resolution while Velayati was in the area, lest the connection with Iran look too obvious. Then Zarif called me on June 2 to say that Akhtari had agreed to my proposal to work for the release of the first German hostage. But I had to wait for my meeting with Abdel Hadi Hammadi for a couple more days. I went to Milan to sign—in total secrecy—my new contract with the multinational corporation I would join after leaving the United Nations. I had not yet set a departure date; Boutros-Ghali would get my resignation only after the release of the German hostages.

That same day, I flew back to Damascus. Aboard the plane I realized to my shock that the flight would be making a stop in Beirut. My anxiety level rose when a passenger who had no documents delayed our departure. We finally boarded, I took my assigned seat, and a man with a mustache on his rather surprised face greeted me in English. I had no idea who he was, but when he was walking down the aisle to get off in Beirut, he stopped by my seat and said, "Hostages, right?" Then he walked out. There was probably an innocent explanation for this mysterious stranger, but I never found out what it was, and the plane could not take off quickly enough to suit me.

In Damascus, the situation had not clarified. A German official informed me that Velayati, who had gone from Damascus to Beirut, had remained there longer than expected to do all he could. Then Zarif called to say he had tried to reach me before I left Milan to tell me not to return to Damascus because "complications" were developing despite the presence of his foreign minister. I told him, "This is the end of the line for me, Javad. I will have to take the consequences, whatever they may be." The next day Zarif said that Velayati understood my predicament but the situation in Beirut was out of control and there was no reason for me to remain in Damascus.

I cabled Petrovsky:

As of Friday, 5 June, the situation can be summarized as follows: On the basis of the meeting between the SG and Rafsanjani, the Iranian side has sent to the area at different phases the Deputy Foreign Minister, a personal envoy of the President and the Foreign Minister himself. On their suggestion I came to the area on the 21st of May to pursue the matter which had already been on the table for some time. The German authorities at all levels, both in Bonn and in Teheran, have indicated full support for the UN. The family [the Hammadis] involved has tried to renegotiate the package but now has taken a very emotional and even aggressive posture. On 5 June Velayati conveyed to me that despite all efforts we were not there yet. It is my assessment that eventually this case, which is more complicated than others because it is "less political," will be solved and that SG will be used. Hopefully, a solution will be found within a reasonable time frame but not tomorrow or the day after. The objective is the release of the two live, repeat two live, persons. The family involved is neither a diplomatic interlocutor nor a political one. My speculation is that the Iranians fear that pushing forward at this moment might be dangerous to the health of the two German hostages. SG efforts should continue, and I believe that Iran will say as much in public soon.

Then I laid it on the line to Zarif, calling him to say that my usefulness now was in question and I would return to New York and take the only decision open to me, which at least would make its small contribution to streamlining the Secretariat. From now on, I said, it was up to him. I then told the Germans that I would play my last card in a few days but did not tell them what it was. In the back of my mind, I left the Middle East with thoughts about writing my letter of resignation to Boutros-Ghali. I needed one week to draft it, polish it, and sleep on it. That would bring us to mid-June, by which time I figured the German hostages would be freed. If they were, I would be, too.

The first news that greeted me when I returned home was Petrovsky's warning, conveyed with a deep friendship that still exists between us, that this might be the end of the road for me. I could not approach Boutros-Ghali directly anymore but should work through him.

On June 9, Zarif called to say that my threat to resign and abandon the hostages had come to Rafsanjani's attention. He now suggested I return to the Middle East so they could start up the process again on the basis of my letter to the Hammadis in April, in which I had offered to serve as guarantor for the two brothers' prison conditions. It seemed, I was told, that "the Hammadis have been cracked." Zarif gave me a message from his foreign minister to the secretary-general asking that I be dispatched to Damascus yet again. The same request was made by the foreign minister of Germany through his ambassador in New York.

By this time, the strain that existed between Boutros-Ghali and me was apparent to everyone. But the secretary-general had been roughed up by Helmut Kohl at a recent international conference—the German chancellor telling Boutros-Ghali to "let Picco do his work"—and on June 11, Petrovsky told me another trip to Damascus had been approved. "I hope that this time when you go, you come back with the two hostages . . . for your own good," my Russian friend told me before adding, "and for the good of the office."

Before I left for Damascus, I sealed the envelope containing my resignation and gave it to my secretary, Crystel de Casson, without telling her what was in it. Judy Karam had trained her in our tradition of silence or death, and I told her, "Crystel, keep this until you receive a call from me. Then you will do exactly what I tell you over the phone." She delivered the letter to Boutros-Ghali's chief of staff at 9:15 A.M. on June 19. On June 19, another round of negotiations with the Iraqis on the proposal to swap oil for humanitarian supplies was scheduled in Vienna, but I could hardly say I might not be able to attend because I was resigning. The countdown to the last hostage had begun.

When I arrived in Damascus on June 14, Akhtari said that for two days he had tried to persuade the Hammadis to come to his embassy but had failed. "Mr. Picco, I don't know how you are going to do this, but you cannot go to Beirut. They really want you dead." It was the first time he had shown any real concern about my health in the Lebanese capital. But then he added, "You know, with the help of God, we can work miracles."

Meanwhile, an intelligence team headed by Bernd Schmidbauer, secretary of state to the chancellor and head of the German intelligence services, had come from Bonn, an arrival widely noted by the press.

Schmidbauer and I met several times on June 14 and 15, and each day he said their information indicated that a release was due within hours. Early on June 16, I told him that I was going to Beirut and would let him know when to come so that he would indeed be present at the release of the hostages.

Lebanon's capital posed a much higher hurdle than before. We were really down to the wire, and going to Beirut now meant that I would be testing the validity of the theory of the "last hostage." Butch Waldrum, the Canadian chief of staff of UNDOF, who had been looking after my security in Damascus, had vetoed my going to Lebanon at this late stage of the game. But his twenty-four-hour absence from Damascus made it easier for me to convince a UN staff driver to take me to Beirut.

Once there, I had a flurry of meetings with Lebanese officials, who all wanted to take part in the release of the last hostages. I met with the Iranian chargé a number of times. He suggested a meeting with an unknown group of Shiite Lebanese because of the recent bombing of south Lebanon by the Israelis. There was no indication from him that Abdel Hadi Hammadi would still be opposed to freeing the German hostages, given the growing momentum for their release, but the chargé made it clear that Hammadi might turn them over to the Lebanese authorities rather than to Syrian intelligence.

By late in the evening of June 16, I was quite sure the hostages would be released the following day, Wednesday, June 17. And they were: Kemptner and Struebig, in captivity for three years, walked out of the Lebanese prime minister's office with a triumphant Schmidbauer before a huge throng of reporters, clicking cameras, and TV Minicams. When it was time to go, or so I thought, the prime minister suddenly said, "Mr. Picco, you and the minister of state of Germany are now expected at the house of the president for a meeting of congratulations."

I climbed into the front seat of my jeep and was surrounded by photographers and journalists. They asked me if my work was finished, and I said, "The work of the UN is not finished. I am very glad this has happened, but the job is not over and the UN will continue working. The UN has a commitment to continue working for the rest." I chose my words carefully, and as I did so, I knew this was my farewell to Beirut.

Schmidbauer, the hostages, and I remained at the apartment of President Elias Harawi for only a few minutes. The president personally thanked me in the name of Lebanon and said, "We have just met, but I have followed your work for a long time and I know how much you have done for us. The nightmare of Lebanon is over." He was brief and precise.

We went downstairs and sped to the airport under heavy protection. Two German government jets were waiting. As the plane took off, I looked back at the receding Mediterranean shoreline and the city that would remain carved in my memory. But I must admit that I did not feel safe until we were well over water and had picked up enough altitude to be out of the range of handheld missiles. Now, as far as I was concerned, it was over.

The last cable I sent to Petrovsky read, "Leaving Beirut. Am on the move, cannot be contacted. Two German hostages in Lebanon were released in the prime minister's office in Beirut at 10 A.M. local time on 17 June '92 in the presence of the Lebanese prime minister, German Minister Schmidbauer, and myself. After the release the delegation made a brief courtesy visit to the president of Lebanon. Personal, from Picco: Dear Mr. Petrovsky, it is with great satisfaction that I report to you that the mission has been accomplished. Please thank the Secretary General, from me, for his confidence."

We landed in Crete, where Kemptner and Struebig were reunited with their families. A few hours later, we arrived at Frankfurt Airport and taxied to the military part of it, where the press was waiting. I had asked the German authorities to arrange for a car to meet me on the tarmac and to drive me to the civilian terminal to catch a flight out of Germany. I declined the invitation to join Schmidbauer at the press briefing. As the plane came to a stop, I could see the press and the cameras maybe fifty yards away, waiting for the hostages to descend the stairs. I let everybody else deplane. Schmidbauer and the two former hostages approached the fences holding back the press. I observed the scene from the plane window. As the attention shifted to them, I slipped out of the plane unnoticed and walked under the aircraft and across the tarmac to a waiting car. Within seconds I was gone.

Out of the Shadows

I had had an incredible run. When I was a young man, my father told me that if I wanted never to work a day in my life, I should do what I liked most. I did. Not coincidentally, when I left the United Nations, I was told that finally I would have to work out there in the real world.

To a large extent, our world is very much the legacy of Voltaire—the triumph of reason, logic, professionalism, and technocracy. Institutions in particular represent a triumph of Voltairean logic since they are supposed to reflect a common rationality that can keep the irrationality of the individual at bay. Yet over and over again, the human factor is at the basis of crises and the individual at the source of solutions. Defenders of reason believe that a new structure can always be created to deal with the latest crisis. In fact, the one that has just exploded is already old and the new one is unknown. International institutions reform to adapt to what has happened; they cannot do so for what has yet to occur. Only individuals can do that.

So a good reform is not one that takes into account only what has happened. A good reform also leaves enough room for an individual to maneuver in a world of unforeseen events. The Charter set out at the United Nations' inception in San Francisco gave the secretary-general that kind of wiggle room. It recognized that human creativity, ultimately, is what matters.

Some individuals hide behind institutions to cover their own mistakes. Others want the individual to disappear as a potential irrational component in a rational structure. Either way, it means that individuals have no accountability or responsibility—a sure prescription for bureaucratic mediocrity.

The Bosnia debacle is the most proximate case in point: everybody ran for cover, and at the end of the day the "institution" was blamed—by the UN leadership itself! But leadership was not and is not an anonymous entity. The names behind the offices were and are well known.

In 1993, a journalist asked Secretary-General Boutros Boutros-Ghali to define the United Nations' objective in Bosnia. Boutros-Ghali replied, "That of the member states." It was politically shrewd but also wrong, an answer unworthy of the leader of the United Nations. Once Bosnia was recognized by the UN General Assembly as an independent state, the moral objective of the institution derived directly from the Charter: to defend Bosnia's integrity not only as a state but as a multicultural, multireligious, multiethnic society. That is the very core of the United Nations itself—the belief that diversity, not homogeneity, is the foundation of the world body. When the multicultural Bosnia died, a piece of the United Nations died with it.

The most important achievement of the United Nations of the last six years, I believe, has been the creation of the war-crimes tribunals for the former Yugoslavia and for Rwanda. For the first time, such tribunals are being called upon to judge not just the vanquished but the victors as well. This breakthrough, impossible to conceive of only a few years earlier, is a qualitative step forward in the ethics of international civil society. It happened on Boutros-Ghali's watch and was spearheaded by a handful of British Foreign Ministry diplomats.

There are many more actors on the international stage today than ever before—more governments, more nongovernmental organizations (NGOs), more large multinational corporations. As a result, most of what engages our world comes from entities not traditionally represented at the table of diplomacy. Today, individuals can play a role in international affairs, NGOs can reach peace agreements, and companies and public opinion groups can set the international agenda. Information and access to it, and the capacity to disseminate one's ideas can make even private individuals powerful in a modern world moving at lightning speed, provided they have credibility.

Is the United Nations ready for that? One night in Beirut, I asked Abdullah about his family. He wanted a better world for his children, he told me. Isn't that what Mrs. Arad sought? Isn't it what we all seek?

From Afghanistan to Cyprus to Lebanon, I always heard about the "enemy"—the existential necessity. In fact, our entire human journey through the millennia has been headed by a long line of leaders who could not lead without enemies. The most dangerous enemy I encountered over the years, however, was not a state, a person, a religion, an ethnic group, or a corporation, but the fear of difference. Call it intolerance, manifest in the growing number of violent acts against undefended civilians. Here, on the threshold of a new century, it is becoming the great enemy of all we should cherish. If the United Nations is looking for a new mission, perhaps it should raise the banner against intolerance in all corners of the world. John Hume, the Nobel laureate for 1998, the real peacemaker of the conflict in Northern Ireland, said it best: The mind-set of war is to see difference as a threat; instead, difference is the very essence of growth.

Still, it would be difficult for an institution such as the United Nations to capture the imagination of the younger generations and become the flag of hope, courage, and human dignity through institutional change alone. That can be achieved only through the contributions of individuals, and especially through the leadership of the secretary-general. Lenin called them the vanguard, Adam Smith called them the elite, Christian doctrine calls them witnesses, and Chairman Mao called them flowers. They all mean the same thing: exemplary role models. Bureaucracy is no role model.

An organization of ten thousand individuals may not need more than a hundred commandos to carry, to pull, to attract others to work for the same cause—providing the cause is right and the tools are ethical. One hundred people who believe deeply that principles should be the guiding light of the United Nations can alter the course of human events and make a difference for future generations. The rewards are worth any price.

I was ill fit for a bureaucracy. Bureaucrats offered me advice based on "precedents." I was attracted instead by what had not been done before. I was often told that "the time is not ripe," but I felt that the worst of times were actually the best of times because they offered opportunities for new, creative approaches. Others preached that might often makes right. I am convinced that we can be better than that. What's right needs no payback because it carries its own gratification. I also learned that money is not the ultimate reward for everyone and that death is not the ultimate threat. It no longer is for me.

Governments and groups have to show a "return" for their actions, either because of domestic opposition or because it is important to flex political muscles and squeeze something out of the other side. It is hard to convince a government to do something just because it is the "right" thing to do, irrespective of what the other side would do. The more violent a regime, the more this is true. I was frustrated by those who did not act and take responsibility because they seemed to lack the courage of their convictions. But those who chart a path for their national interests have all my admiration because they are the ones who eventually have to make decisions and live by what they have done. The ability and courage to make decisions commands respect.

The secretary-general of the United Nations and his staff can afford to act on the basis of principles even without "return." They are in a unique position to do so. I know that many of my former colleagues will agree with me when I say that the gratification of doing so was beyond that of any experience we had ever had. It was more than I could have expected. It was life at its peak.

Cast of Characters

Abdullah: Nom de guerre of the main spokesman for the kidnappers of the Western hostages in Lebanon.

Akhtari, Mohammed Hassan: Iranian ambassador to Syria from 1986 to 1998, subsequently elevated to the religious rank of ayatollah.

al-Assad, Hafez: President of Syria.

al-Shaara, Farouk: Foreign minister of Syria since the mid-1980s.

Anderson, Terry: AP journalist in Beirut at the time of his kidnapping in 1985. He was released as part of the UN operations in 1991.

Arad, Ron: Israeli navigator shot down during a military operation in Lebanon in 1986. Though his case became pivotal in the UN efforts, no news about his whereabouts has been ascertained as of this writing.

Arens, Moshe: Israeli defense minister during the time of the author's hostage operations in Beirut.

Aziz, Tariq: Deputy prime minister of Iraq since 1993. Prior to that, he served as foreign minister. A member of the Christian minority in Iraq, he has served as an international spokesman for the regime of Saddam Hussein over the last two decades.

Azkari, Mohammed Hassan: Pasdaran leader and commander of the Iranian Guard contingent in the Bekaa Valley since 1982. He was allegedly the last person to see the Israeli MIA Ron Arad in 1989.

Badruddin, Mustafa: Lebanese Shia from south Lebanon. Brother-in-law of Imad Moughniya and one of the Dawa Seventeen prisoners arrested in Kuwait in 1983 for the terrorist attack against the emir and the French and American ambassadors to Kuwait.

Bandar bin Sultan, Prince: Saudi ambassador to the United States.

Barak, General Ehud: Presently the leader of the Labor party in Israel. He was chief of staff of the Israeli Army during the time of the author's operations in Beirut. He remains the most decorated military officer in Israel.

Bjornsson, Steiner: UN staff member and chief administrative officer of UNDOF in Damascus during the author's hostage operations in Beirut.

Boutros-Ghali, Boutros: Secretary-general of the United Nations from January 1992 to December 1996. Prior to this position, he had served as adviser to President Anwar Sadat during the Camp David negotiations, and minister of state for foreign affairs in Egypt from 1980.

Buckley, William: U.S. officer and alleged CIA chief of station in Beirut, he was kidnapped in March 1984, tortured, and subsequently killed. His body was retrieved by the United Nations on December 27, 1991.

Burleigh, Peter: U.S. diplomat who dealt with the Afghanistan crisis in the early 1980s.

Casson, Crystel de: Author's secretary from 1989 to 1992.

Cicippio, Joseph: Comptroller at the American University of Beirut, abducted in West Beirut in 1986 and freed in 1991 as a result of the UN operations.

Collett, Alec: British national working for the United Nations Relief and Works Agency (UNRWA) when he was kidnapped in Beirut in 1985. Tapes of his alleged hanging were not conclusive. His fate is undetermined as of this writing.

Cooper, Roger: English technician taken prisoner by the Iraqi government in 1990 and released in 1992.

Cordovez, Diego: UN under secretary for political affairs, appointed personal representative to the secretary-general during the Afghan crisis in March 1982. An Ecuadorian national, he became foreign minister of Ecuador in 1990.

Denktash, Rauf: Leader of the Turkish-Cypriot community and vice president of Cyprus from 1960 to 1963.

Dost, Mohammed Shah: Foreign minister of the pro-Soviet regime in Afghanistan from 1980 to 1986.

Dostum, Abdul Rashid: A general from the Uzbek part of Afghanistan. He was a strong supporter of the Communist regime until 1992. He has since joined the new government coalition there.

Durani, Mustafa: Lebanese Shia kidnapped by the Israelis in Lebanon in 1994 and allegedly the keeper of Ron Arad until 1989.

Evren, General Kenan: President of Turkey from 1981 to 1986.

Fadlallah, Mohammed Hussein: Lebanese Shia clergyman who founded the Al Dawa movement (the precursor of Hizbollah in Lebanon).

Fawzil, Darwish: Currently general of the Syrian Army. He was previously the liaison between the Syrian Army and UNDOF.

Fink, Joseph: Israeli soldier taken in Beyth, in the Yahoun area of south Lebanon, together with his comrade Rhamin al-Sheikh by Islamic militants in 1986. Hizbollah claimed responsibility. Proof of their death was finally obtained by the author, via the United Nations, in September 1991, although the bodies were returned only in 1997.

Foley, James: AP photographer (and friend of Terry Anderson) who was in Beirut at the time of Terry Anderson's kidnapping.

Gavrilov, Nikolai: Soviet diplomat and shadow negotiator for the USSR during the UN-sponsored negotiations on Afghanistan at the time of the leadership of Yuri Andropov. He died of a heart attack in 1983.

Goulding, Marrack: UN under secretary for political affairs from 1986 to 1996. A British career diplomat.

Hammadi, Abbas: Imprisoned by the German authorities for his role in the smuggling of explosives into Frankfurt in 1989. Brother of Mohammed Ali and Abdel.

Hammadi, Abdel Hadi: Leading figure of the Lebanese Shia Hammadi family which, together with the Moughniya clan, ran the security apparatus of Hizbollah. He was also allegedly a member of the core group of kidnappers in Lebanon. Brother of Abbas and Mohammed Ali.

Hammadi, Mohammed Ali: Imprisoned by the German authorities for his role in the hijacking of TWA Flight 847 and the murder of a passenger in June 1985. Brother of Abbas and Abdel.

Heinzerling, Larry: AP journalist during the Terry Anderson kidnapping who served as a full-time point man for the company's efforts to release his colleague.

Higgins, William: A U.S. Marine Corps lieutenant colonel, abducted in Lebanon in 1988. He was apparently hanged a few months later. His body was recovered by the United Nations in Beirut in 1991.

Holopainen, Timo: Finnish lieutenant colonel who served with UNTSO (UN Truce and Supervision Organization), detached from OGB (Observer Group Beirut).

Jacobi, Hans: Swiss under secretary of state for foreign affairs.

Jacobson, David: U.S. hostage freed through the Iran-contra arms delivery to Iran.

Jenco, Lawrence: Kidnapped in 1985 and released in 1986 as part of the second round of the Iran-contra operations.

Karam, Judith: UN staff member, served as the author's assistant in most of his political assignments at the United Nations.

Karmal, Babrak: Founder of the Communist party of Afghanistan. He became president of that country in 1979.

Kazempour, Ardebili: Iranian official, at different times deputy foreign minister, deputy minister of oil, ambassador to Tokyo, and adviser to President Khatami.

Keenan, Brian: Professor at Beirut University since 1985. He was taken hostage in 1986 and released in 1990. Born Irish, he was taken hostage as part of the British contingent.

Kemptner, Thomas: German aid worker kidnapped and released in May 1989. He was kidnapped again that same month and released as a result of the UN operations in 1992.

Kharrazi, Kamal: Foreign minister of Iran since 1997. He served as Iranian ambassador to the United Nations from 1990 to 1997.

Khoei, Ayatollah Abu al Qasim al Mussawi al: Major religious figure in Shiism and an opponent of President Saddam Hussein.

Khorasani, Rajaie: Iranian ambassador to the United Nations from 1984 to 1987, he subsequently became a member of the Majlis.

Kinkel, Klaus: Foreign minister of Germany from 1992 to 1998. Prior to holding this position, he served as Germany's justice minister.

Kittani, Ismat: Iraqi ambassador to the United Nations at the time of the end of the Iran-Iraq war in 1988. Prior to this, he served as a UN staff member under Secretaries-General U Thant and Kurt Waldheim.

Kozyrev, Nikolai: Soviet diplomat mandated by Gorbachev to push forward negotiations with the United Nations on the resolution of the Afghan crisis.

Lahad, Antoine: Lebanese Christian leader of the South Lebanese Army (SLA), the pro-Israeli entity established after the Israeli invasion of Lebanon.

Larajani, Javad: Deputy foreign minister of Iran in the 1980s; subsequently secretary of the National Security Council of Iran and a member of the Majlis.

Leyraud, Jérôme: French aid worker kidnapped in Beirut in 1991 and released that same year, allegedly after Hizbollah executed the perpetrators for challenging the group's decision to continue the releases within the context of the UN operations.

Lubrani, Uri: Israeli chief negotiator with Lebanon for the peace process; former Israeli ambassador to Iran during the time of the Shah. Responsible for the operation that led to the transfer of the Felasha (Ethiopian Jews) to Israel during the 1980s.

Mahallati, Mohammed Jafar "Amir": Chargé d'affaires of the Islamic Republic of Iran to the United Nations from 1987 to 1988. He paid dearly for his activities in favor of peace by his subsequent purge from the government of Iran.

Mann, Jackie: British retired RAF pilot kidnapped in Beirut in 1989 and released in 1991 as a result of the UN operations.

Mavrommatis, Andreas: Greek-Cypriot negotiator for the UN-sponsored talks with the Turkish-Cypriot side.

McCarthy, John: British journalist kidnapped in Beirut in 1986 and released in 1991 as part of the UN operations.

Mohtashemi, Ali Akhbar: Former Iranian interior minister and ambassador to Syria. He was credited as being the *éminence grise* of the creation of Hizbollah in Lebanon.

Molinari, Alberto: Italian citizen who spent most of his life in Lebanon and was kidnapped during the civil war. Attempts by the United Nations to locate him and secure his release have been unsuccessful as of this writing.

Moughniya, Imad: Lebanese Shia, alleged to be the key figure in implementing the kidnapping operation in Beirut. He was a leader of the SSA (Special Security Apparatus) of Hizbollah.

Mussavi, Hussein: Lebanese Shia and head of the Amal militia in the Bekaa Valley during the early 1980s, a forerunner of the Hizbollah militia.

Mussawi, Abbas: Elected secretary-general of Hizbollah in 1986 and holder of this position until his assassination by the Israelis in 1992. Cousin of Hussein Mussavi.

Najibullah, Nasrullah: President of Afghanistan from 1986 to 1992. He lived as a de facto prisoner at the UN compound in Afghanistan from 1992 to 1996, after which he was hanged in the public square in Kabul by the Taliban.

Nasserallah, Hassan: Secretary-general of Hizbollah since 1992; educated under the tutelage of Ayatollah Khomeini.

Nasseri, Cyrus: Ambassador of the Islamic Republic of Iran to the United Nations in Geneva from 1986 to 1997.

Nielsen, Jens: Danish military officer who served in the OGB during the author's hostage operations in Beirut.

Obeid, Abdul Karim: Shia leader of south Lebanon, abducted by Israeli forces in 1989.

Palme, Olof: Prime minister of Sweden, he became a special envoy to the secretary-general with regard to the Iran-Iraq war and retained that position until his assassination in Stockholm in 1986.

Panigatti, Angelo: Chaplain at the Italian embassy in Afghanistan from the late 1960s to the late 1980s and unofficial Vatican envoy.

Pérez de Cuéllar, Javier: UN secretary-general from 1982 to 1991.

Petrovsky, Vladimir: Former Soviet diplomat with the rank of deputy foreign minister of the USSR during the Gorbachev era. He later became under secretary-general of the United Nations in 1992.

Pickering, Thomas: U.S. under secretary of state since 1997. Prior to holding this position, he served as U.S. ambassador to Moscow, New Delhi, the United Nations, Israel, and Jordan. A career diplomat.

Polhill, Robert: U.S. educator kidnapped in Beirut in 1987 and released in 1990.

Rafsanjani, Ali Akbar Hashemi: President of Iran from 1989 to 1997.

Reed, Frank: U.S. educator kidnapped in Beirut in 1986 and released in 1990.

Riza, Iqbal: Pakistani diplomat who became a UN official in 1984. He has served as UN secretary-general Kofi Annan's *chef de cabinet* since 1997.

Ross, Chris: U.S. ambassador to Syria at the time of the author's hostage operations in Beirut.

Saltik, Ertugrul: Commander of the Turkish forces in Cyprus from 1976 to 1977 and member of the military junta that rose to power in Ankara in 1981.

Sanbar, Samir: Director of the UN information office in Beirut during the Lebanese civil war in the 1970s and 1980s.

Saud al-Faisal, Prince: Saudi minister of foreign affairs.

Scowcroft, Brent: U.S. national security adviser from 1989 to 1992.

Seurat, Michel: French sociologist kidnapped in West Beirut in 1985 and killed while in captivity in 1986.

Sevan, Benon: UN under secretary-general. Worked with the author on the Afghan crisis after the Soviet withdrawal.

Shamsheddin, Mohammed: Vice president of the higher Shia assembly of Lebanon.

Sherry, George: A leading player in the UN secretary-general's political efforts in the Cyprus affair.

Shevchenko, Arkady: Highest-ranked Soviet ever to defect to the West. Allegedly a double agent until 1977, when he defected to the United States and served as under secretary-general for political and security council affairs at the United Nations.

Shihabi, Samir: Ambassador of Saudi Arabia to the United Nations in New York throughout the 1980s. He was subsequently named president of the General Assembly in 1991.

Slonim, Ori: Israeli lawyer and consultant to the Israeli government on the matter of the Israeli MIAs. He resigned from this position in 1991.

Steen, Alann: Educator abducted in West Beirut in 1987 and freed in 1991 as a result of the UN operations.

Struebig, Heinrich: German aid worker kidnapped in 1989 and released in 1992 as a result of the UN operations.

Sutherland, Thomas: U.S. educator kidnapped in 1985 and freed in 1991 as a result of the UN operations.

Tickell, Crispin: British ambassador to the United Nations in the mid-1980s.

Tokhteh, Sayed: Iranian diplomat who served as a political counselor at the embassies of the Islamic Republic of Iran in Beirut, New York, and Damascus.

Tracy, Edward: U.S. citizen kidnapped in 1986 and released in 1991 as a result of the UN operations.

Treiki, Ali Abdul Salaam: Libyan ambassador to the United Nations, subsequently made foreign minister of Libya.

Turner, Jesse: U.S. educator kidnapped in 1987 and released in 1991 as a result of the UN operations.

Urquhart, Brian: Under secretary-general of the United Nations and founder of the UN's peacekeeping operation.

Vadset, Martin: Norwegian commander of the UN Truce and Supervision Organization and the UN Interim Force in Lebanon.

Vaezi, Mahmoud: Deputy foreign minister of Iran in charge of European and North American affairs. Accordingly, he was responsible for the "Swiss Channel" for the hostage release efforts.

Velayati, Ali Akhbar: Foreign minister of Iran from 1982 to 1997.

Vergau, Hans-Joachim: Deputy permanent representative of Germany to the United Nations at the time of the author's work in Lebanon.

Vorontsov, Yuri: Deputy foreign minister of the Soviet Union at the time of the author's work in Afghanistan and Lebanon. Played a major role in the closure of the Afghan crisis in 1988.

Waite, Terry: British clergyman kidnapped in Beirut in 1987 and released in 1991 as part of the UN operations.

Waldrum, Butch: Brigadier general of the Canadian army and chief of staff to UNDOF between Syria and Israel in Damascus during the time of the author's hostage operations in Beirut.

Weir, Benjamin: The third U.S. hostage to be released upon the delivery of weapons to Iran; in this case, one hundred TOW missiles.

Zamania, Amir Hossein: Iranian diplomat who served at his country's mission to the United Nations in New York and at its embassies in Beirut and Damascus.

Zarif, Javad: Deputy foreign minister of Iran for international organizations since 1994, Iranian diplomat since 1980. Deputy permanent representative of Iran to the United Nations in New York during the time of the author's hostage operations in Beirut.

Selected Bibliography

Abu-Amr, Ziad. *Islamic Fundamentalism in the West Bank and Gaza.* Bloomington: Indiana University Press, 1994.

Ahmed, Akhbar S. *Discovering Islam: Making Sense of Muslim History and Society.* London: Routledge and Kegan Paul, 1988.

Anderson, Terry. *Den of Lions: Memoirs of Seven Years.* New York: Crown Publishers, 1993.

Arjomand, Said Amir. *The Shadow of the Hidden Imam: Religion, Political Order and Societal Change in Si'ite Iran from the Beginning to 1890.* Chicago: University of Chicago Press, 1984.

Arnó, Fiammetta. *Prigionièri del Jihad.* Milan: Guerrini e Associati, 1998.

Avi-Ran, Reuven. *The Syrian Involvement in Lebanon Since 1975.* Boulder, Colo.: Westview Press, 1991.

Bakhash, Shaul. *The Reign of the Ayatollahs: Iran and the Islamic Revolution.* New York: Basic Books, 1984.

Cicippio, Joseph, and Richard W. Hope. *Chains to Roses: The Joseph Cicippio Story.* WRS Publishing, 1993.

Coughlin, Con. *Hostage: The Complete Story of the Lebanon Captives.* London: Little, Brown and Company, 1992.

Dietl, Wilhelm. *Staats Affare: Hinter den Kulissen der Geheimdienste.* Stuttgart, Germany: Deutsche Verlags-Anstalt, 1997.

Fisk, Robert. *Pity the Nation: Lebanon at War.* Oxford: Oxford University Press, 1991.

Friedman, Alan. *Spider's Web: The Secret History of How the White House Illegally Armed Iraq.* New York: Bantam Books, 1993.

Hanf, Theodor. *Coexistence in Lebanon: Decline of a State and Rise of a Nation.* London: Centre for Lebanese Studies and I. B. Tauris, 1993.

Hourani, Albert. *A History of the Arab Peoples.* New York: Warner Books, 1992.

Hume, Cameron R. *The United Nations: Iran and Iraq, How Peacemaking Changed.* Bloomington: Indiana University Press, 1994.

Jaber, Hala. *Hezbollah: Born with a Vengeance.* London: Fourth Estate, 1997.

Keenan, Brian. *An Evil Cradling.* London: Hutchinson, 1992.

Kepel, Gilles. *La Revanche de Dieu.* Paris: Éditions de Seuil, 1991.

Levin, Sis. *Beirut Diary: A Husband Held Hostage and a Wife Determined to Set Him Free.* Chicago: Intervarsity Press, 1989.

Lewis, Bernard. *Islam and the West.* Oxford: Oxford University Press, 1992.

————*The Middle East: A Brief History of the Last 2000 Years.* New York: Scribner, 1995.

McCarthy, John, and Jill Morrell. *Some Other Rainbow: Their Own Story.* New York: Bantam Books, 1993.

Pérez de Cuéllar, Javier. *Pilgrimage for Peace: A Secretary General's Memoir.* New York: St. Martin's Press, 1997.

Ranstorp, Magnus. *Hizb'allah in Lebanon: The Politics of the Western Hostages.* New York: St. Martin's Press, 1997.

Rubin, Barnette R. *The Search for Peace in Afghanistan: From Buffer State to Failed State.* New Haven: Yale University Press, 1995.

Salabi, Kamal. *A House of Many Mansions: The History of Lebanon Reconsidered.* Berkeley: University of California Press, 1988.

Sutherland, Tom, and Joan Sutherland. *At Your Own Risk: An American Chronicle of Crisis and Captivity in the Middle East.* Golden, Colo.: Fulcrum Publishing, 1996.

Uz-Zaman, Waheed. *Iranian Revolution: A Profile.* Islamabad, Pakistan: Institute of Policy Studies, 1985.

Waite, Terry. *Taken on Trust.* New York: Harcourt, Brace and Company, 1993.

Index

C

About the Author

GIANDOMENICO PICCO was born in the northeastern Alps of Italy and was educated at the University of Padua, the University of California at Santa Barbara, the University of Prague, and the University of Amsterdam. He joined the United Nations Secretariat in the early 1970s and worked there until 1992, ending his UN career as the assistant secretary-general for political affairs. Picco has since joined the private sector as the founder and president of GDP Associates, an international consulting firm in New York City, and continues his work in conflict resolution through the Geneva-based Non-Governmental Peace Strategy Project, which he also founded. He writes for a variety of foreign-policy publications about Middle East, Persian Gulf, and Caspian affairs.